Blackstone's Guide to the

BANK OF ENGLAND ACT 1998

Blackstone's Guide to the

BANK OF ENGLAND ACT 1998

Michael Blair, QC

General Counsel to the Board of the Financial Services
Authority; Treasurer, General Council of the Bar of England and Wales

Ross Cranston, MP, Barrister

Visiting Professor of Law at the University of London,
London School of Economics and Political Science

Christopher Ryan

Professor and Head of the Department of Law at
City University, London

Michael Taylor

Reader in Financial Regulation, ISMA Centre,
University of Reading

Foreword by the Rt. Hon. Alistair Darling, MP

Chief Secretary to the Treasury

BLACKSTONE
PRESS LIMITED

First published in Great Britain 1998 by Blackstone Press Limited,
Aldine Place, London W12 8AA. Telephone 0181-740 2277

ISBN: 1 85431 847 0

British Library Cataloguing in Publication Data
A CIP catalogue record for this book is available from the British Library.

Typeset by Montage Studios Limited, Horsmonden, Kent
Printed by Ashford Colour Press, Gosport, Hampshire

Contents

Foreword

The Bank of England Act 1998 marks an important milestone in the government's reform of the financial system. Our reforms build on the best features of the existing system but improve and extend it in important ways.

The government's reforms in this area are founded on the principles of transparency and accountability, by setting out a clear division of responsibilities. So the Act makes clear the Bank's operational responsibility for monetary policy decisions, to meet the government's inflation target. The new Bank of England will be one of the most open and accountable central banks in the world.

The Act also transfers responsibility for banking supervision to the Financial Services Authority (FSA). When the process of regulatory reform is complete, the FSA will supervise all aspects of financial supervision and regulation — a move that will put the UK in the forefront of regulation, and ensure the industry is ready to meet the needs of the 21st century.

The government is committed to putting into place the highest standards of regulation for the financial services industry, to serve the public and ensure the sector remains internationally competitive.

This Guide is a useful commentary on the new Act. All those interested in the conduct of economic policy, and in the health and effectiveness of the financial sector, will find the Guide of value in explaining what we have done in this first phase of our reforms, and why we have done it.

The authors intend to produce a similar guide to the second stage of the reform. I look forward to seeing the results of those efforts also, just as I am looking forward to completing the task of putting in place a modern legislative framework for an industry which is a major employer in this country and is an acknowledged world leader.

The Rt. Hon. Alistair Darling, MP
Chief Secretary to the Treasury
April 1998

Chapter 1
Introduction and Overview
Michael Blair, QC[1]

The Bank of England Act 1998 arrived in a somewhat unexpected way. It sprang from two very early announcements by the present government, in the first month following the general election. While the first of these, on the establishment of a Monetary Policy Committee in the Bank of England, had been foreshadowed by opposition spokesmen before the 1997 election, it had not generally been expected to lead to legislation, at any rate on the urgent footing that eventually transpired. And the second announcement, on transfer of banking supervision from the Bank of England to the body now known as the Financial Services Authority (then the Securities and Investments Board), took almost everyone by surprise.

THE COMMON THREAD AND THE MAIN THEMES

Although the Act has a common thread, it is probably best to think of it as one that achieves four or possibly five separate but overlapping aims. The common thread accordingly has to be stated at quite a high level of generality: it is the modernisation of the United Kingdom's central financial institutions, so as to enable them, through greater transparency, accountability and orderliness, to perform well in the modern and increasingly international world of finance.

The main themes, in descending order of importance, are as follows:

(a) independence of the Bank of England from government and from political influence, for the purposes of operational responsibility for monetary policy;

(b) transfer from the Bank of England to the Financial Services Authority (FSA) of responsibility for banking supervision, and allied supervisory tasks;

(c) reconstitution of the internal structure for governance for the Bank of England;

---

[1] Chapter 1 represents Mr Blair's personal views, and should not be taken as an expression of the views or policy of the Financial Services Authority.

(d)   a statutory framework for transparency in relation to the Bank of England's financial arrangements; and

(e)   the merger of the National Savings Stock Register into the Bank of England Registrars' Department, alongside the (non-statutory) transfer of responsibility for debt management from the Bank of England to the Treasury.

To set against those main themes in the legislation, five concerns emerged in Parliament in the course of its examination of the Bill for the Act. These were as follows:

(a)   concern about the transfer of monetary policy operations from 'democratic control' into the hands of a non-elected 'quango', and the resulting problems associated with reconciling conflicts between different economic instruments (e.g., interest rates, fiscal policy and rates of exchange);

(b)   questions about external approval, e.g., by the House of Commons or a select committee of that House, of senior appointments in the Bank of England;

(c)   issues, in part at least semantic, about the relationship between the statutory objective of maintaining price stability and the apparently subordinate objective of supporting the government's economic policy, including growth and employment;

(d)   concern about the costs of regulation and supervision, and about the putting into place of machinery to bear down upon those costs; and

(e)   in relation to the transfer of banking supervision, unease at the constraints involved in the Bill, in that it proposed no more than a transfer of functions, without any real opportunity to make substantive improvements in relation to the responsibilities being transferred.

This book offers some comment and analysis on concerns (a), (c) and (d).

Returning to the common thread, the Act is a first and incomplete part score: it is to be followed relatively soon by a further, more fundamental, piece of legislation about modernisation of our central financial institutions. That second Bill will integrate in greater or lesser measure the regulatory regimes for banking supervision, for securities supervision (including retail investment matters) and for insurance. Accordingly, a large part of the Bank of England Act 1998 will have a short life, as the material relating to transfer of supervisory functions will almost certainly be repealed in the ensuing Act. The long-term survivors in this Act will therefore be Part I on the constitution of the Bank, Part II on monetary policy and a few sections in Part IV so far as they relate to matters not connected with banking supervision. About half of the Act, accordingly, can be seen as temporary, with the other half remaining on the statute book over the longer term.

THE THEMES TACKLED IN THIS BOOK

After a description of the historical background, in chapter 2, the subsequent four chapters deal, in the order set out in the Act, with four of the five main themes mentioned above:

Chapter 3 (governance and constitution of the Bank) deals with the third of the main themes above, that is, reconstitution of the governance of the Bank of England.
Chapter 4 deals with the cardinal theme, independence for the Bank in relation to monetary policy.
Chapter 5 covers the second most important theme, that of transfer of responsibilities for banking supervision, with some additional related material to be found in chapter 7.
Chapter 6 handles the other transfers of responsibilities and minor improvements in relation to stock registration and gilts management, the last of the five main themes.

This leaves, without specific treatment hereafter, the fourth of the main themes, statute-based transparency for the Bank of England's finances, which straddles two parts of the Bill: some account of it is therefore given in this introductory chapter.

MAIN CHARACTERISTICS OF THE ACT: BALANCE AND REDISTRIBUTION

Viewed in the round, this Act can be described as achieving a finely struck *balance*, and as effecting a workmanlike *redistribution* of functions.
The balance is most clearly seen in the first two Parts of the Act. These deal with an internal balance within the governance of the Bank of England, including the new Monetary Policy Committee, and with an external balance as between the Bank of England (or specific parts of its working), on the one hand, and the Treasury and Treasury ministers, on the other. The redistribution of functions is most clearly seen in Part III, which transfers to the FSA responsibility for banking supervision: but there is an important sub-theme running through that Part, and in Part II, which deals with the redistribution of the power to raise revenue to meet the costs of carrying out the functions concerned.
This chapter attempts an overview of both of these aspects.

THE BALANCING ASPECT

Balance in connection with monetary policy

Under the Act, there is now a Monetary Policy Committee, set up by s. 13 as a committee of the Bank of England. It consists of nine persons, that is, the Governor, the two Deputy Governors, two Bank of England 'insiders' (one a monetary policy analyst and one skilled in monetary policy operation), together with four 'outsiders' who are, nonetheless, made 'servants' of the Bank of England once appointed. The Governor, or in his absence the relevant Deputy Governor (the one responsible for monetary policy), has a casting vote. Accordingly, there is an in-house majority of five against four external experts, though early experience of the informal Monetary Policy Committee (operating in advance of the commencement of the Act) suggests that divisions in the committee, when they occur, result from differences in relative weight given to the various economic indicators rather than to 'in-house' or 'external' status.

The Act achieves a balance of power and responsibility as between the court of directors of the Bank, on the one hand, and the Monetary Policy Committee on the other. The court manages the Bank's affairs (other than the formulation of monetary policy). This includes determining the Bank's objectives with the aim of ensuring the efficient discharge of the Bank's functions. By contrast, the Monetary Policy Committee 'shall have responsibility within the Bank for formulating monetary policy' (s. 13).

It seems clear from the Act that, while the Committee deals with the formulation of monetary policy, it does not deal with or direct the execution of monetary operations, though, by s. 14, the decision against which those operations are to be conducted is one taken by the Committee. Section 14 sets out the machinery for publishing the decisions of the Monetary Policy Committee (on whether or not the Bank should change interest rates, or whether it should intervene in the financial markets). Publication is for the Bank, and in such manner as the Bank thinks fit, with the duty to publish arising as soon as practicable after each meeting of the Committee. But the decision whether publication should be delayed (because of the risk of impeding or frustrating a decision to intervene in the financial markets) rests with the Committee. So the Committee is a kind of pawl in the ratchet of the Bank's obligation to publish a decision. The minutes of Committee meetings (s. 15), normally to be published within six weeks, are subject to a similar delaying provision. Quarterly reports are also similarly balanced: the Bank is to prepare and publish the reports, including a review of the monetary policy decisions published by the Bank in the quarter, but the report needs the approval of the Monetary Policy Committee under s. 18(5).

Balance within the court

Within the court of directors, there is a carefully crafted balance as between the Governor and the two Deputy Governors, on the one hand, and the 16 non-executive directors, on the other. For instance, the court of directors has, by s. 16, to keep the procedures followed by the Monetary Policy Committee under review, with particular reference (because of the Bank's branch and agency network) to collection of regional, sectoral and other statistics. But this function is by statute delegated to the non-executive directors and does not rest with the court as a whole. The Act is not specific on the question of finance for carrying out monetary policy functions: the responsibility to provide belongs to the court, and the question whether the court has any obligation to supply the Committee with the necessary policy-making resources is not specifically regulated in the Act (though see below as to the functions of the non-executive directors).

The Act makes a new set of distinctions between the functions conferred on the court as a whole, and those that are referred, in accordance with modern notions of corporate governance, to a sub-committee of non-executive directors of the Bank, now numbering 16. These functions, mainly in ss. 3 and 16, involve review of performance, monitoring of the meeting of objectives, internal financial control, remuneration, and procedures of the Monetary Policy Committee, particularly in relation to statistics.

Although the Bank has two Deputy Governors, they, under the statute, are required to work exclusively for the Bank (sch. 1, para. 1(2)) and, accordingly, the search for a senior non-executive figure has to go outside. The Act chooses, for this purpose, the chairman of the non-executive sub-committee established by Section 3, who is designated by the Chancellor of the Exchequer. That person is the deputy chairman of the court, in the sense that he or she takes the chair of the court if the Governor is not present (sch. 1, para. 13(3)).

The Act goes to some lengths to ensure that all the 16 appointments of non-executive directors are available to Her Majesty on the date of coming into force of the Act by requiring existing appointees to vacate their office. While, no doubt, some reappointments can be envisaged, this ensures that The Sovereign, through her ministers, has the power to establish a new set of non-executive directors who are ready and willing to operate under the new machinery.

Balance between the Bank and the Treasury

This aspect is the one that has attracted the greatest amount of public attention. So far as the law is concerned, s. 10 removes from the Treasury the power to give directions to the Bank in relation to monetary policy. That said, the Treasury have, as is described in chapter 2 below, important powers to condition the general strategy in relation to monetary policy. Critically, s. 12 enables the Treasury to specify what price stability is to be taken to consist of, and what the government's economic policy is to be taken to be. These are the two elements, and the only two elements, of the Bank's statutory objectives in relation to monetary policy, though the second of them contains a subsidiary reference to objectives for growth and employment. The internal balance in s. 11 itself as between price stability, on the one hand, and supporting the economic policy of the government, on the other, is described in chapter 2 below: suffice it to say that the section makes it plain that price stability is 'trumps'.

Further, there are in s. 19 carefully drawn and balanced reserve powers, which enable Treasury directions to be given, in the public interest and in 'extreme economic circumstances', with respect to monetary policy. Consultation with the Governor is required, though the question whether the directions are required in the public interest and by extreme economic circumstances is one for the Treasury. The use of the word 'they' in s. 19(1) does not include the Governor, since, in this Act as in legislation generally, the Treasury are a plural noun (see, for example, ss. 12(3) and 19(2)). The order has to be laid before Parliament and is subject to the affirmative resolution procedure for its continued effect after 28 days.

By schedule. 3, para. 13, the Treasury have an observer on the Monetary Policy Committee. A Memorandum of Understanding between the Treasury, the Bank of England and the Financial Services Authority, which is set out in full in appendix 5, carefully delineates the respective functions of the three authorities, particularly in relation to issues of systemic difficulty, such as the collapse of a major bank.

There is a good deal of careful balancing in the new provisions, described in greater detail below in this chapter, for the new arrangements for financing the Bank of England. Although the Treasury have the power to fix the parameters against which the banks and building societies are required to deposit cash with the Bank, the Act stops short of giving the Treasury full budgetary control over the process: instead, sch. 2, para. 11, provides that in exercising the critical power, 'the Treasury shall have regard to the financial needs of the Bank'. This implies that it is for the Bank to state what its financial needs are, rather than for the Treasury, though the process of having regard to such an assessment implies a certain measure of oversight.

THE REDISTRIBUTIVE ASPECT

The main element to mention under this heading is the transfer of banking supervision, though other, lesser transfers, inwards to and outward from the Bank of England, have also been mentioned above. The transfer of banking supervision is the first half of a wider reform announced by the incoming government in May 1997. The Financial Services Authority, which is to become the widely based financial regulator in the United Kingdom, is emerging in two stages, with banking supervision forming the first of those stages. Unification of securities regulation, including retail investment regulation, insurance supervision, and the oversight of building societies and other mutual organisations will appear in the second phase, currently expected in 1998–9. This first phase in the more widespread reform has been welcomed, not only in its own right, but also as the first part of the wider, overall, approach.

As chapter 5 below makes plain, this element of the Act is largely an exercise in the transfer of functions, and thus in the redistribution of part of the Bank's existing portfolio of functions. The Act, in this aspect, does very little more than a sheer transfer of functions, together with matters inescapably related to that transfer. Examples of those essential concomitants are the power to charge fees, the creation of new gateways for the supply of information, and provisions enabling the transfer of rights and liabilities. An example of a non-essential change related to this transfer is in s. 31, which modifies the arrangements for appointment to the board of the Financial Services Authority (removing the Governor as a co-appointor): this is a desirable change, but not one that is necessarily driven by the transfer itself. A second was introduced in the House of Lords to change the constitution of the Board of Banking Supervision: initially the Bill had proposed that the chairman of the FSA should chair the Board, but, after amendment, the Act requires the independent members to elect one of their number to chair it (s. 28).

The effect of this redistribution on the Bank

The areas of influence of the Bank, as stated in the Memorandum of Understanding (see appendix 5) are as follows:

(a)   overall stability of the financial system as a whole, and, in particular,

(b) stability of the monetary system;

(c) financial system infrastructure, especially payments systems;

(d) broad overview of the (financial) system as a whole;

(e) ability to conduct what loosely may be described as official support operations; and

(f) efficiency and effectiveness of the financial sector, with particular regard to international competitiveness.

In terms of legislative provisions, it emerges from the Act, principally in s. 36 and sch. 7, para. 2, that two specific functions of the Bank are recognised by statute, e.g., for the purposes of exchange of information. These are:

(a) its functions as a monetary authority; and

(b) its functions as a supervisor of systems for the transfer of funds between credit institutions and their customers.

The Registrar's Department of the Bank has a statutory existence. Other statutory functions now include operational responsibility for interest rates, functions relating to the currency and the operation of the exchange equalisation account. These, albeit important, are less than the full breadth of the Bank's areas of expertise, interest and influence.

The Bank has, under this Act, gained its (qualified) independence as a monetary authority, and additional (relatively limited) functions in relation to registration of gilts. By contrast, it has lost the supervision of banks (and allied supervisory responsibilities) and, through executive action, its operational role in the debt management area.

It has also gained two new statutory benefits. First, it now has a statutory power to obtain information for monetary policy purposes, and, second, it now enjoys a *statutory* source of income, as opposed to one based on custom and practice, with the scope now extended to include building societies as well as banks. But a concomitant of the extra security of the statutory backing is the power of the Treasury to fix the relevant framework for the collection by the Bank of the necessary revenue to meet its 'financial needs'.

When banking supervision left the Bank of England on commencement of the Act on 1 June 1998, about 500 staff were transferred to the Financial Services Authority, though most of them will remain physically located in the Bank of England's buildings until nearly the end of 1998. Treasury debt management adds a few further staff to the transfer list, while, by contrast, an estimated 60 jobs, presently in National Savings, will be transferred to the Bank of England or saved.

By contrast with its European analogues, the Bank of England is already a relatively small central bank. In part this is because it has fewer functions than in some other member States, and many fewer agencies and branches. Nonetheless, it is striking that countries with a similar population to the United Kingdom, such as France and Italy, have substantially more staff in their central banks. France tops the

list with 16,500 staff, followed by Germany (now a somewhat larger member State
than the United Kingdom) with 16,000, and by Italy with 9,400. The United Kingdom
ranks roughly on a par with Spain with 3,200 staff. If the 500 banking supervisors are
abstracted, the UK central bank probably drops to seventh position, below Spain,
Greece and Belgium.[2]

Redistribution in relation to finance

Until the Act came fully into force on 1 June 1998, the Bank of England had been
financed by a variety of sources and importantly a system of voluntary cash ratio
deposits. Stemming historically from early arrangements to secure the solvency and
liquidity of the banking system, these deposits have been placed with the Bank of
England on an interest-free footing. The Bank has then been able to discharge its
public functions by spending the interest earned by the deposits made by the banking
institutions. The percentage amount of these cash ratio deposits has diminished over
the years, and until recently stood at 0.35% of sterling eligible liabilities, with a
disregard for banks with less than £10 million in such liabilities.

Section 6 of, and sch. 2 to, the Act now place on a statutory basis the arrangements
for the placing of cash ratio deposits with the Bank. The structure to enable the Bank
to call for these deposits is established on the footing of decisions made by the
Treasury, to define eligible liabilities, to specify value bands and ratios etc. The Bank
will hereafter give each institution, including in the future building societies, a call
notice specifying the amount of deposit required. The arrangement is enforceable,
with penal rates of interest for shortfall, and powers to obtain information.

Overall, this system should be more transparent than the present financing
arrangements. Not only is the amount of the deposits to be derived from instruments
which have been laid before and in some cases approved by Parliament, but the Act,
in ss. 4 and 7, requires the Bank to keep and to publish accounts, which are also to
be laid before Parliament. In fact the Bank has in recent years published its accounts,
so the main change here will be in the Parliamentary aspect.

To return to the theme of redistribution, until commencement of the Act, banking
supervision was effectively paid for out of the voluntary cash ratio deposits. Hereafter,
however, banking supervision is to be paid for by a system of fees charged by the
Financial Services Authority, pursuant to regulations made by it under sch. 6 to the Act.
That Schedule is modelled largely on the pre-existing arrangements whereby the
Financial Services Authority charges fees in relation to investment business supervision.
Under the consultative paper issued in February 1998 by the Financial Services
Authority, all banks will be expected to pay something, at a flat rate, but with a minimum
for very small institutions and with a special tapering provision for the very large banks.
This arrangement will produce a highly transparent source of revenue for the FSA.

---

[2] For the figures, see the House of Commons written answers for 4 March 1998, in response to a question
from Sir Nicholas Winterton MP (question 31947).

The Government's expectation, almost certain to be borne out in practice, is that the overall cost to business under the new arrangements in respect of cash ratio deposits and fees taken for banking supervision will be no greater than under the pre-existing arrangements. The percentage was reduced to 0.25% earlier in 1998 and is expected to drop again to 0.15% on 1 June 1998. The fees for the FSA are not expected to exceed the equivalent of 0.10%.

In other words, here is an exercise in redistribution without increase, and with the prospect of economies over time as the benefits of reorganisation and, perhaps, greater transparency begin to outweigh the costs of achieving the transition itself.

Chapter 2
Central Bank Independence: The Policy Background
Michael Taylor

MONETARY POLICY AND CENTRAL BANK INDEPENDENCE

The Bank of England Act of 1998 amounts to one of the most significant changes to the Bank's governance, role and functions in its 300-year history. It is certainly the most significant legislative change to affect the Bank since its nationalisation in 1946. But whereas the latter was a consequence of the then Labour government's desire to obtain control of the main levers for influencing the economy, the 1998 Act reflects a new policy consensus in favour of taking the conduct of monetary policy out of direct political control.

There had been a growing consensus in favour of granting the Bank of England monetary policy independence for a long period prior to the new Act. The resignation speeches of two recent Chancellors of the Exchequer, Nigel Lawson and Norman Lamont, both expressed support for the concept, with the former revealing that in 1988 he had prepared a plan to grant the Bank its independence. In addition, a committee chaired by Lord Roll of Ipsden had recommended in a 1993 report for the influential Centre for Economic Policy Research (*Independent and Accountable: A New Mandate for the Bank of England*) that the Bank be made independent, and the House of Commons Treasury and Civil Service Select Committee also expressed sympathy for similar changes. Added to this policy consensus was support from across the economics profession, including many leading academic economists.

However, the policy consensus in the UK is only part of a wider international trend. Prior to 1989 only three countries — the United States, Germany, and Switzerland — had established independent central banks. The decade since then has witnessed what might be described as a revolution in central banking, with countries from Chile to the Philippines, from France to Argentina, and from New Zealand to Spain, legislating to grant their central banks independence. With the Bank of England Act 1998 the United Kingdom has joined this growing list.

While the worldwide trend towards central bank independence has its roots in a number of factors, the most fundamental is a change in economic orthodoxy. The original nationalisation of the Bank of England took place against a policy background which largely accepted the need for governments deliberately to stimulate demand in the economy to ensure constant high levels of output and employment. This policy was largely inspired by the economic theories of John Maynard Keynes, and hence became known as Keynesian demand management, or 'Butskellism' after its two most famous exponents as Chancellor of the Exchequer, Hugh Gaitskell and R. A. Butler. In the first few decades of the post-war era governments sought to use their power to tax, borrow and spend ('fiscal policy') to ensure that unemployment stayed low. Inflation was not seen as a serious threat, and a modest amount could be accepted as the price of protecting jobs. Thus monetary policy was regarded as subsidiary to fiscal policy as the main lever for influencing the level of economic activity, and interest rates were deliberately kept down to stimulate investment. In this environment it was natural to expect the central bank to play a subordinate role to government, and to follow policies which supported the broad policy objective of ensuring against the return to the mass unemployment of the 1930s. An editorial in the *Daily Herald* summed up the spirit of the times when, commenting on the nationalisation of the Bank, it said that 'the lives of our people shall never again be at the mercy of the restrictionist financial ideas which once ruled us so banefully'.

This orthodoxy began to break down in the early 1970s. Governments throughout the developed world were then faced by both rising unemployment *and* rising inflation, something the Keynesian model of the economy failed to predict. The failure of demand-management policies permitted the emergence of a new economic orthodoxy which stressed the importance of controlling inflation as the key to ensuring successful long-term economic performance. According to this view there is a 'natural rate' (to use Milton Friedman's term) of unemployment in the economy. The term 'natural rate' is a little misleading as the unemployment rate is not fixed for all time, but can be changed over the medium to long term by encouraging the efficiency of markets and competitiveness on the 'supply side' of the economy, for example, by making it easier for firms to hire and dismiss workers, or by improving the skills of the labour force through education and training initiatives. However, the important point is that the unemployment rate cannot be altered by changes in government spending and borrowing. At best increases in government spending will achieve a brief, temporary reduction in unemployment. In the medium term unemployment will return to its 'natural rate' and the only effect of the increased government spending will be to push inflation ever higher. It follows that governments can no longer spend their way to full employment, and they should focus instead on price stability as the ultimate objective of economic management. Stable prices matter because they provide the right environment in which individuals and firms can make the decisions which determine the productivity and success of the supply side of the economy. Thus this economic model reverses the old Keynesian emphasis on government borrowing and spending decisions and its comparative neglect of interest rates. Instead, monetary policy now assumes centre stage as the main instrument for delivering price stability, and fiscal policy is reduced to an exercise in prudent housekeeping.

The movement towards central bank independence is one practical consequence of this new economic orthodoxy. Once controlling inflation is recognised as the primary goal of policy, attention can focus on the mechanisms by which this can be delivered. Although they may disagree about the best mechanism for controlling inflation, most academic economists agree on the need for a rule-based monetary policy, which is best delivered by an independent central bank able to treat monetary policy as a technical matter free of the pressures of the political process.

The case for central bank independence is derived from a number of sources, both theoretical and empirical. Supporters of central bank independence sometimes cite the theory of the political business cycle, which assumes that politicians aim to maximise their own welfare, especially short-term electoral gain, rather than the public good. It also assumes that voters feel the immediate benefits of government attempts to stimulate the economy, but that they do not experience the inflationary consequences for up to two years later. These factors mean that politicians have a natural tendency to prefer economic expansion, and their attempts to stimulate the economy generate economic cycles in which the boom periods are timed to coincide with elections, with the bust inevitably following afterwards. This natural tendency means that as long as politicians have control of the money supply they will be tempted to use it to promote economic expansion and hence inflation.

Another theoretical argument stresses the importance of the authorities giving a credible and binding commitment to a particular monetary discipline which they are unable to vary under political or electoral pressures. Credibility in this context means ensuring that firms and individuals ('economic agents' in economists' terminology) believe in the authorities' commitment to doing whatever is necessary to achieving a low level of inflation. If the authorities' commitment to fighting inflation is not believed then economic agents will expect inflation to be higher, which has a tendency to be a self-fulfilling prophecy. Hence the lack of credibility in monetary policy will in turn give rise to higher inflation, which will further undermine the credibility of policy, and so on in a vicious circle.

One way for the authorities to achieve credibility is to commit themselves irrevocably in advance to a certain course of action (known as 'precommitment' by economists). In effect, the authorities bind themselves to taking whatever measures are necessary to reduce inflation, no matter how unpopular and no matter whether or not they wish to do so. This removes the possibility that politicians might be tempted to relax their commitment to fighting inflation. Handing decisions on monetary policy over to a central bank which enjoys a substantial measure of independence from short-term political pressures is widely regarded as a way of providing such a commitment by governments. Putting monetary policy in the hands of those who are given an explicit objective of maintaining low inflation or stable prices is a way of ensuring that inflationary expectations, and hence inflation, will be low.

Empirical studies of central bank independence have purported to show that the more independent a country's central bank, the lower its inflation rate has tended to be. However, these studies have been challenged on a number of grounds. The first is that the sample of independent central banks is relatively small, since only those of the United States, Germany and Switzerland can be regarded as having been genuinely independent before 1989. Of the central banks which have been granted their independence since then, the evidence is more mixed, although in most cases the experience of independence has simply been too short to draw any meaningful conclusions. Furthermore, these empirical studies often do not clearly distinguish between correlation and causation, and it has frequently been pointed out that Japan enjoys an excellent record on inflation notwithstanding the political dependence of its central bank. (It is worth noting, however, that as part of the 'Big Bang' financial liberalisation reforms, the Bank of Japan will also win a substantial measure of monetary policy independence.) Conversely, however, mere independence alone cannot guarantee price stability. Other factors, including the commitment of the community at large to the goal of price stability, are at least as important, as the popular attitude to inflation in Germany well illustrates. The anti-inflationary temper of the German electorate helps reinforce the Bundesbank's independence by giving it a legitimacy which it might lack in more inflation-prone countries.

Whatever the strength of the academic case, there remains one immensely important practical factor favouring the international trend towards central bank independence, at least within the European Union. This factor is the 1992 Treaty on European Union, a significant part of which enshrines the concept of central bank independence in European law. The Treaty on European Union was clearly influenced by the theoretical arguments discussed above, but is also a testament to the example for the rest of Europe provided by the stable currency presided over by the German Bundesbank. Thus, within the EU, many member States have legislated for central bank independence to comply with their Treaty obligations in preparation for economic and monetary union.

MODELS OF CENTRAL BANK INDEPENDENCE

Although there may be broad support for the general concept of central bank independence, there are several ways of legislating to give effect to it. Examples of an explicit constitutional provision enshrining the independence of central banks are relatively rare, although Chile and the Philippines have both used this method. Most countries have instead merely enacted laws to make their central banks independent, with some — most notably New Zealand — also employing a formal contract between government and central bank.

'Strong' independence: the Federal Reserve, Bundesbank and European Central Bank

Germany and the United States provide the leading examples of independent central banks, and there are several notable similarities between the arrangements existing in these two countries. Both have federal governmental systems and the structure of their central banks reflects this. The Federal Reserve System (Fed) comprises 12 regional Federal reserve banks, ranging from New York to San Francisco and from

Minneapolis to Atlanta. Each regional bank is headed by a president, who is elected by its member (commercial) banks. In addition, there is a Federal Reserve Board of seven members headed by a chairman, all of whom are nominated by the President subject to Senate confirmation. Important decisions on monetary policy are taken by the Federal Open Market Committee (FOMC), which comprises the seven members of the Federal Reserve Board plus the president of the New York Fed, with four of the other regional Presidents serving on a rotating basis for one-year terms. The Bundesbank is similarly composed of regional ('*Land*') central banks, the main difference from the Fed being that all the regional presidents serve on the crucial committees concerning monetary policy. The similarity in structure of the two central banks is largely a product of the fact that the Bundesbank was promoted by the US occupation authorities after the Second World War. However, an especially important point is that although both Germany and the United States have written constitutions, neither has enshrined central bank independence in them.

It is widely assumed that the Bundesbank is the creation of the German constitution, but all that the relevant article (art. 88) requires is the establishment of a Federal note-issuing and currency bank; it is silent as to its status and relationship with other governmental institutions. The Bundesbank is instead the creature of statute, the *Bundesbankgesetz* of 1957. This states:

> Without prejudice to the performance of its functions, the Deutsche Bundesbank shall be required to support the general economic policy of the Federal government. In exercising the powers conferred on it by this Act it shall be independent of instructions from the Federal government.

The Bundesbank has taken the phrase 'without prejudice to the performance of its functions' to imply that it alone has the right to interpret what this obligation requires. In practice, this has meant that it has pursued the goal of price stability. Thus although it is also subject to the 1967 Act on stability and economic expansion, which requires it to take into account a high rate of employment, the trade balance and economic growth in addition to the goal of price stability, the Bundesbank has unambiguously pursued the objective stated in art. 3 of the *Bundesbankgesetz* which refers to 'the aim of safeguarding the currency'. In this respect it is, in the words of former German Chancellor Konrad Adenauer, 'fully sovereign in its relationship with the government; it is responsible only to itself'.

The legal independence of the Federal Reserve is less clear-cut. As with the Bundesbank there is no constitutional provision which creates the Federal Reserve Board, it being instead the creation of the 1913 Federal Reserve Act. The Constitution in fact vests in Congress the power to 'coin money' and to 'regulate the value thereof'. (US Constitution, art. I, s. 8). Moreover, whereas the Bundesbank has a clearly defined policy goal in its legislation, the Fed is required instead to:

> maintain long-run growth of the monetary and credit aggregates commensurate with the economy's long-run potential to increase production, so as to promote

effectively the goals of maximum employment, stable prices and moderate long-term interest rates.

Thus, unlike the Bundesbank, the Federal Reserve faces a number of competing objectives, and it must also submit twice-yearly reports to Congress explaining its plans and their relationship to goals stated in the President's Economic Report. This contrasts with the position of the Bundesbank, which, although its annual report is presented to parliament, has no formal accountability to either the upper or lower house. In fact, the Fed's position as an 'independent' central bank is largely a consequence of the way in which successive chairmen have interpreted their role, especially since the so-called 'accord' between the Treasury Department and the Fed in 1951. However, this document had no legal status, and merely stated that they had 'reached full accord with respect to debt-management and monetary policies to be pursued in furthering their common purpose to assure the successful financing of the government's requirements and, at the same time, to minimise monetisation of the public debt'. The strongest safeguard of the Fed's independence has been its ability to exploit to the full the structural tension between Congress and President which is built into the US Constitution, and this is an essentially political skill. Perhaps its greatest exponent in recent times was Paul Volcker, chairman from 1979 until 1987.

Hence the Federal Reserve's independence is largely a consequence of its skill, and especially its chairman's skill, as a political actor, whereas the Bundesbank has a stronger legal guarantee of its independence. Nonetheless, the independence of both institutions is underwritten by a number of specific provisions, including the appointments process for senior executives, their terms of office and provisions for dismissal, and the institutions' financial autonomy from government. For example, members of the Bundesbank's general council are appointed in most cases for an eight-year period by the Federal President; nominations are made by the Federal government after consultation with the general council. The president and vice-president are similarly appointed, but for an indefinite period and with no specific provisions for removal. However, the Bundesbank's independence is qualified by a provision which permits members of the Federal government to attend meetings of the general council and to propose motions. Although they have no right to vote, they may require decisions to be deferred for up to two weeks.

Since 1935 the Fed's board of governors has had no corresponding provision allowing government representatives to participate in its deliberations. Members of the board are appointed by the President (subject to Senate confirmation) for 14-year terms, although the chairman and vice-chairman are appointed for only four-year terms (this compares with a five-year term for the Governor of the Bank of England.) The Fed does, however, enjoy considerable budgetary autonomy, and is not subject to the appropriations process or to the Office of Management and Budget. This gives it a substantial degree of independence from either the Congress or the President. The Bundesbank also has considerable financial autonomy, with art. 26 of the *Bundesbankgesetz* conferring on it the power to prepare and approve its own accounts.

The 1992 Treaty on European Union (TEU) demonstrates clear evidence of the influence of the Bundesbank model. It establishes, *inter alia*, the European System of Central Banks (ESCB) which comprises the European Central Bank (ECB) plus the national central banks of the EU member States. Like the *Bundesbankgesetz* the Treaty and its associated Protocol on the Statutes of the ESCB and of the ECB accord the ESCB a precise and specific objective: 'The primary objective of the ESCB shall be to maintain price stability' (EC Treaty, art. 105(1) inserted by the TEU, art. G(25)). In an echo of the wording of the *Bundesbankgesetz*, the same paragraph also states that 'without prejudice' to this objective the ESCB shall support the economic policies of the Community. Article 107 of the EC Treaty enshrines the legal independence of the ESCB in a way which goes beyond either the Federal Reserve Act or the *Bundesbankgesetz*:

> When exercising the powers and carrying out the tasks and duties conferred upon them by this Treaty and the Statute of the ESCB, neither the ECB, nor a national central bank, nor any member of their decision-making bodies shall seek or take instructions from Community institutions or bodies, from any government of a member State or from any other body.

Article 108 of the EC Treaty requires member States to legislate to give effect to the required independence in respect of their national central banks.

A Protocol annexed to the Treaty on European Union sets out the statutes of the ESCB and ECB in greater detail. Here, too, the influence of the Bundesbank model is apparent, although the European Central Bank will enjoy even greater institutional autonomy than that currently available to the German central bank. The President, Vice-President and the four other members of its Executive Board will be appointed for a non-renewable eight-year term, while the Governors of the national central banks, who with the Executive Board collectively constitute the ECB's Governing Council, are required to have a minimum term in office of five years. Nominations to the Executive Board of the ECB will be by the Council of the European Union, after consultation with the European Parliament and the Governing Council of the ECB. These officers will be appointed by the heads of State or government of the member States acting in common accord. Members of the Executive Board will also enjoy considerable security of tenure, and can be removed only by the Court of Justice acting on an application from either the Governing Council or Executive Board (Protocol on the Statute of the European System of Central Banks and the European Central Bank, art. 11.4). No other Community institution or member State is empowered to remove a member of the Executive Board. The ECB will also enjoy substantial financial autonomy, with most decisions on the allocation of its profits being decided by the Governing Council, subject to the rules set out in arts. 26–33 of the Protocol.

Thus the Federal Reserve, Bundesbank and European Central Bank display a basic similarity of structure. Although not themselves creatures of a written constitution, each is set up within a system in which there is a fundamental law which restricts and separates the powers of government (or Community competence in the case of the ECB). Moreover, each also reflects a system in which there is considerable geographical dispersion of power, whether in the form of an explicitly federal constitution or in the form of the European Union's principle of subsidiarity. None of these features is present in the case of the United Kingdom, which, besides a unitary State and an unwritten constitution, must also accommodate the doctrine that no parliament may bind its successors. These conditions mean that central bank independence on the Federal Reserve or Bundesbank model would be difficult to import into the British constitution.

The New Zealand model

For this reason, the New Zealand model of central bank independence has appeared to be an attractive model for many British proponents of the concept, since it has been developed in a country which shares many constitutional features in common with the UK. The Act establishing the independence of the New Zealand Reserve Bank (1989 No. 157) explicitly recognises the Crown's continuing right 'to determine economic policy', but also introduces the notion of a contract between the government and the central bank's Governor, which has the effect of precommitting the authorities to pursue the goal of price stability. It is a mechanism which might be characterised as 'contractually based independence' or 'independence with instructions'. The government sets the broad policy parameters, but the central bank is free to achieve them in whatever way it sees fit.

The New Zealand Act resembles the *Bundesbankgesetz* to the extent that it accords the Reserve Bank the single policy objective of formulating and implementing 'monetary policy directed to the economic objective of achieving and maintaining stability in the general level of prices'. (s. 8). However, whereas both the Fed and Bundesbank models accord the responsibility for formulating monetary policy to a committee of central bankers, the New Zealand model empowers the finance minister to determine, in consultation with the Governor of the Reserve Bank, what is to constitute 'price stability' by setting an explicit, formal policy target. When the Reserve Bank Governor is appointed, the finance minister must 'fix, in agreement with that person, policy targets for the carrying out by the Bank of its primary function during that person's term of office, or next term of office, as Governor' (s. 9(1)). However, the choice of means to achieve the target is left to the Governor, whose personal responsibility it is to ensure that the policy target is followed (s. 11). The inadequate performance of the Governor in pursuit of the policy target provides one of the grounds for his or her removal from office, which can be accomplished by Order in Council made by the Governor-General, acting on the advice of the finance minister (s. 49(2)(d)). Thus the essence of the New Zealand model is the personal accountability of the Governor of the Reserve Bank for meeting the policy target.

In setting the policy target the New Zealand finance minister is precommitted to following a particular anti-inflationary path. Although the policy target can be reviewed during the Governor's tenure of office, the Act makes clear that any such changes must be a joint decision between the minister and Governor (s. 9(4)) and an additional buttress to the Governor's independence is that the Reserve Bank's price stability objective can be overridden only by Order in Council made by the Governor-General acting on the minister's advice (s. 12). (This would appear to be intended as a reserve power to be used in exceptional economic circumstances.) A further guarantee of central bank independence is the public nature of the policy target and of any attempt by the government to override it. The Reserve Bank Governor is required to publish a semi-annual policy statement which, *inter alia*, specifies the policy and means by which the Bank intends to seek its objectives, the reasons for adopting those policies and means, and a review of the implementation of monetary policy during the previous period (s. 15). This statement is laid before the New Zealand House of Representatives and its relevant committees.

OTHER BANK OF ENGLAND FUNCTIONS

The Bank of England has historically exercised a wide range of functions in addition to its role in monetary policy. It has been responsible for managing the government debt and for intervening in foreign exchange markets on behalf of the government, has operated banking services for the government, and has functioned as the supervisor of the banking system. The Bank of England Act 1998 (together with associated administrative action) has the effect of removing two of these important functions, debt management and banking supervision, from the Bank.

There are arguments both for and against separating banking supervision and management of the government debt from the central bank, but greater weight now appears to be attached to the consideration that both functions can potentially conflict with a central bank's overriding monetary policy objective. The grant of central bank independence is intended to permit the pursuit of price stability without extraneous influence, and both management of the government debt and banking supervision can give rise to these influences.

Management of the government debt

Although the management of the government debt might seem to be a technical and relatively unimportant function, it has been one of great significance for the Bank. The Bank was established in 1694 with the primary purpose of managing the national debt. It is thus a function which is closely bound up with its history, and in which the Bank has built up considerable expertise over a long period. It involves deciding the pricing and timing of government bond issues, the term structure of the debt (for example the relative merits of long versus short-term borrowing), and managing the public debt portfolio. These activities in turn require a close knowledge of market conditions, on which the Bank has always prided itself. Thus the removal of the debt management function, although it may have captured few headlines, will have struck the Bank as a heavy blow to its prestige.

Nonetheless, there are sound economic arguments for separating monetary policy and debt management functions. In particular, it avoids potential conflicts of interest between monetary policy and debt management, which might otherwise compromise the central bank's independence. For example, a central bank which also manages the government debt may be reluctant to raise interest rates to control inflationary pressures because such a move would adversely affect the value of its debt portfolio (when interest rates rise the value of bonds falls, and vice versa). In addition, it might be tempted to manipulate financial markets to reduce the interest rates at which government debt is issued. For example, it might expand the money supply prior to a large issue of government debt in order to inject liquidity into the market and thus make it easier to place the debt. It might also be prepared to accept higher levels of inflation as these will reduce the value of government debt in real terms.

Several countries have accordingly separated the monetary policy and debt management functions to avoid these conflicts of interest. In the United States debt management has always been the direct responsibility of the Treasury Department, not the Federal Reserve System, and in Germany it is the function of a specialised directorate within the Ministry of Finance. However, other countries have further moved to separate debt management from their finance ministries by the creation of autonomous debt management offices (DMOs). The rationale for setting up DMOs has been the desire to render the management of the public debt credibly independent of political pressures, and to signal to financial markets a commitment to a more transparent, even-handed and accountable debt management policy. In 1988 New Zealand created a DMO as part of the package of reform measures which led to independence for the Reserve Bank. Although the Reserve Bank continues to act as the agent of the DMO, the latter is responsible for managing the public debt. Similar arrangements have been put in place in Ireland, Sweden and Austria.

The package of reforms resulting from the Bank of England Act 1998 includes the creation of a Debt Management Office, which, as an Executive Agency, does not itself require legislation. Treasury ministers will set the annual remit for the agency, published in the Debt Management Report each March. The Chief Executive will report regularly to Treasury ministers on the delivery of the remit requirements, and agree any changes required to the remit during the year. The precise relationship of the DMO to the Treasury will be set out in a published framework document. The DMO will be responsible for decisions on auction stocks and sizes, taps of stock and any secondary market transactions within the terms of the remit. The current policy of publishing an annual borrowing programme with a quarterly auction schedule will be continued, and it is expected that the DMO will continue to operate in secondary markets in the same way as the Bank has done.

Banking supervision

In contrast to the debt management function, the Bank's role in banking supervision was acquired in a formal sense only as recently as the Banking Act 1979. Nonetheless, its informal oversight of the financial system can be traced back much further, at least to the Bank's attempts to ensure orderly conditions in the mid-nineteenth century market for bills of exchange. As a central bank, the Bank has long maintained that it needs to play an active role in supervising the banking system, since this is the mechanism through which its monetary policy is transmitted to the wider economy. Moreover, the central bank is uniquely placed to act as 'lender of last resort' in the sense of providing emergency liquidity support to a troubled bank. If it is to perform this function adequately, it is argued that the central bank will require access to supervisory information, since this alone can provide it with a basis on which to make an informed decision about which banks to support and which not to support. These considerations have in the past been taken as grounds for combining banking supervision and core central banking functions within a single institution.

Arguments for the separation of these functions have gained greater weight as the movement towards central bank independence has grown. As with the separation of debt management and monetary policy, the separation of banking supervision and monetary policy is intended to avoid conflicts of interest which might potentially undermine the independence of the central bank. It is argued that a central bank might be inclined to exercise forbearance in taking needed monetary policy action out of concern for the health of the banking system which it is also responsible for supervising. The central bank may not wish to raise interest rates, for example, if to do so would trigger a number of bank failures for which it could be blamed. Seen from another perspective, bank failures which are blamed on the central bank can damage its reputation and standing, and hence can serve to undermine the credibility of monetary policy. Hence the separation of these functions from the central bank is quite consistent with the rationale for granting it independence in respect of monetary policy, and can be viewed as an extension of the principle that monetary policy should be pursued without extraneous influences.

The arguments for separation are finely balanced, and in practice separation and combination are found in equal measure. Thus the Bundesbank lacks direct supervisory responsibilities, these being discharged by a separate governmental agency, the Banking Supervisory Office. Nonetheless, the Bundesbank continues to take an active interest in the banking system and in the formulation of supervisory policies. Banking Supervisory Office regulations must be agreed in advance with the Bundesbank, and the monthly supervisory reports filed by German banks are available to both institutions. The Federal Reserve is directly responsible for the supervision of bank holding companies and state-chartered member banks. This close involvement is probably inevitable for any central bank, whatever the range of its formal responsibilities, for reasons already cited in support of the combination of supervisory and monetary policy functions. Thus although the Bank of England may have lost its formal supervisory responsibilities under the Banking Act 1987, it will need to remain close to the supervisory process, as is evidenced by the memorandum of understanding agreed between the Treasury, Bank, and Financial Services Authority.

CONCLUSION

The institutional structure created by the Bank of England Act 1998 exhibits elements of each of the forms of central bank independence discussed in this chapter. The model of independence within a policy objective set by the Chancellor obviously owes something to the New Zealand experience, although it differs from it to the extent that responsibility for meeting the target is not the Governor's personal responsibility. The Bank's new Monetary Policy Committee is to some extent modelled on the US Federal Open Market Committee, although its method of appointment evidently gives it much less independence from government than the latter, and the FOMC is able to determine for itself what inflation target to pursue.

The separation of banking supervision from the Bank of England follows the Bundesbank model rather than that of the Federal Reserve. The separation of debt management from monetary policy accords with the practice in both the United States and Germany, but most closely follows the New Zealand approach, in that one component of the package of reforms, beyond the Act itself, involves the creation of an autonomous Debt Management Office. The reforms are self-evidently a hybrid arrangement, born out of an attempt to introduce central bank independence into British constitutional practice.

Chapter 3
Governance and Constitution of the Bank
Michael Taylor

Part I of the Bank of England Act 1998 makes important changes to the constitution of the Bank, the composition and functions of its court (the Bank's board of directors), and to the Bank's financial arrangements. Although a few of these changes are a direct consequence of the decision to grant the Bank monetary policy independence, the majority of them are unrelated to it. They should be regarded instead as being part of a package to introduce greater transparency into the Bank's operations, of which the enhanced transparency of monetary policy, resulting from the monetary policy target and publication of the minutes of Monetary Policy Committee meetings, is only one aspect. In a number of respects these changes can also be seen as the completion of an agenda left unfinished at the original nationalisation of the Bank. The Treasury have taken the opportunity provided by the new Act to implement changes in the Bank's governance which they had first proposed in 1946 but which the Bank had then successfully resisted. The changes also have the effect of formalising many aspects of the Bank's relationship with the Treasury which have previously been governed only by informal arrangements. This is the case, for example, with s. 8 of the Act, which contains provisions for payments by the Bank to the Treasury in lieu of dividend.

THE BANK'S CONSTITUTIONAL HISTORY

From its foundation in 1694 to its nationalisation in 1946 the Bank of England functioned as a private joint stock company, incorporated under Royal Charter, in which it was styled 'the Governor and Company of the Bank of England'. As Walter Bagehot pointed out in *Lombard Street*, his classic work on the London money markets published in 1873, direction of this company was in the hands of a board of directors who were not themselves bankers. Instead:

> The mass of the Bank directors are merchants of experience, employing a considerable capital in trades in which they have been brought up, and with which

they are well acquainted. Many of them have information as to the present course of trade, and as to the character and wealth of merchants, which is most valuable, or rather is all but invaluable, to the Bank. Many of them, too, are quiet serious men, who, by habit and nature, watch with some kind of care every kind of business in which they are engaged, and give an anxious opinion of it. Most of them have a good deal of leisure, for the life of a man of business who employs only his own capital and employs it nearly always in the same way, is by no means fully employed.

Collectively, this board of directors was — and still is — referred to as the 'court' of the Bank of England. The court of Bagehot's era was self-electing, without a fixed term, and when a vacancy occurred through the death of a member, the whole board was involved in choosing the successor from among 'the names of the most attentive and promising young men in the old-established firms in London'. The Governorship and Deputy Governorship in this period were filled by rotation; each Governor was succeeded by his Deputy, and the latter was usually the oldest Director who had not previously been in office. The tenure of the Governorship was only two years.

Bagehot was critical of the 'amateur' nature of the Bank's governance, and in particular of the shortness of the Governor's tenure, which he believed deprived the Bank's policies of any clear continuity. He believed that these features of the Bank's governance had contributed to its failure adequately to resolve the tension inherent in its status as a private company discharging a public duty (its control over interest rates). While the latter tension was not resolved until the Bank of England Act 1946, which nationalised the Bank, the Governorship became a permanent appointment much earlier. Montagu Norman, whom many regard as its greatest Governor, occupied the position for 25 years from 1919 until his death just before the Bank's nationalisation.

The Act of 1946 transformed membership of the court (including the Governor and Deputy Governor) into Crown appointments (s. 2(1)). In practice appointments to the court continued to reflect Bagehot's description of 'merchants of experience' (with the addition of a few industrialists and the occasional trade unionist), but public ownership did nonetheless result in significant changes. In the first place, fixed terms for members of the court were introduced. The term for the Governor and Deputy Governor was set at five years — the Bank had initially sought a seven-year term — with the possibility of renewal, and that of the other members of court at four years, also with the option of renewal (sch. 2, paras 1–3.) In addition, the 24 pre-nationalisation directors were reduced to 16 by the Act (s. 2(1)). Of these 16 directors, the Act made provision for a maximum of four of them to be 'employed to give their exclusive services to the Bank' (sch. 2, para. 6), in other words for them to serve as executive directors. (In the light of the 1998 Act it is significant that the Treasury's original proposal had been for a court of 12, with no executive directors.)

The Act of 1946 continued to provide the Bank with a large measure of the operational and institutional independence from government it had enjoyed as a private company, and the court was permitted wide discretion in running the Bank.

Subject only to the power under s. 4(1) for the Treasury to give directions to the Bank, 'the affairs of the Bank shall be managed by the court of directors in accordance with such provisions (if any) in that behalf as may be contained in any charter of the Bank for the time being in force and any byelaws made thereunder' (s. 4(2)). Moreover, even the Treasury's power of direction in s. 4(1) was further moderated by the provision that it was to be used only after consultation with the Governor.

In essence, the relationship between Bank and Treasury enshrined in the 1946 Act simply transposed into statute the practice of the preceding decades. The Bank of this period neither expected nor sought 'independence' in the sense of the monetary policy independence discussed in chapter 2. Even as formidable a Governor as Montagu Norman was content to declare in 1937 that in this respect 'I am an instrument of the Treasury'. The pre-nationalisation Bank accepted the Treasury's right to determine 'policy', regarding itself instead as a confidential monetary and financial adviser to the government, its most important customer. 'Independence' in this context meant the Bank retaining control over its internal affairs, and not being subsumed into the Civil Service. The 1946 Act did indeed leave the Bank to enjoy a considerable element of autonomy in its internal affairs, and included the specific provision that a civil servant could not serve on the court (sch. 2, para. 4(a)).

Although the 1946 legislation made comparatively few changes to the Bank's governance arrangements, in practice the post-nationalisation years saw the role of the court become substantially attenuated. In particular, the court's role was significantly eroded following the 1957 Bank Rate Inquiry when one of the directors was accused of having benefited from a premature leak of a change in Bank rate. The ensuing tribunal recommended that the Bank should no longer share sensitive information with the court, which effectively ended its role as a policy-making body. The evidence of the Bank's Governor, Gordon Richardson (now Lord Richardson of Duntisbourne), to the 1979 Committee to Review the Functioning of Financial Institutions (the Wilson Committee) made clear that the court no longer had any direct involvement in decisions relating to the Bank's monetary policy advice to government. Indeed, he made it plain that he did not believe that oversight of this important aspect of the Bank's functions was the prerogative of the court. A further diminution of the role of the court occurred with the passage of the Banking Act 1987, which created a Board of Banking Supervision with a separate membership to that of the court. The function of this Board was to oversee the Bank's supervisory function and to provide expert advice to the banking supervisors, both functions which might have in the past been considered part of the function of the court. Thus the impression certainly existed in many quarters that the post-nationalisation court had struggled to define its role, and therefore a review of the Bank's governance arrangements had become necessary.

THE NEW CONSTITUTIONAL ARRANGEMENTS FOR THE BANK

The 1998 Act makes a number of significant changes to the Bank's governance. One of the most obvious of these is that it provides for the appointment of a second Deputy

Governor (s. 1(1)). Throughout the Bank's history, the Governor has been supported by only one Deputy. A second Deputy was proposed by the Treasury at the time of nationalisation but was successfully resisted by Lord Catto, the Bank's Governor, on the grounds that 'in the absence of the Governor all his powers devolve on the Deputy Governor.... If there were two Deputy Governors the question would arise as to which one acted in the absence of the Governor: plainly only one could so act'. The then Chancellor accepted this argument, and the 1946 Act provides for only one Deputy. The new Act changes this by creating a second Deputy Governor. It is intended that one Deputy will support the Governor on monetary stability matters and the other on financial stability (the Chancellor's letter to the Governor, 6 May 1997). Both will serve on the Monetary Policy Committee, although the latter will serve additionally on the Board of the Financial Services Authority.

In addition to the Governor and the two Deputy Governors, the Act makes provision for 16 non-executive members of court, all of whom will be Crown appointments, as now (s. 1(2)). In future, however, with the exception of the Governor and his two Deputies, the board will be exclusively non-executive. There is thus no provision for the four executive directors to continue to serve on the court. To all intents and purposes this is the model of governance initially proposed by the Treasury in 1946 for the post-nationalisation Bank (albeit with four fewer non-executive directors than now). In addition, the 16 non-executive members of the court will be appointed for three years rather than the present four, with scope for appointments initially to be made for shorter or different periods so as to secure that appointments expire at different times (sch. 1, para. 1(2)). However, the Governor and his two Deputies will continue to be appointed for five-year terms, this being the minimum tenure necessary to comply with the provisions of the Treaty on European Union (see chapter 2). There is also provision for the reappointment of the Governor, the two Deputies and non-executive members of the court. The conditions for their removal from office are set out in sch. 1, para. 7. Among these are that a member of the court has become a minister of the Crown or has been absent from meetings of the court for more than three months without the court's prior consent; that he has become bankrupt; and that he is unable or unfit to discharge his functions as a member. Unlike the New Zealand legislation discussed in chapter 2, the Governor cannot be removed from office on the grounds of having failed to meet the inflation policy target set by the Chancellor.

The 1998 Act is much more prescriptive about the responsibilities of the court than that of 1946. It assigns to the court the responsibility for managing the Bank's affairs, other than the conduct of monetary policy. These functions will include, in particular, determining the Bank's objectives (including objectives for its financial management) and strategy. In setting the objectives and strategy, priority is to be given to ensuring the Bank's effectiveness in the discharge of its functions and, subject to that, to ensuring the most efficient use of the Bank's resources. In a new departure, and signalling the court's more active involvement in the Bank's corporate governance, the Act establishes a sub-committee of the non-executive directors which will be responsible for keeping the Bank's performance under review, monitoring the Bank's financial management, and keeping the Bank's internal financial controls under review. This sub-committee, akin to the audit committee of a commercial enterprise, is also charged with acting as a remuneration committee, determining the remuneration and pension arrangements of the Governor and his two Deputies (s. 3(2)). Although the court has previously operated a number of sub-committees, including an audit committee, none has previously enjoyed a statutory basis. Moreover, the chairman of this sub-committee will be appointed by the Chancellor rather than by the Governor. Thus the intention is clearly to subject the powers wielded by the Governor to greater external check than has hitherto been the case, and the intention appears to be that the sub-committee of court will be more closely involved in the Bank's day-to-day affairs than has any of its predecessors.

The court will continue not to have a direct involvement in the formulation of monetary policy (s. 2(1)). However, the non-executive members will be responsible for reviewing the performance of the Bank as a whole, including the Monetary Policy Committee. That committee will report to the monthly meeting of the court as part of the latter's responsibility to review its performance. The non-executive members of the court are also required to have particular regard to whether the Bank is collecting proper regional and sectoral information for the purposes of conducting monetary policy, perhaps reflecting a suspicion that the Bank has in the past displayed a tendency to overemphasise City interests at the expense of regional or industrial ones. In his 6 May 1997 letter to the Governor, the Chancellor stated that it is his intention to ensure that the court 'will be representative of the whole of the United Kingdom'. It is proposed that the non-executive members will be appointed for their expertise, and will be drawn widely from industry, commerce and finance. The non-executive members of court will themselves be expected to provide regional or sectoral information relating to their area of expertise.

FINANCIAL ARRANGEMENTS

Part I of the Act also makes important changes to the Bank's financial arrangements. Section 4 places its annual report on a statutory basis. The Bank's report will in future be required to contain a report on the functions carried out by the sub-committee of the court, a balance sheet and profit and loss account, and the rates of remuneration of directors. The report will be published and the Chancellor will lay copies before Parliament. In addition, for the first time the Bank is made subject, by s. 7(3) and (9), to requirements corresponding to those of the Companies Act 1985 as they relate to the preparation of accounts by a banking company.

Prior to nationalisation the Bank had published no accounts other than the weekly, and largely uninformative, Bank Returns. Following nationalisation the Bank had published an Annual Report which was laid before Parliament; however, the need for 'operational secrecy' had been used to justify the disclosure of comparatively little financial information. This began to change following a recommendation of the House of Commons Select Committee on Nationalised Industries in 1969–70, which resulted in the publication of much more extensive accounts, including a balance sheet, profit and loss account, and rates of remuneration for directors. However, the Bank remained exempt from the Companies Act, and in particular the provisions of the Act relating to the preparation of accounts by a banking company. The Bank has used this privilege to disclose less of the detail of the constituent elements of its profit and loss account, particularly of interest income and expenses and provisions for bad and doubtful debts, than would be required under both the Companies Act and applicable Financial Reporting Standards. This practice has been justified by the Bank on the grounds that it is sometimes necessary to preserve secrecy or confidentiality when it has provided lender of last resort facilities to financial institutions in difficulty. Full disclosure might jeopardise these support operations by damaging confidence in the institutions thus supported. Notwithstanding s. 7(3) and (9), s. 7(4) of the Act permits the Bank to continue this practice, and leaves to the Bank the decision not to disclose, although s. 7(7) provides for a Treasury override. In effect, the Treasury can by notice in writing instruct the Bank to disclose details of any lender of last resort operations in which it may have been involved. This is moderated by s. 7(8), which obliges the Treasury to consult the Bank before giving notice under s. 7(7), but there should be no doubt that this provision explicitly gives the Treasury a power to require disclosure which previously existed only implicitly in s. 4(1) of the 1946 Act, if at all.

Another significant change to the Bank's financial arrangements is contained in s. 6 of and sch. 2 to the Act, which for the first time place its funding on a statutory basis. The primary source of the Bank's revenue is cash ratio deposits: these are non-interest bearing deposits which banks are required to place with the Bank. Cash ratio deposits are the legacy of the Bank's pre-1971 mechanism for controlling the growth of credit, which required the clearing banks to hold in either cash or non-interest bearing accounts with the Bank of England £8 for every £100 of deposits they took (this 8% ratio was known as the 'cash ratio'). The competition and credit control regime introduced in 1971 went some way to liberalising this arrangement: it applied to all banks doing sterling business, not just the clearing banks, and introduced a reserve ratio of 12.5%, of which non-interest bearing deposits at the Bank were simply one component, along with call money at the discount market, Treasury and eligible bank bills, and short-term gilts. Ten years later, in 1981, the Conservative government abandoned the attempt to control the growth of credit by the reserve ratio, and decided to rely instead on market forces. The banks were no longer required to place large sums interest-free with the Bank.

This raised the question of how the Bank was to be funded. The Bank's limited number of customers could not yield the kind of income it required to sustain its operations as the UK's central bank. The existence of a source of income in the form of non-interest bearing accounts (which the Bank was able to reinvest in the money markets) had given it an independence of the government which it could not enjoy if it were funded from the general government budget, and the Bank regarded the maintenance of a dedicated funding source as being integral to its standing and prestige as a central bank. In the event it was arranged that the whole banking community in the UK should place non-interest bearing deposits with the Bank, in a prescribed ratio to their deposits. The broadening of the community of institutions to which the cash ratio deposits applied permitted the cash ratio to be set initially at 0.5%, a proportion which has been progressively cut to the present 0.15% on eligible liabilities over £400 million. However, this arrangement was not previously backed by statute, except to the extent that the institutions from which the Bank levied cash ratio deposits were also subject to its supervision under the Banking Act 1979 (and its 1987 successor). With the removal of the Bank's supervisory powers, it was clearly necessary to place its ability to levy cash ratio deposits on a more secure legal foundation.

Schedule 2 to the Act sets out the arrangements for the levy of cash ratio deposits. It defines eligible institutions more broadly than hitherto, encompassing all those categories of financial institution which are classed as 'credit institutions' under the relevant EU Directives. These comprise banks authorised under the Banking Act 1987; European authorised institutions within the meaning of SI 1992/3218 (i.e., institutions authorised by another member State of the European Economic Area using the 'passport' conferred by the Second Banking Coordination Directive); and building societies authorised under the Building Societies Act 1986. The 1998 Act itself does not define eligible liabilities, beyond the provision that they can comprise liabilities denominated in both sterling and foreign currency (sch. 2, para. 2(1)). It confers on the Treasury the power to make orders which determine the definition of eligible liabilities, the value bands used for calculating the cash ratios, and the actual ratios levied. These are all matters which the Bank has previously decided for itself, although in consultation with the Treasury. The Bank's discretion remains only in the precise manner of calculation employed for each institution's liability (sch. 2, para. 4(2)). Although para. 10 of the schedule requires the Treasury to consult the Bank before making an order under the schedule, there is a similar requirement to consult persons who are 'representative of persons likely to be materially affected by the order', i.e., the trade associations representing the banking community. Thus, while the immediate purpose of these changes is to place the Bank's funding on a more secure statutory basis, their effect is to remove the discretion the Bank has previously enjoyed in setting its cash ratio deposits, to permit the Treasury to determine much more directly the Bank's funding arrangements, and presumably also to exercise tighter control of its budgets. An important consequence is that it will be more difficult in future for the Bank independently to vary the cash ratio deposit to raise additional funds for its operations, as occurred, for example, in the rescue of Johnson Matthey Bankers in 1984. In future, such operations will need the Treasury's explicit approval in the form of an order to vary the cash ratio deposit rate.

The Act empowers the Bank to issue notices to an eligible institution specifying the amount of cash ratio deposit it is expected to have on deposit with the Bank during a specified period. In the event that an institution does not have on deposit with the Bank its notified depositable amount, the Bank may by notice in writing require a payment in lieu of deposit, which is to be calculated by applying a penal rate of interest (4 per cent over the benchmark rate) to the average shortfall for the period in respect of which the requirement is made (sch. 2, para. 6(3)). The schedule also grants the Bank the power to obtain information from eligible institutions 'which the Bank considers it necessary or expedient to have for the purposes of its functions under this Schedule' — i.e., for the calculation of each institution's liability for cash ratio deposits (sch. 2, para. 9(1)). It should be noted that under this rubric the Bank will continue to be empowered to collect a substantial amount of information from deposit-taking institutions which duplicates that available to the Financial Services Authority as the prudential supervisor of these institutions. (The Bank's information-gathering powers for the calculation of cash ratio deposits are independent of its powers to gather information for monetary policy purposes. See the discussion of s. 17 in chapter 4.)

The third and final reform which the new Act initiates in the Bank's financial arrangements relates to the amounts payable to the Treasury in lieu of a dividend on Bank stock. When the Bank was nationalised, the Bank's existing stockholders were compensated by a simple exchange of Bank stock for government stock, and it was agreed that the Bank would pay annually to the Treasury an amount sufficient to service the new stock or such other sum as they might between them agree. Following the recommendation of the House of Commons Select Committee on Nationalised Industries in 1969–70, it was agreed that the Bank would pay over to the Treasury the post-tax profits of the Banking Department, net of provisions for reserves and working capital, as what became known as 'the agreed provision'. However, the precise amount of agreed provision payable to the Treasury remained a matter of dispute, and a final settlement was not reached until 1984, with an agreement to split the Bank's profits equally between the government and the Bank. Section 8 of the 1998 Act formalises this arrangement: in lieu of agreement between the Bank and the Treasury on the payment of dividends, s. 8(1) requires the Bank to pay a sum equivalent to 50% of the Bank's post-tax profits for the previous financial year, in two instalments in April and October. This replaces the specific figure cited in the 1946 Act, s. 1(4), which has long since ceased to have effect.

Overall, therefore, the effect of these changes to the Bank's governance, constitution and financial arrangements is to introduce greater transparency and the potential for greater public scrutiny into its operations. For its part the Bank has lost some of the discretion and the ability to conduct its operations in secrecy, which it has jealously prized for much of its history. These changes, it should be stressed, are not directly connected to the grant of monetary policy independence, in the sense that it was possible for the latter to have occurred without the former.

Chapter 4
Monetary Policy
Ross Cranston, MP

INTRODUCTION

There is a worldwide move to greater independence for central banks in the conduct of monetary policy. Thus in the European Community, as a result of the Maastricht Treaty (the Treaty on European Union), the proposed European Central Bank will be independent of political direction (see the Treaty Establishing the European Community, especially art. 108). Under art. 109 of the EC Treaty, member States must ensure that their own central banks are similarly independent. Thus both the Bundesbank and Banque de France have very general objectives, they enjoy full operational independence, and there is no provision for the government to override their decisions. Britain has the option to decide whether to be bound by this Treaty obligation although if it becomes part of the single European currency it will need to do so.

After the Bank of England Act 1998, the Bank of England will still not have a sufficient degree of independence to be compatible with the criteria set out in the Maastricht Treaty. This illustrates the point that independence is an elastic concept: there is a continuum running from legal subordination through to complete goal and operational independence. Under the 1998 Act, while the Bank has operational independence, the government can set its objectives in a fairly specific manner, and in emergency situations the government can override its decisions.

The policy arguments for greater independence for the Bank of England were set out in a statement by the Chancellor of the Exchequer, Gordon Brown, on 6 May 1997, shortly after the election of the new government. Further details were set out in a letter from the Chancellor to the Governor of the Bank of England on the same date (see House of Commons, Treasury Committee, *First Report, Accountability of the Bank of England* (House of Commons Papers, Session 1997–98, 282), annexes 1 and 2). In summary, greater independence for the bank is one part of the government's policy of establishing a modern and lasting framework to deliver stability for long-term economic growth. While the government thought it must remain responsible for setting the objectives of economic policy — in particular, the targets for monetary policy — the only way to achieve a fully credible monetary policy was if decisions about how those targets were fulfilled were guided by long-term economic, rather than short-term political, considerations.

There are more theoretical arguments as well. There is evidence suggesting that in the medium to long term inflation does not contribute to positive economic performance (e.g., C. Goodhart, *The Central Bank and the Financial System* (London: Macmillan, 1995), pp. 60 ff.). There is also evidence that in some countries the average rate of inflation has been lower with an independent central bank (A. Cukierman, *Central Bank Strategy, Credibility and Independence: Theory and Evidence* (Cambridge, Mass: MIT Press, 1992), ch. 19–23; C. Briault et al., 'Central bank independence and accountability: theory and evidence', *Bank of England Quarterly Bulletin*, vol. 36, No. 1 (February 1996)). However, this positive relationship may reflect third factors such as fiscal restraint and political stability (see R. Lastra, *Central Banking and Banking Regulation* (London: FMG, 1996)). As well as these factors in Germany is the way hyperinflation seared itself into the public consciousness, which led to the almost universal determination to keep inflation low.

Sections 10–12 of the Bank of England Act 1998 constitute for the Bank of England what has been described as 'operational independence'. Economists sometimes describe this as 'instrument independence', in that the Bank has discretion in the use of monetary policy instruments to reach its goal. Monetary policy instruments are used to influence short-term interest rates, which in turn have an effect (with time lags) on inflation. The Bank does not have 'goal' or 'target independence': s. 11 of the Act specifies the objectives of the Bank in relation to monetary policy. Under s. 12 the Treasury are obliged to give notice to the Bank as to what these objectives entail. Within these constraints, however, the Bank is free from the political direction to which it was theoretically subject under the 1946 Act. There is an exception in s. 19, for emergency situations, where the Treasury have a reserve power.

OPERATIONAL RESPONSIBILITY FOR MONETARY POLICY

Under the Bank of England Act 1946, the Bank was legally subordinate to political direction in the shape of the Treasury. The Treasury were empowered under s. 4(1) of the 1946 Act to give such directions to the Bank as they thought necessary in the public interest. This very wide discretion could only be exercised after consultation with the Governor of the Bank. In fact a direction under this section has never been given (T. Daintith, 'Between domestic democracy and an alien rule of law? Some thoughts on the ''Independence'' of the Bank of England' [1995] *PL* 118). Moreover, the long history of the Bank and its pre-eminent position in the City of London have meant that its views on monetary policy have had an authority and weight belied by the legal position.

The legal position, whereby the Bank lacked any autonomy in monetary policy, is amended by s. 10 of the 1998 Act, which provides that the power to give directions under s. 4(1) of the 1946 Act may not be used in relation to monetary policy. By itself, this provision would be sufficient to confer operational responsiblity for monetary policy on the Bank. Nonetheless, the following sections of the 1998 Act provide a structure for how this is to be exercised. The Treasury can trench on the operational independence of the Bank in relation to monetary policy only in the open and accountable way set out in these sections.

THE BANK'S MONETARY POLICY OBJECTIVES

The current trend is that price stability should be the paramount objective for monetary policy. This is coupled with the cause of central bank independence. An independent central bank, with the primary goal of price stability, will promote confidence in its monetary policy and dampen inflationary expectations. The Bundesbank provides the model: it must use its monetary powers with the aim of safeguarding the currency although, without prejudice to that, it must also support the general economic policies of the federal government (*Bundesbankgesetz*, arts. 3 and 12). Since 1 January 1994 the Banque de France has been obliged by law to formulate and implement monetary policy with the aim of ensuring price stability, although it is to carry out these duties 'within the framework of the government's overall economic policy'. The European System of Central Banks will have as its primary objective the maintenance of price stability although, without prejudice to that objective, it shall support the general economic policies in the Community with a view to contributing to the broad goals which the Community has set for itself (EC Treaty, art. 105(1)).

However, other central bank laws, moulded by the Keynsianism of the immediate period after the Second World War, place an emphasis on goals additional to price stability, such as maximum employment (e.g., the US Federal Reserve; see 12 United States Code, §225a). Where a central bank has such multiple goals there is a potential difficulty that in particular circumstances they may be in conflict, at least in the short term. One consequence is that it becomes more difficult to call the bank to account for a failure to achieve its goals, unless the goals have been placed in some sort of hierarchy. Even if the legislative mandate does not establish a priority between different goals, inevitably the central bank will need to do so. This has happened in the United States, where the Federal Reserve has acted as if price stability was its single objective. As a matter of law there is no necessary obstacle to this since, as so widely expressed, the goals are exhortatory rather than justiciable.

The objectives of the Bank of England's monetary policy set out in s. 11 of the Bank of England Act 1998 are to maintain price stability (the primary objective) and, subject to that, to support the government's economic policy, including its objectives for growth and employment (the secondary objective). Price stability as the primary objective is more precise than the objective for the Bundesbank of safeguarding the currency. The latter raises the issue of whether the Bundesbank must simply maintain the domestic value of the currency, or must also take into account its external value vis-à-vis other currencies. Price stability as a goal concentrates on the domestic value of the currency: it connotes low inflation. One justification for this these days is that while monetary policy is an important factor in the nominal exchange rate, as a result of speculative attacks in international markets the external value of a currency may not be clearly related to a country's economic performance. While desirable, then, a stable and competitive exchange rate is not a primary goal for the Bank, although as part of the government's economic policy it may be a secondary goal.

Price stability as the primary objective is something to be achieved over the medium to long term. Pursuing short-term inflation targetting could destabilise the real economy. For example, were there to be very high inflation it is clear that the Bank might not be able to reduce it immediately. Similarly, if there were to be an external shock to the economy, such as a dramatic rise in oil prices or a fall in the stock market, it might be damaging to deflate the economy in order to achieve quickly the goal of price stability.

Price stability is the primary goal. The goal of supporting the government's economic policy is 'subject to that'. In the Chancellor's announcement of 6 May 1997 the phraseology used was 'without prejudice to' price stability, which is the expression used in art. 105 of the EC Treaty in relation to the European System of Central Banks. The phrase 'subject to' is a more regular feature of United Kingdom legislation than 'without prejudice to', although it is difficult to discern any difference in meaning between the two phrases.

In essence, the Bank must pursue price stability, and in so far as this is not inconsistent with the government's economic policy, must act in a way supportive of that. Were there to be an incompatibility between the objectives of price stability and supporting government economic policy, as a matter of law the latter would need to give way. In practice the two are inextricably linked: as the Chancellor's statement of 6 May 1997 makes clear, the government sees price stability as a precondition of high and stable levels of growth and employment, which in turn will help to create the conditions for price stability on a sustainable basis.

The wording of the secondary objective for the Bank is 'to support the economic policy of Her Majesty's Government, including its objectives for growth and employment' (s. 11(b)). Clearly growth and employment are not the only aspects of government economic policy to which the Bank must give attention. 'Economic policy' is an all-encompassing phrase, including other aspects of fiscal policy such as taxation and public expenditure, but also extending to matters such as the exchange rate, European monetary union, the private finance initiative and financial regulation. In so much as the latter are less central to economic policy, however, they will have less relevance for the Bank's decisions on monetary policy. While 'growth and employment' are but illustrative, their mention indicates that they are at the top of the government's agenda for economic policy. As indicated earlier, price stability, i.e., low inflation, is being regarded as a precondition for the ultimate goal of economic policy — the highest possible growth of output and employment.

REMIT FOR THE BANK

Under the Bank of England Act 1998 the government must specify for the Bank what it means by 'price stability' and what its 'economic policy' is taken to be. Without specification, the Bank would be largely unaccountable for whether it had met its objectives. Section 12(2)(b) requires the Treasury to specify what the objectives mean at least once every 12 months. The obvious time to do this will be in the budget statement. Under the Act the notice containing these matters must be in writing and must be laid before Parliament. The Treasury have a discretion as to how otherwise they will publish it. Already the government has set an inflation target, which the Bank must meet by setting short-term interest rates. In his June 1997 Mansion House speech, the Chancellor set the target for inflation as 2 ½ per cent, as defined by the 12-month increase in the retail price index excluding mortgage interest payments (*Equipping Britain for Our Long-Term Future. Financial Statement and Budget Report* (House of Commons Papers, Session 1997–98, 85), para 1.15).

Under s. 12 the government must set the inflation target once every 12 months. In this sense the Bank does not have the goal or target independence of some central banks such as the Bundesbank. The arguments against goal independence relate to democratic accountability. Rather the Bank has operational independence to reach the inflation target set by government. By virtue of the section, however, the government can reset the target in its discretion. Were it to do this too frequently, the Bank's operational independence would be affected. Thus time lags before changes in short-term interest rates take effect in the economy would mean uncertainty about whether the Bank had ever hit the government's targets.

THE TREASURY'S RESERVE POWER

Section 19 of the Act sets out the reserve power for the Treasury to direct the Bank with respect to monetary policy if satisfied that such action is required by the public interest and by extreme economic circumstances. The reserve power is exercisable only after consultation with the Governor of the Bank and in accordance with the special precedures applying to an order under the section. Basically these are that the order must be laid before Parliament, and it lapses if not approved by resolution of both Houses within 28 days of being made (s. 19(3)–(5)). An order may include consequential modifications of the legislation (s. 19(2)) but cannot have effect for a period of more than three months (s. 19(6)). If the reserve power is exercised, the monetary policy objectives, set under statute for the Monetary Policy Committee, cease to have effect: s. 19(7).

These overarching powers are one reason that, as a matter of law, the legislation is not compatible with the criteria for independence in the Maastricht Treaty. However, the reserve power will be rarely exercisable. Extreme economic circumstances were said, by the minister representing the government in standing committee, to include war or a major catastrophe which affected the nation and had an impact on economic circumstances, or a major catastrophe which affected another economy closely related to the British economy. The minister went on to say that there had not been extreme economic circumstances, within the terms of the Act, in the previous 25 years: neither the Gulf War nor the cessation of British membership of the European exchange rate mechanism in 1992 qualified (Hansard, HC, Standing Committee D, 2 December 1997, cols 256, 261–2).

MONETARY POLICY COMMITTEE

The Bank exercises its operational independence through the Monetary Policy Committee. The Committee has responsibility within the Bank for formulating monetary policy by deciding on short-term interest rates. The Chancellor announced the establishment of the Committee in his 6 May 1997 statement: it has been operating on a non-statutory basis prior to the legislation. Section 13 constitutes the Committee, which comprises the Governor, the two Deputy Governors and six other members, two of whom are the Bank officials responsible for monetary policy analysis and monetary policy operations respectively. These two are appointed by the Governor, after consultation with the Chancellor. The Chancellor appoints the remaining four members of the Committee. Before appointing these persons, the Chancellor must be satisfied that they have knowledge or experience which is likely to be relevant to the Committee's functions. The appointment of these outsiders ensures that a broader range of opinion and expertise determines monetary policy than if the decisions were left within the Bank alone. The recommendation of the House of Commons Treasury Committee, that the appointments be subject to confirmation by it (*Accountability of the Bank of England*, op. cit., para. 47), was rejected by the government pending consideration of confirmatory hearings for senior government appointments in general.

Schedule 3 sets out details relating to membership and operations of the Monetary Policy Committee. Notably appointments are to last three years, except initially when some appointments may be for a shorter period so that the appointments do not all expire at the same time (para. 1). Members may be removed only if they are absent for more than three months without leave, have become bankrupt or are insolvent, or are otherwise unable or unfit to discharge their functions (para. 9). Appointments to similar positions in other central banks are longer, so as to reduce any pressure on persons to toe a political line. For example, in the proposed European Central Bank, there will be eight-year terms of appointment for the president, vice-president and other members of the executive board, coupled with the protection that they can be removed only for cause found by the European Court of Justice. Certainly the three-year terms are on the low side, but the procedures for appointment to and operation of the Committee are relatively transparent, so that any outside influence will readily be detected. Moreover, it is not certain at this stage in the life of the Committee whether membership for any longer period will be sufficiently attractive to suitable candidates.

The Committee must meet at least once a month (para. 10) and decisions are taken by a majority vote (para. 11). A Treasury representative may attend and speak at any meeting of the Committee (para. 13), an efficient method of conveying the government's latest views on the economy.

Section 16 obliges the sub-committee of the court of directors of the Bank, constituted under s. 3 of the Act, to keep under review the procedures followed by the Monetary Policy Committee. In particular they must determine whether the Committee has collected the regional, sectoral and other information necessary for the purposes of its monetary policy functions. There is no doubt that in making monetary policy, central banks need an extensive network of information gathering. Information must not only come from the banking sector, but from companies and elsewhere. The Bank's agents around the country collect such information.

TRANSPARENCY IN DECISION-MAKING

The Bank must publish, as soon as practicable after each meeting of the Monetary Policy Committee, a statement as to what action was decided on (s. 14(1)). The exception is if the decision was to meet the monetary policy objectives through interventions in financial markets, and immediate publication would impede or frustrate such intervention. Nonetheless, as soon as practicable after the Committee has decided that publication would no longer have that market-sensitive quality, the Bank must publish details of its decision on such intervention (s. 14(4)).

As well as publication of decisions, the Act also provides for publication of minutes of meetings of the Monetary Policy Committee, no more than six weeks later, with members' voting preferences indicated (s. 15(i)). The delay of up to six weeks is to prevent financial markets pre-empting the Committee's decisions by using the minutes of one meeting to draw conclusions about what will be decided at the next. Again there is an exception in the case of market-sensitive information about intervention in financial markets, although in line with s. 14 this information must be published within six weeks of any statement of the relevant decision under that section. The policy behind the section is greater accountability: observers and commentators will be able to see the reasoning behind particular decisions on monetary policy and how each member voted.

INFORMATION AND REPORTS

Section 17 enables the Bank to obtain information about the relevant financial affairs of an undertaking needed for the exercise of its monetary policy functions. The provisions mirror in large part the powers in s. 82 of the Banking Act 1987, relevant in the context of financial regulation. The information may be required in a particular form or manner, at particular times, and in relation to particular periods. The Treasury may by order specify which financial affairs of an undertaking are relevant for the purposes of the section. The undertakings from which the information may be sought are listed in s. 17: banks; building societies; money market managers; deposit-taking institutions such as penny savings banks and friendly societies; residential land mortgage institutions; financial institutions with a bank as a subsidiary and other subsidiaries which are either exclusively or mainly banks or financial institutions and institutions which have issued (or their agents which have arranged or managed the issue of) specified debt securities. The list is subject to amendment by order. Orders under the section can only be made after wider consultation.

The government has said it will take into account the cost to institutions of requiring the information, as required under the current code of practice for Bank of

England statistics. The specific information that will be collected is likely to include: the financial assets and liabilities of an undertaking; off-balance-sheet financial assets, liabilities and commitments, such as guarantees; transactions in income and expenditure accounts and capital expenditure; interest rates and other fees and commissions charged for the provision of financial services; agency business on behalf of customers; assets and liabilities, financial transactions and changes to ownership associated with direct investment; and insurance and redemptions of relevant debt securities (Hansard HC, Standing Committee D, 2 December 1997, col. 237). The information that will be specified in the order will be generalised information about specific financial transactions of the institutions themselves (ibid).

The Bank must publish quarterly reports on its conduct of monetary policy — reviewing its decisions, assessing inflation over the period, and indicating its expected approach to meeting its monetary policy objectives (s. 11(1)-(3)). The reports must have the approval of the Monetary Policy Committee (s. 18(5)).

CASH RATIO DEPOSITS

Until the Act, the settlement banks maintained voluntary cash deposits at the Bank of England. The Bank acts as banker and the deposits are used to settle payments between the banks on clearing. Because the deposits have been interest free, the Bank has made a profit by investing them, and has used the profit to fund itself. To improve transparency and accountability, s. 6 and sch. 2 puts this system of cash deposits on a statutory basis. Paragraph 1 of sch. 2 applies the system to: all institutions authorised under the Banking Act 1987; to institutions authorised elsewhere in the European Economic Area with deposit-taking branches in the UK; and to building societies. The Treasury can amend this list by order. All banks are now included in the new scheme, even those without accounts at the Bank of England. The reasoning is that they base their liquidity management on their holdings of liquid assets and credit facilities with the settlement banks, which in turn depend on the liquidity provided by the Bank. Building societies are not included in the present voluntary scheme, but the Act includes them because of the important role they play in the economy and the benefit they also receive from the liquidity which the Bank provides. Schedule 2 goes on to provide for how the level of deposit for each eligible institution is to be calculated. This is to be on the basis of eligible liabilities, which the Treasury can define by order. The Treasury can also specify by order value bands of eligible liablities and the ratios applicable to the institutions. The amount which each institution must deposit is then the amount produced by multiplying the appropriate ratio by its average eligible liabilities which fall within the value band to which the ratio relates. Levels are set for six monthly periods and set out for institutions in call notices.

If a bank does not have on deposit with the Bank, in a specially designated account, the amount so calculated, it must make a payment in lieu of deposit. This is calculated at a penal rate of interest — for the time being LIBID (the London interbank sterling deposit rate, calculated in the manner set out in the Schedule) plus four per cent on the average shortfall for the period.

Chapter 5
Transfer of Banking Supervision to the Financial Services Authority
Christopher Ryan

INTRODUCTION

Prior to the Bank of England Act 1998 the Bank's core purposes and strategy included monetary stability, monetary analysis, monetary operations, banking activities, financial stability, supervision and surveillance. Part III of the 1998 Act transfers responsibility for banking supervision and surveillance from the Bank to the Financial Services Authority (FSA). The FSA has now acquired the powers, previously exercised by the Bank, to supervise banks, listed money market institutions (as defined in the Financial Services Act 1986, s. 43) and related clearing houses (as defined in the Companies Act 1989, s. 171).

History of banking supervision

The Banking Act 1987 complements the Financial Services Act 1986 and the Building Societies Act 1986. The primary narrow concern of the Banking Act is the supervision of banks in the interests of depositors. The first statutory framework for the authorisation and supervision of deposit-taking business under the aegis of the Bank of England was set out in the Banking Act 1979. The effectiveness of the original framework was called into question by the prodigous growth in the banking sector and the need to rescue Johnson Matthey Bankers in October 1984. The 1979 Act provided a two-tier system of supervision and regulation based on whether an institution or body was classified as a recognised bank or a licensed deposit-taker. Johnson Matthey Bankers as a recognised bank was subject to less stringent statutory controls than those imposed on licensed deposit-takers.

The report of a Committee on the System of Banking Supervision chaired by the Governor of the Bank (Cmnd 9550, 1985) and a government White Paper, *Banking Supervision* (Cmnd 9695, 1985), led ultimately to the current 1987 banking legislation. The 1987 Act introduced a new Board of Banking Supervision to assist with advice on the Bank's supervisory duties; subjected all authorised institutions to the same regime for authorisation, supervision and regulation; required authorised institutions to report large exposures to the Bank; increased cooperation between supervisors and auditors of authorised institutions; and gave the Bank enhanced powers to gather information and to disclose information.

The 1987 Act provided for detailed supervision by the Bank and meant that deposit-takers had to satisfy the Bank that they were fit and proper and financially adequate before they could commence operating. The Act regulated advertising and provided depositors with protection, if a bank went into insolvency, through a Deposit Protection Fund. In short, the Bank's supervisory functions were extended without altering the traditional flexibility with which they had been applied.

Causes of change

Several developments have led to the transfer of these supervisory functions to the FSA. First, despite the Banking Act 1987 and the Financial Services Act 1986, the City continued to be rocked by financial scandals such as Maxwell, BCCI and Baring Brothers. In relation to BCCI, in particular, the Bank's supervision was found wanting by an independent report by the Board of Banking Supervision. Secondly there had been considerable intervention from Europe that required change: the Second Banking Coordination Directive, the Investment Services Directive, and the Capital Adequacy Directive. Thirdly there had been a shift of responsibility for regulating the financial services industry from the DTI to the Treasury in June 1992 with the aim of giving a single department of State control over the regulation of both securities and banking business. Fourthly, increasing internationalisation and conglomeration of the industry have necessitated a new initiative in relation to authorisation, regulation, surveillance and supervision of banking and financial services.

CHANGES

Part III of the Bank of England Act 1998 makes some consequential changes to the Banking Act 1987, in particular to provide for funding of banking supervision and for the transfer of relevant Bank staff to the FSA. The FSA, from 1 June 1998, will exercise the intervention powers in relation to banks governed by the Banking Act 1987. The 1998 Act does not change any of the relevant statutory provisions (Banking Act 1987 or Financial Services Act 1986) but the FSA will now adopt a common policy and approach to the task of investigating and dealing with illegal deposit-taking (before this Act, carried out by the Bank) and unauthorised investment business which it has itself carried out since 1988. In order to minimise disruption and maximise operational effectiveness, the FSA aims to maintain broad continuity of individual firms' and banks' relationship with regulatory and supervisory staff. One of the keys to the successful transfer of functions is the Memorandum of Understanding between the Treasury, the FSA and the Bank (see appendix 5 below).

This document explains how the three authorities will work together towards the common objective of financial stability and describes the responsibilities to be undertaken by each.

The division of responsibilities is based on:

(a) transparent accountability for non-duplicated functions and
(b) cooperative information exchange.

The FSA, as a consequence of this Part of the Act, will be responsible for:

(a) the authorisation and prudential supervision of banks, and investment firms;
(b) the supervision of financial markets and of clearing and settlement systems.

TRANSFER OF BANK FUNCTIONS

 Section 21 transfers from the Bank to the FSA the Bank's former banking supervision functions under the Banking Act, and banking supervisory functions under s. 101(4) of the Building Societies Act 1986, the Banking Coordination (Second Council Directive) Regulations 1992 and similar functions relating to the listing of money market institutions and of persons providing settlement arrangements. These banking aspects involve (a) regulating the acceptance of deposits in the course of a deposit-taking business, (b) the Deposit Protection Scheme, (c) banking names and descriptions, (d) overseas institutions with representative offices, and (e) the gathering and disclosure of information.

The Second Banking Coordination Directive was issued on 15 December 1989 and is one of several aimed at facilitating the establishment of the single internal market. It aimed to coordinate the law, regulations and administrative provisions relating to the taking up and pursuit of the business of credit institutions. Its aim is harmonisation and especially the mutual recognition of authorisation and prudential supervision systems. The intention was to facilitate the recognition of a single licence throughout the Community and of home member State prudential supervision in relation to certain listed activities in the fields of banking and financial services. Member States are required to allow listed credit activities to be carried on within their territorial boundaries by any credit institution authorised and supervised by the recognised competent authority in another member State. This Directive's requirements became part of our law by the Banking Coordination (Second Council Directive) Regulations 1992.

CONTINUITY, TRANSFER OF STAFF AND PROPERTY

Section 22 brings into effect sch. 4 to the Act, which specifies in detail provisions:

(a) to maintain the continuity of supervision and regulation during the process of transferring functions from the Bank to the FSA;

(b)   to provide for the transfer of staff from the Bank to the FSA;

(c)   to provide for the transfer of some of the Bank's property, rights and liabilities to the FSA.

The transfer of functions under this Act shall not affect the validity of anything done prior to the transfer day (i.e., 1 June 1998, the day this Act comes into force) by the Bank in performing the functions which are now transferred to the FSA.

Anything commenced by the Bank prior to the transfer day can be continued by the FSA if it relates to any of the functions transferred to it. Any banking requirement complied with prior to the transfer day will be treated as having been complied with, after that day and so on (sch. 4, para. 1).

Schedule 4 treats the transfer of functions as though it was a transfer of all or part of an undertaking in terms of the Transfer of Undertakings (Protection of Employment) Regulations 1981 (SI 1981/1794), which implements Directive 77/187/EEC and which was construed by the House of Lords as giving full effect to it in *Litster* v *Forth Dry Dock and Engineering Co. Ltd* [1990] 1 AC 546. This means that employees are protected by recognising the continuation of the enterprise but providing them with rights to payment for redundancy or unfair dismissal if they are not kept on. This is the same whether there is a transfer of an undertaking or change of controlling shareholdings (Employment Rights Act 1996, s. 218, Transfer of Undertakings (Protection of Employment) Regulations 1981 (SI 1981/1794) and the Collective Redundancies and Transfer of Undertakings (Protection of Employment) (Amendment) Regulations 1995 (SI 1995/2587)) or as here the transfer of Bank functions to the FSA (Bank of England Act 1998, sch. 4, para. 2).

In so far as the necessary transfer of Bank property, rights and liabilities is concerned, sch. 4 requires the Bank to make a scheme to transfer whatever appears appropriate in consequence of the transfer of functions. This scheme must have the consent of the FSA before it is submitted to the Treasury for their formal approval. The Treasury also may, after consulting both the Bank and FSA, make such a transfer scheme if the Bank does not produce a scheme within the Treasury's time frame or the scheme produced is not acceptable to the Treasury. The Bank is required to provide the Treasury with all the necessary information. The scheme may provide for the Bank to retain an interest in some of the property transferred and likewise for the FSA to have an interest in property retained by the Bank. It may also provide in connection with those transfers for the FSA to be treated as the same person in law as the Bank; that references to the Bank in any agreement, deed, bond or other instrument or document be treated as a reference to the FSA; that proceedings commenced by or against the Bank be continued by or against the FSA; and that both the Bank and the FSA cooperate in connection with the scheme (sch. 4, paras 3–6).

STATUS

The FSA in carrying out any of the transferred functions is not a Crown organ or body nor are its officers and employees Crown servants (s. 24).

This section recognises that the FSA is a registered, private, limited liability company, limited by guarantee.

LIABILITY

Amendments made by the Bank of England Act 1998, s. 25 and sch. 5, para. 2(c), extend to the FSA and its personnel the same immunity from suit in relation to the transferred functions as was given to the Bank. The FSA already has similar immunity in relation to its investment business function under s. 187(3) of the Financial Services Act 1986.

The immunity is confined to liability in damages (usually in the form of an action for negligence), but it does not mean that the Bank (or the FSA) is above the law. There is no immunity provided for acts or omissions shown to be in bad faith. There is as yet no binding authority on the meaning of bad faith in this context, but it is likely to include knowingly acting contrary to the *Wednesbury* principle, i.e., acting unreasonably or perversely (*Associated Provincial Picture Houses Ltd* v *Wednesbury Corporation* [1948] 1 KB 223). No exemption is given from proceedings for judicial review, e.g., for failure to comply with the provisions of the Act, any consequential delegated legislation or the rules of natural justice such as giving notice, an unbiased hearing, reasons for decisions etc. or for unreasonable or perverse decisions. Judicial review proceedings will not produce damages but can be an avenue for redress (*R* v *Panel on Take-overs and Mergers, ex parte Datafin plc* [1987] QB 815). The reason for granting immunity to supervisors, such as the Bank and the Financial Services Authority, is so that their governing bodies and staff are not inhibited about taking any necessary action, in the interests of the banking system, depositors and the financial services industry respectively, through fear of legal proceedings for damages.

POWER TO CHARGE FEES

The FSA is empowered to charge application fees and periodic fees in connection with its new role as a banking supervisor. Schedule 6, para. 1, empowers the FSA to make regulations specifying its banking application fees, periodic supervision fees and fees necessary for incidental purposes.

The regulations must specify the time when fees are to be paid but the FSA is given a wide degree of flexibility and discretion in relation to the use of scales of fees, abatement of fees and the making of different provision for different cases (para. 1(4)).

The FSA is required to consult those likely to be affected and to invite and consider their representations about the proposed fees before making the regulations, although that procedure may be circumvented if the FSA considers the delay involved would prejudice the interests of depositors (para. 2.).

The regulations are to be made by written instrument stating that they are made in compliance with sch. 6 to the Act and they are to be printed and made available to the public (paras 3 and 4). No application fee for authorisation will be payable if the fees regulations were not available at the time the fee was payable (para. 4(2)).

A printed copy of the fees regulations endorsed by a certificate signed by an officer of the FSA verifying the copy and the date they were made available to the public will be prima facie or sufficient evidence of the facts stated in the certificate. Anyone wishing to cite the fees regulations in any legal proceedings may require the FSA to provide a copy endorsed with such a certificate (para. 5).

Section 27 enables the collection of information by the FSA to be carried out by an agent. This is intended to enable the Bank to continue to collect statistical information and supply it to the FSA, until the staffing in that area is reorganised in due course.

BOARD OF BANKING SUPERVISION

Section 28 reiterates that the Board of Banking Supervision continues under that name but that it now will consist of two ex officio members from FSA (whereas formerly there were three members from the Bank) and six independent members with no executive responsibility in the FSA, jointly appointed by the Chancellor of the Exchequer and the Chairman of FSA. The Chairman of this Board will now be an independent member of the Board chosen by the independent members (whereas previously it was chaired by the Governor of the Bank).

The discussion prior to the implementation of the Banking Act 1987 had concluded, at that time, that the Bank rather than some separate body should continue to be the supervisor of banks. That Act, however, did establish a new Board of Banking Supervision which brought in independent commercial banking experience and expertise to assist the Bank in this function. The current legislation moves the supervisory function to the FSA with a corresponding change in its composition to reflect that change and to create an independent chairmanship, but otherwise the Banking Act 1987, s. 2, which established the original Board, is unaffected.

Consequently the Chancellor of the Exchequer still must be informed in writing by the ex officio members of the Board if the advice of the independent members is not followed and the independent members may inform the Chancellor of their reasons for their advice. The Board is required to give an annual report which now is to be incorporated into the FSA Annual Report. The same immunity from suit for damages as is given to the FSA, its directors and officers is extended to the Board's members.

Schedule 1 to the Banking Act 1987, suitably amended to reflect FSA responsibility, continues to apply. It contains detailed provisions in respect of terms of appointment, removal from office, increasing or decreasing the size of membership, Board procedure and the remuneration of independent members.

DEPOSIT PROTECTION BOARD

The Banking Act 1987, s. 51, continued the scheme established by the 1979 Act of a Deposit Protection Board and a Deposit Protection Fund to try to ensure that if an authorised institution (a bank) became insolvent then, up to the limit defined in ss. 59–60 of that Act (which is currently £20,000 or the sterling equivalent of 22,222 ecus), a sum equivalent to nine-tenths of the amount of any protected deposit would be paid out of the Fund. All UK and European authorised and participating institutions are liable to contribute to this fund. They are known as 'contributory institutions'. The system provides for initial, further or special contributions. The Board is required to levy an initial contribution on contributory institutions and the 1987 Act specifies how the Board shall calculate such contributions and fixes the minimum initial contribution at £10,000 (Banking Act 1987, s. 56(1)). If the Fund contains less than £3 million at the end of the financial year then the Board may, with Treasury approval, levy further contributions which, when combined with the initial contribution must not, in the case of any one institution exceed £300,000 (Banking Act 1987, s. 56(2)), to bring the fund up to a figure between £5 million and £6 million. There is a further power in the Board, with Treasury approval, to levy special contributions to meet the fund's commitments. Calculations, by reference to a deposit base, are provided to limit the total contributions that any one institution can be required to pay. According to s. 64 of the 1987 Act and the Deposit Protection Board (Increase of Borrowing Limits) Order 1991 (SI 1991/1684) the Board has power to borrow up to £125 million if it appears desirable, and under s. 65 the Board has power to require information and documents from institutions in order to determine their contributions.

If a UK or participating institution goes into insolvency the Board must as soon as practicable and in any event within three months of the insolvency, pay from the Fund to depositors with protected deposits in that institution, nine-tenths of their protected deposit subject to the maximum limit outlined above. For further details see ss. 58–60 of the Banking Act 1987.

Section 29 of the Bank of England Act 1998 simply amends the composition of the ex officio membership of the Deposit Protection Board as set out in sch. 4 to the Banking Act 1987. It makes the FSA Chairman the Chairman of the Board and requires him to nominate another FSA officer to Board membership. The section also gives Board membership to the Deputy Governor of the Bank responsible for financial stability.

These three members are empowered to appoint alternates to stand in for them and perform their duties in their absence as members of the Board. The two FSA members must choose an alternate from within the FSA and the Bank representative must appoint as an alternate someone from within the Bank.

Section 29 also requires the FSA Chairman to appoint three ordinary Board members chosen from the ranks of the directors, controllers or managers of contributory institutions and an unspecified number of his own FSA officers or employees. The terms 'director', 'controller' and 'manager' are extensively defined in s. 105 of the Banking Act 1987.

Chapter 6
Debt Management and Gilts Management
Ross Cranston, MP

DEBT MANAGEMENT

In his letter to the Governor of the Bank of England on 6 May 1997 the new Chancellor of the Exchequer announced the government's decision that the Bank's role as the government's agent for debt management, the sale of gilts, oversight of the gilts market and cash management would be transferred to the Treasury. A consultation document was published on 29 July, and Treasury officials held extensive discussions with market participants, representative bodies and the Bank of England. On 22 December the new arrangements were announced. From 1 April 1998 the United Kingdom Debt Management Office will take day-to-day operational decisions over the management of the government's debt. Debt management will continue to be within a published annual borrowing remit set by Treasury ministers.

As well as the management of government debt, the new Debt Management Office under the Treasury will take over Exchequer cash management sometime after October 1998. However, a major innovation will be required in the government's operations in the sterling money markets if the Exchequer's cash position is to be managed separately from the Bank of England's monetary policy operations. The new Office must smooth the seasonal changes in the Exchequer's cash flows through changing the size and maturity of the Treasury bill tender programme. The Office will then take the daily forecast of the Exchequer's cash position and seek to trade in the sterling monetary markets each day so as to eliminate any effect on the government's accounts at the Bank of England, which will continue to provide the central government's banking facilities. The Office will not speculate over the outcome of the Bank's Monetary Policy Committee meetings, but will aim to smooth the daily changes in cash flow. Ultimately the Bank will freeze the current 'ways and means' overdraft facility provided to the Exchequer and the balance will be repaid. Under Article 104 of the EC Treaty, the ways and means facility must be abandoned.

Section 32 of the Bank of England Act 1998 is a technical amendment to the Financial Services Act 1986, which will facilitate these new arrangements for management of government debt. Under s. 43 of the 1986 Act those involved in the wholesale money markets must be on a list which has been maintained by the Bank of England, though responsibility for it will be transferred to the Financial Services Authority by s. 21 of the 1998 Act. Schedule 5 to the 1986 Act details transactions which institutions on that list may undertake without being authorised under that Act. As a result of the amendments to sch. 5 by s. 32 of the 1998 Act, listed institutions will be able to enter into these transactions with the Treasury.

GILTS MANAGEMENT

Transfer of gilts from the National Savings Stock Register

The Bank of England, through its Central Gilts Office, provides a book entry system whereby deals in gilts (government securities) can be settled. Ultimately this system may be merged with CREST, which provides the settlement system for equity and debt securities used by companies.

The aim of s. 33 of the Bank of England Act 1998 is to provide for the transfer of the National Savings Stock Register to the Bank of England, which is already the main registrar for gilt-edged stock. Until now, individual savers could buy and sell gilts at the Post Office using the register kept by National Savings. However, the register has been running at a loss. The transfer will allow economies of scale, in that there will be only one register for gilts.

The Treasury are empowered by s. 33 of the 1998 Act to end the registration of gilts in the National Savings Stock Register and transfer such registration from the Director of Savings to the Bank of England. Provision is made for the transfer of the entries of holders' names from the National Savings Stock Register to the books of the Bank and for the transfer of the Director of Savings' rights and liabilities in relation to the registration of gilts to the Bank. The Treasury may by statutory instrument make the necessary consequential and incidental orders to facilitate this transfer of functions.

Brokerage services for gilts registration

Currently the Director of Savings provides a brokerage service with fixed fees to small-scale investors wishing to buy and sell gilts which are registered in the National Savings Stock Register. When the registration of gilts is transferred from the Department of National Savings to the Bank, the Treasury will also transfer the residual brokerage function from National Savings to the Bank and s. 34 of the 1998 Act provides for regulations to be made specifying the commission and fees chargeable by the Bank for that service. The regulations may also place limits on the amount that any person may buy or sell on any day. When Standing Committee D of the House of Commons was considering this provision, the Paymaster General stated that the current daily limit for purchase is £25,000 per person, per stock and that there is no current limit on the amount of stock that can be sold by any one person on any day. He also stated that there are no plans to alter those limits.

Chapter 7
Miscellaneous Provisions
Christopher Ryan

DESIGNATED AGENCY

The Financial Services Authority remains the designated agency under the Financial Services Act 1986 charged with the responsiblity for regulation and supervision of the financial services industry. The Bank of England Act 1998 enlarges the FSA's functions to include banking supervision. In consequence, the governance of the authority has been changed. Now, the governing body (consisting of the Chairman and other members) must be persons appointed, and liable to removal from office, by the Treasury. Originally this appointing function was performed by the Secretary of State and the Governor of the Bank acting jointly. Section 31 removes the Governor of the Bank from this function and all of the Secretary of State's functions were transferred to the Treasury by the Transfer of Functions (Financial Services) Order 1992 (SI 1992/1315). It is the Treasury that will oversee and approve the composition of the FSA board.

PAPERLESS TRADING IN BEARER SECURITIES

Section 35 of the 1998 Act is completely separate from the main thrust of the Act. It in no way relates to transfer of functions between the Bank and the Financial Services Authority. This Act simply provided a convenient vehicle to bring into line the law concerning the modes of transfer available for bearer securities with those for registered securities. Now provision may be made to permit bearer securities to be transferred without delivery (i.e., by a computer entry transfer), as is the case with registered securities.

The Companies Act 1989, s. 207, conferred power on the Secretary of State to make provision for a paperless system for recording title to and transfer of securities (i.e., shares, stock, debentures, debenture stock, loan stock, bonds, units of a collective investment scheme within the meaning of the Financial Services Act 1986 and other securities of any description).

The Uncertified Securities Regulations 1995 (SI 1995/3272) have been made under the power in the 1989 Act in connection with the introduction of CREST in July 1996. This is a system in which shares can be transferred by alterations in computer records which serve as evidence of title, so that share certificates are unnecessary.

The Bank of England Act 1998, s. 35, inserts a new subsection (10) in the Companies Act 1989, s. 207, providing that regulations under s. 207 may enable the transfer of bearer securities without delivery.

DISCLOSURE OF INFORMATION

Introduction to restrictions in banking environment

The laws restricting disclosure of information by the Bank which are contained in part V of the Banking Act 1987 are amended to apply to the Bank and the FSA to take account of their new functions under the 1998 Act. Part V of the 1987 Act deals with the issue of confidentiality of information which is obtained under, or for the purposes of, the Act and relating to the business or other affairs of any person. It places restrictions or prohibitions on the disclosure of such information but relaxes the restrictions to encourage the exchange of information between supervisory authorities. Both the Financial Services Act 1986 (ss. 179 to 182) and the Building Societies Act 1986 (ss. 53 to 54) have similar provisions restricting disclosure of information and also create a number of exceptions.

General exemptions

There is a blanket restriction on disclosure by persons who receive information under or for purposes of the Banking Act 1987 or by any person who received it from them unless consent has been obtained from the person to whom the information relates and also from the person from whom the information was obtained.

Without specific consent, disclosure may be made if the information has already been made public or the information is in such an abbreviated form that the business or affairs of any particular person cannot be identified by the disclosure.

The Bank and other supervisory authorities (which now includes the FSA) are not precluded from disclosing information for facilitating the discharge of their functions. These now include the Bank's enhanced function as a monetary authority or supervisor of systems for the transfer of funds between credit institutions and their customers. Also included are the FSA regulatory functions under the Financial Services Act 1986, Banking Act 1987 and in relation to certain money markets under the Companies Act 1989, s. 171 (e.g., those settlement processes run by individuals who are on the list which has been maintained by the Bank of England with the approval of the Treasury, but for which responsibility is to be transferred to the FSA).

Part IV of sch. 5 to the 1998 Act makes the necessary amendments to the Banking Act 1987, Consumer Credit Act 1974, Insurance Companies Act 1982, Companies Act 1985, Companies (Northern Ireland) Order 1986, Building Societies Act 1986,

Financial Services Act 1986, Companies Act 1989, Courts and Legal Services Act 1990, Friendly Societies Act 1992, Pension Schemes Act 1993, Pension Schemes (Northern Ireland) Act 1993, Pensions Act 1995 and Pensions (Northern Ireland) Order 1995.

Disclosure restrictions in the 1998 Act

Schedule 7 to the 1998 Act restricts the disclosure of information relating to the financial affairs of any undertaking obtained for monetary policy or cash ratio deposit purposes.

The restriction on disclosure is identical to that in the Banking Act 1987, s. 82, and applies to the Bank, its officers and employees or any person obtaining the information directly or indirectly from the Bank. Both enactments make disclosure which is non-exempt a criminal offence punishable on conviction on indictment in the Crown Court by up to two years' imprisonment and an unlimited fine or both or on summary conviction in the magistrates' court by imprisonment not exceeding three months or a fine, currently not exceeding £5,000, or both.

Paragraph 2 of sch. 7 to the 1998 Act exempts the Bank from the restriction on disclosure so that it can perform its functions as a monetary authority or as a supervisor of systems for the transfer of funds between credit institutions and their customers, and so that it can call on eligible institutions to make cash ratio deposits.

Paragraphs 3 and 5 of sch. 7 specify three broad categories of exceptional circumstances in which the Bank may disclose confidential information:

(a)   To enable or assist the performance of functions specified in para. 3(1) by certain other regulatory, supervisory or investigative bodies, namely, the Treasury, company inspectors appointed by the Department of Trade and Industry (to investigate insider dealing or certain insurance or financial services matters), the FSA, the Office for National Statistics, the Friendly Societies Commission, the Building Societies Commission, and the Occupational Pensions Regulatory Author-ity. The Treasury may vary by statutory instrument (after consulting the Bank) the list of persons to whom assistance to perform their functions may be provided by Bank disclosure.

(b)   In order to institute any legal proceedings for payment in lieu of cash ratio deposits or for any criminal proceedings (whether under the 1998 Act or not).

(c)   In order to fulfil any European Community obligation.

Information supply offences

It is a criminal offence under the Bank of England Act 1998, s. 38, for any undertaking to fail, without reasonable excuse, to supply to the Bank acting in its monetary policy role under s. 17, or in any way in relation to calculating, maintaining and enforcing cash ratio deposits under para. 9 of sch. 2 to the Act, information requested about its financial affairs. For this purpose 'undertaking' is defined very broadly by the

Companies Act 1985, s. 259, to include partnerships and other commercial, unincorporated associations as well as companies. Section 17 applies to an undertaking if it has a place of business in the UK and is a bank, a European institution within the Banking Coordination (Second Council Directive) Regulations 1992 which has a public deposit accepting branch in this country, a building society, a financial holding company under art. 1 of Council Directive 92/30/EEC or a non credit monetary financial institution within annex A to Council Regulation (EC) No. 2223/96 or which is not a credit institution within the Banking Coordination (Second Council Directive) Regulations 1992 but grants credits secured on land for residential purposes, or has issued a relevant debt security or has acted as an agent in arranging or managing any such security.

Penalties

An offence under the Bank of England Act 1998, s. 38, is a summary offence triable in the magistrates' court and currently has a maximum fine on conviction of up to £2,500 (level 4 on the standard scale). Continued contravention is a further offence and subject to the same maximum fine. If, however, a person purports to supply the requested information but knows that it is in fact false or misleading in a material particular or recklessly provides such information then the offence is much more serious. It becomes an indictable offence triable in the Crown Court before a jury and on conviction the penalty imposable is imprisonment not exceeding two years, an unlimited fine or both. Alternatively it may be dealt with by summary proceeding where the penalty on conviction is imprisonment up to three months, a fine not exceeding £5,000 (currently the statutory maximum) or both.

Proof of blameworthiness or fault

In relation to the indictable offence the prosecution would usually have to prove beyond reasonable doubt that the person accused of this offence intentionally provided false or misleading information. This has been taken by the courts to mean proof that the accused had as his or her deliberate aim, object or goal the provision of false or misleading information, but in some instances the jury may be invited to infer, having considered all the evidence, that the accused foresaw that the information provided was virtually certain to be false or misleading and from that, that he or she must have intended it to be false or misleading (R v Maloney [1985] AC 905; R v Nedrick [1986] 1 WLR 1025).

The prosecution, however, do not necessarily have to overcome the difficult task of proving, subjectively, intention. This is because, as an alternative, the word 'reckless' is included in the wording of the offence and this will enable a conviction to be achieved if one of two sets of facts can be shown (beyond reasonable doubt). The first is that the accused took a conscious risk that the information was false or misleading (advertent recklessness: R v Cunningham [1957] 2 QB 396). The second is that the accused failed to consider the possibility of there being any risk that the information was false or misleading, in circumstances where, if any thought had been given, the risk would have been obvious to a reasonable person (i.e., 'failure to think about' or inadvertent recklessness: *Metropolitan Police Commissioner* v *Caldwell* [1982] AC 341). The latter method of proving recklessness on the part of an accused is controversial and the Court of Appeal has limited its application by excluding certain recklessness offences from its ambit. At its widest this section could catch the honest but unreasonable supply of false or misleading information required by the Bank for monetary policy or cash ratio deposit purposes.

Offences by bodies corporate and officers

The Bank of England Act 1998, s. 39, makes a provision which is usually made in statutes creating criminal offences regulating economic activity. It provides that the fact that a company, or other corporation, is guilty of an offence under the Act does not preclude prosecution of an individual director, manager, secretary or other such officer of the company who was responsible if the offence occurred with his or her consent or connivance or was attributable to his or her neglect. This means that if an individual has been responsible for a company committing an offence, both he and the company can be convicted as principal offenders in respect of the same act. In a provision like this 'manager' is a person who has the management of the whole affairs of the company, is in a position of real authority and has the power and responsibility to decide corporate policy and strategy (*R* v *Boal* [1992] QB 591).

DELEGATED LEGISLATIVE POWER

The making of amendments by order

In the Bank of England Act 1998 Parliament has legislated in broad terms for the transfer of functions to and from the Bank. Most of the transfers are to the Financial Services Authority. The Treasury are authorised to make orders (often referred to as regulations) to implement the detailed or technical aspects of the transfers. These orders must, by s. 40(1), be made by statutory instrument. The opportunity that delegated law-making provides for abuse in the hands of the executive requires that it be properly controlled. The wider the discretionary power given by the enabling Act the more difficult it is to control. If, however, the Treasury were to make instruments that went beyond the powers given by the Act then the statutory instrument in question can be challenged as *ultra vires* by proceedings for judicial review in the High Court.

Affirmative laying procedure

Section 40(2) specifies that certain orders must be laid before and approved by both Houses of Parliament before they come into effect. They include orders:

(a) specifying what information the Bank may obtain by way of its power under s. 17 to require information and reports from undertakings;

(b) specifying the undertakings or institutions to which requests under s. 17 may be made;

(c) defining eligible institutions for purposes of the liability base for cash ratio deposits;

(d) specifying value bands and applicable ratios for the calculation of depositable amounts;

(e) amending the table of institutions or authorities to which the Bank is able to disclose information.

The government must find time in the parliamentary timetable for an appropriate motion to be passed in each House. Unless the order is controversial any discussion in the Commons will take place in committee and, after a brief report by the committee, the regulations will be approved. There is no power to amend the proposed regulations. Because of the time involved this affirmative laying procedure is reserved for the most important statutory instruments. The use of it in this context indicates awareness or intuition in the Treasury that these are matters of importance or sensitivity where Parliament would expect to keep control in its own hands.

Negative laying procedure

Section 40(3) specifies that certain orders are to be made subject to annulment by a resolution of either House of Parliament. The orders in this category are those made by the Treasury in exercise of their power:

(a) to amend or revoke any statutory instrument as they think necessary in consequence of the transfer of supervisory functions of the Bank to the FSA;

(b) to define eligible liabilities for purposes of calculating cash ratio deposits;

(c) to amend or replace the benchmark rate of interest for call notices requiring eligible institutions to make a cash ratio deposit;

(d) to ensure continuity in the exercise of functions during the transfer from the Bank to the FSA;

(e) to impose conditions on or restrict the permissible disclosure by the Bank to any authority or institution to whom the Bank may disclose information.

Orders made by the Treasury under s. 33 of the Act in connection with the closure of the National Savings Stock Register to gilts and their transfer to the books of the Bank are subject to annulment by a resolution of the House of Commons only (s. 40(4)).

A statutory instrument made subject to this procedure will come into effect when it is made (i.e., signed by a minister), unless a later commencement date is specified in the instrument. Consequently the instrument could be law for some time prior to being annulled by a negative resolution. Annulment is unlikely because the government normally has a majority in the Commons to defeat such a motion.

Special laying procedure

Where the Treasury exercise their reserve powers in the public interest under s. 19 to issue orders to the Bank with respect to monetary policy, the statutory instrument must be laid before Parliament after it is made and must be approved by each House of Parliament within 28 days of its being made or else it ceases to have effect at the end of that period. If it is appropriately approved within that time limit then the life of the order is extended to a maximum period of three months from the date the order was made (not the date it was approved).

Compliance with laying procedures

Where there is a requirement that an instrument be laid before Parliament, the Statutory Instruments Act 1946, s. 4, states that the instrument shall be laid subject to the proviso that if it is essential for an instrument to come into effect immediately, it can be brought into effect before being laid but the Speaker and the Lord Chancellor must be informed of the reasons for doing so.

Failure to comply with the laying requirements may affect the validity of the instrument on the basis of a procedural irregularity. If the omission is challenged in the courts then the instrument's validity will depend on whether compliance with that requirement is considered to be directory or mandatory. Breach of the latter type might result in invalidity.

Scrutiny of orders

Virtually every statutory instrument laid before each House of Parliament is considered by the Parliamentary Joint Committee on Statutory Instruments, consisting of seven members from each House and a chairman drawn from the opposition benches in the Commons.

TRANSITIONAL MATTERS

Immunity

The Bank's supervisory functions and duties prior to the coming into effect of the Bank of England Act 1998 are contained in s. 1 of the Banking Act 1987, which also grants immunity from any legal action for damages to the Bank, its directors, staff and seconded personnel for anything done or omitted in the discharge or purported discharge of the functions of the Bank unless it is shown that the act or omission was in bad faith (s. 1(4)). A similar provision can be found in the Financial Services Act 1986, s. 187, in respect of the FSA, SROs and certain other bodies. This immunity for the Bank and its officers is confirmed by para. 1 of sch. 8 to the 1998 Act, for things done or omitted before the day on which the Act comes into force and thereafter in relation to things done on or after that date in connection with any proceedings arising from things done or omitted before that day.

Schedule 5, discussed in chapter 4 above, transfers this immunity in banking matters to the FSA on taking over the Bank's supervisory role.

Disclosure of information

After the Bank's banking supervision functions under the Banking Act 1987 have been transferred to the FSA, the Bank may still hold confidential information it obtained under the Act. Paragraph 2 of sch. 8 to the Bank of England Act 1998 provides continuing permission to the Bank to disclose such information under part V of the 1987 Act (except ss. 86 and 87) as it was before amendment by the 1998 Act. However, the Bank will not be able to disclose information in order to discharge functions under the 1987 Act itself or as a supervisor of money market and gilt market institutions. Instead it may pass the information on to the FSA for that Authority to discharge such functions. Similarly the Bank will not be able to pass information on to auditors of authorised institutions, but must leave that to the FSA. Accordingly the Bank's power to disclose such information to its professional advisers to enable it to carry out its functions under the 1987 Act is also withdrawn.

Pre-commencement consultation

The Bank of England Act 1998 requries varying degrees of consultation to take place in a number of instances prior to action being taken such as the making of an order by statutory instrument. The ambit of the required consultation varies between the narrow or purely 'administrative' consultation between the Treasury, the FSA, the Bank or some of their organs or officers and wider, 'public' consultation. Wider consultation is required in relation to the making of:

(a) An order in relation to cash ratio deposits (sch. 2, para. 10).

(b) An order specifying the financial information which the Bank may require from undertakings (s. 17(6)).

(c) An order relating to banking supervision fees (sch. 6, para. 2(1)). Consultation here is to embrace all those persons likely to be affected by the order.

Narrow, internal or 'administrative' type consultation is required in relation to the making of:

(a) An order for publication of additional information in relation to the content of the Bank's annual accounts (s. 7(8)).

(b) A scheme for the transfer of such of the Bank's property, rights or liabilities to the FSA as appear appropriate (sch. 4, para. 3(5)).

(c) An order whereby the Treasury exercise their reserve power to direct the Bank's monetary policy in extreme economic circumstances (s. 19).

(d)   An order restricting disclosure by the Bank of information it has obtained under s. 17 (for monetary policy purposes) or sch. 2, para. 9 (to calculate cash ratio deposits) (sch. 7, para. 3(4)).

According to sch. 8, para. 6, any such consultation of either type which takes place before the 1998 Act comes into force will be deemed to satisfy the consultation requirement under the Act.

Membership of the Deposit Protection Board

The terms of a person's appointment as an ordinary member of the Deposit Protection Board prior to the commencement of the 1998 Act will not be affected by the coming into force of the Act: the FSA and its Chairman are substituted for the Bank and its Governor in relation to the appointments of such Board members (sch. 8, para. 7).

REPEALS

Schedule 9 to the Bank of England Act 1998 repeals various parts of sections in the Bank of England Act 1946, the Financial Services Act 1986, the Banking Act 1987 and the Courts and Legal Services Act 1990 and revokes parts of regulations in the Banking Coordination (Second Council Directive) Regulations 1992 and the Investment Services Regulations 1995, primarily to remove references to the Bank of England.

EXTENT AND COMMENCEMENT

The Bank of England Act 1998 extends to England and Wales, Scotland and Northern Ireland (s. 44) and it comes into force on a date to be appointed by the Treasury (s. 45) in a statutory instrument (s. 40). Section 45 provides for only one commencement date for the whole Act and does not make the usual allowance for different provisions to be brought into force on different days. On 24 April 1998, a commencement order was made appointing 1 June 1998 as the day for the coming into force of the Act.

Appendix 1
Bank of England Act 1998

CHAPTER 11
ARRANGEMENT OF SECTIONS

PART I
CONSTITUTION, REGULATION AND FINANCIAL ARRANGEMENTS

Constitution and Regulation

PART II
MONETARY POLICY

Role of the Bank

Monetary Policy Committee of the Bank

General

Final provisions

SCHEDULES:

BANK OF ENGLAND ACT 1998
CHAPTER 11

An Act to make provision about the constitution, regulation, financial arrangements and functions of the Bank of England, including provision for the transfer of supervisory functions; to amend the Banking Act 1987 in relation to the provision and disclosure of information; to make provision relating to appointments to the governing body of a designated agency under the Financial Services Act 1986; to amend Schedule 5 to that Act; to make provision relating to the registration of Government stocks and bonds; to make provision about the application of section 207 of the Companies Act 1989 to bearer securities; and for connected purposes.

[23 April 1998]

BE IT ENACTED by the Queen's most Excellent Majesty, by and with the advice and consent of the Lords Spiritual and Temporal, and Commons, in this present Parliament assembled, and by the authority of the same, as follows:—

PART I
CONSTITUTION, REGULATION AND FINANCIAL ARRANGEMENTS

Constitution and regulation

1. Court of directors

(1) There shall continue to be a court of directors of the Bank.

(2) The court shall consist of a Governor, 2 Deputy Governors and 16 directors of the Bank, all of whom shall be appointed by Her Majesty.

(3) On the day on which this Act comes into force, all persons who are, immediately before that day, holding office as director of the Bank shall vacate their office.

(4) Schedule 1 shall have effect with respect to the court.

2. Functions of court of directors

(1) The court of directors of the Bank shall manage the Bank's affairs, other than the formulation of monetary policy.

(2)   In particular, the court's functions under subsection (1) shall include determining the Bank's objectives (including objectives for its financial management) and strategy.

(3)   In determining the Bank's objectives and strategy, the court's aim shall be to ensure the effective discharge of the Bank's functions.

(4)   Subject to that, in determining objectives for the financial management of the Bank, the court's aim shall be to ensure the most efficient use of the Bank's resources.

3.   Functions to be carried out by non-executive members

(1)   The functions mentioned in subsection (2) shall stand delegated to a sub-committee of the court of directors of the Bank consisting of the directors of the Bank.

(2)   The functions referred to are—

(a)   keeping under review the Bank's performance in relation to the objectives and strategy for the time being determined by the court of directors of the Bank,

(b)   monitoring the extent to which the objectives set by the court of directors of the Bank in relation to the Bank's financial management have been met,

(c)   keeping under review the internal financial controls of the Bank with a view to securing the proper conduct of its financial affairs, and

(d)   determining how the functions under paragraph 14 of Schedule 1 (remuneration and pensions etc. of executive members of the court) should be exercised.

(3)   At a meeting of the sub-committee the quorum shall be 7.

(4)   The Chancellor of the Exchequer may designate one of the directors to chair the sub-committee.

(5)   If a member of the sub-committee has any direct or indirect interest in any dealing or business with the Bank which falls to be considered by the sub-committee—

(a)   he shall disclose his interest to the sub-committee when it considers the dealing or business, and

(b)   he shall have no vote in proceedings of the sub-committee in relation to any question arising from its consideration of the dealing or business, unless the sub-committee has resolved that the interest does not give rise to a conflict of interest.

(6)   In any proceedings of the sub-committee, a member shall have no vote in relation to any question arising which touches or concerns him but shall withdraw and be absent during the debate of any matter in which he is concerned.

(7)   Subject to subsections (3) to (6), the sub-committee shall determine its own procedure.

(8)   The sub-committee may delegate any of its functions to two or more of its members.

4.   Annual report by the Bank

(1)   As soon as practicable after the end of each of its financial years, the Bank shall make to the Chancellor of the Exchequer a report on its activities in that year.

(2)   A report under this section shall, in particular, contain—

(a) a report by the directors of the Bank on the matters for which the sub-committee constituted by section 3 is responsible, and

(b) a copy of the statement for the year prepared under section 7(2) and the report of the Bank's auditors on it.

(3) The report mentioned in subsection (2)(a) shall, in particular, include a review of the Bank's performance in relation to its objectives and strategy, as determined by the court of directors of the Bank, in the financial year to which the report under this section relates.

(4) A report under this section shall also contain—

(a) a statement of the rate or rates at which directors of the Bank have been remunerated in the financial year to which the report relates, and

(b) a statement of the Bank's objectives and strategy, as determined by the court of directors of the Bank, for the financial year in which the report is made.

(5) The Bank shall publish every report under this section in such manner as it thinks appropriate.

(6) The Chancellor of the Exchequer shall lay copies of every report under this section before Parliament.

5. Custody and use of the seal

(1) The court of directors of the Bank shall have custody of the Bank's seal.

(2) The seal shall only be affixed to an instrument if the affixation has been authorised by the court or by a sub-committee of the court acting in exercise of delegated authority.

(3) The affixing of the seal shall be attested by the signature of—

(a) two members of the court,

(b) one member of the court and the secretary to the court, or

(c) two other officers of the Bank authorised by the court for the purpose.

Financial arrangements

6. Cash ratio deposits

Schedule 2 (which makes provision about the maintenance of cash deposits with the Bank by certain financial institutions) shall have effect.

7. Accounts

(1) The Bank shall keep proper accounts and records in relation to the accounts.

(2) The Bank shall prepare for each of its financial years a statement of accounts consisting of—

(a) a balance sheet as at the last day of the year, and

(b) a profit and loss account.

(3) In preparing accounts under subsection (2), the Bank shall be subject to requirements corresponding to the relevant Companies Act requirements, except insofar as the accounts relate to the Issue Department.

(4) The Bank may disregard a requirement to which it is subject under subsection (3) to the extent that it considers it appropriate to do so having regard to its functions.

(5)   The Bank shall appoint an auditor or auditors to audit its accounts, including any statement under subsection (2).

(6)   As soon as practicable after receiving the report of its auditors on a statement prepared under subsection (2), the Bank shall send a copy of—

(a)   the report, and

(b)   the statement,

to the Chancellor of the Exchequer.

(7)   The Treasury may by notice in writing to the Bank require it to publish in such manner as it thinks fit such additional information relating to its accounts as the Treasury may specify in the notice, including information which the Bank has excluded under subsection (4) from a statement under subsection (2).

(8)   The Treasury shall consult the Bank before giving a notice under subsection (7).

(9)   In subsection (3), the reference to the relevant Companies Act requirements is to the requirements to which the directors of a company which is a banking company for the purposes of the Companies Act 1985 are for the time being subject under that Act (except section 232) in relation to the preparation of accounts under section 226(1) of that Act.

8.   Payments in lieu of dividends

(1)   In section 1 of the Bank of England Act 1946, in subsection (4), (amount payable to Treasury in lieu of dividends on Bank stock), for the words from 'the sum' to the end there is substituted 'a sum equal to 25 per cent. of the Bank's net profits for its previous financial year, or such other sum as the Treasury and the Bank may agree'.

(2)   In that section, at the end there is inserted—

'(6)   In subsection (4) of this section, the reference to the Bank's net profits for its previous financial year is to the profits shown in the audited accounts for that year less the amount of the tax charge so shown.'

(3)   In Schedule 1 to that Act (supplemental provisions), after paragraph 11 there is inserted—

'11A.—(1)   If, when a payment falls to be made under section 1(4) of this Act, the Bank's accounts for the previous financial year have not been audited, the payment shall be made on the basis of the Bank's estimate of the relevant amounts.

(2)   If an amount estimated under sub-paragraph (1) of this paragraph differs from the amount shown in the audited accounts, an appropriate adjustment shall be made to the next payment under section 1(4) of this Act to be made after the difference becomes apparent.'

(4)   In that Schedule, for paragraph 14 there is substituted—

'14.   Any sum paid by the Bank to the Treasury in lieu of dividends shall be allowed as a deduction in assessing the Bank to corporation tax for the accounting period by reference to which the payment is calculated.'

Supplementary

9.   Consequential amendments

(1)   In section 14 of the National Debt Reduction Act 1786 and section 32 of the Life Annuities Act 1808, for 'deputy governor' there is substituted 'deputy governors'.

(2)   In section 55 of the National Debt Act 1870, the first reference to the Deputy Governor of the Bank of England shall be treated as a reference to a Deputy Governor of the Bank of England.

(3)   In section 3(3) of the Bank of England Act 1946, after 'this Act' there is inserted 'and the Bank of England Act 1998'.

PART II

MONETARY POLICY

Role of the Bank

10.   Operational responsibility

In section 4(1) of the Bank of England Act 1946 (power of the Treasury to give directions to the Bank), at the end there is inserted ', except in relation to monetary policy'.

11.   Objectives

In relation to monetary policy, the objectives of the Bank of England shall be—

(a)   to maintain price stability, and

(b)   subject to that, to support the economic policy of Her Majesty's Government, including its objectives for growth and employment.

12.   Specification of matters relevant to objectives

(1)   The Treasury may by notice in writing to the Bank specify for the purposes of section 11—

(a)   what price stability is to be taken to consist of, or

(b)   what the economic policy of Her Majesty's Government is to be taken to be.

(2)   The Treasury shall specify under subsection (1) both of the matters mentioned there—

(a)   before the end of the period of 7 days beginning with the day on which this Act comes into force, and

(b)   at least once in every period of 12 months beginning on the anniversary of the day on which this Act comes into force.

(3)   Where the Treasury gives notice under this section they shall—

(a)   publish the notice in such manner as they think fit, and

(b)   lay a copy of it before Parliament.

Monetary Policy Committee of the Bank

13.   Monetary Policy Committee

(1)   There shall be a committee of the Bank, to be known as the Monetary Policy Committee of the Bank of England, which shall have responsibility within the Bank for formulating monetary policy.

(2)   The Committee shall consist of—

(a)   the Governor and Deputy Governors of the Bank,

(b)   2 members appointed by the Governor of the Bank after consultation with the Chancellor of the Exchequer, and

(c)   4 members appointed by the Chancellor of the Exchequer.

(3)   Of the 2 members appointed under subsection (2)(b)—

(a)   one shall be a person who has executive responsibility within the Bank for monetary policy analysis, and

(b)   the other shall be a person who has executive responsibility within the Bank for monetary policy operations.

(4)   The Chancellor of the Exchequer shall only appoint a person under subsection (2)(c) if he is satisfied that the person has knowledge or experience which is likely to be relevant to the Committee's functions.

(5)   Schedule 3 shall have effect with respect to the Committee.

14.   Publication of statements about decisions

(1)   As soon as practicable after each meeting of the Monetary Policy Committee, the Bank shall publish a statement as to whether it was decided at the meeting that the Bank should take any action, other than action by way of intervening in financial markets, for the purpose of meeting its objectives under section 11 and, if it was, what the action is.

(2)   If, at any meeting, the committee decides that the Bank should intervene in financial markets, it shall also consider at the meeting whether immediate publication of the decision would be likely to impede or frustrate the achievement of the intervention's purpose.

(3)   If the Committee decides under subsection (2) that immediate publication of a decision would not have the effect mentioned there, the Bank shall, when it publishes a statement under subsection (1) about the meeting, publish a statement as to what action by way of intervening in financial markets the Committee has decided the Bank should take.

(4)   If the Committee decides under subsection (2) that immediate publication of a decision would have the effect mentioned there, it shall keep under consideration the question of whether publication of the decision would still have that effect.

(5)   As soon as practicable after the Committee has decided that publication of a decision which has not been the subject of a statement under subsection (3) would no longer have the effect mentioned in subsection (2), the Bank shall publish a statement as to what action by way of intervening in financial markets the Committee decided the Bank should take and when the decision was made.

(6)   Publication under this section shall be in such manner as the Bank thinks fit.

15.   Publication of minutes of meetings

(1)   After each meeting of the Monetary Policy Committee, the Bank shall publish minutes of the meeting before the end of the period of 6 weeks beginning with the day of the meeting.

(2)   Subsection (1) shall not apply to minutes of any proceedings relating to—

(a)   a decision to intervene in financial markets, or

(b)   a decision about the publication of a decision to intervene in financial markets,

unless the Committee has decided that publication of the decision to intervene would not be likely, or would no longer be likely, to impede or frustrate the achievement of the intervention's purpose.

(3)   Minutes of proceedings relating to—

(a)   a decision to intervene in financial markets, or

(b)   a decision about the publication of a decision to intervene in financial markets,

shall, if not required to be published before the end of the period of 6 weeks beginning with the day of the meeting, be published by the Bank before the end of the period of 6 weeks beginning with the day on which a statement about the decision to intervene is published under section 14(5).

(4)   Minutes published under this section shall record, in relation to any decision of the Committee, the voting preference of the members who took part in the vote on the decision.

(5)   Publication under this section shall be in such manner as the Bank thinks fit.

16.   Functions of court of directors

(1)   The court of directors of the Bank shall keep the procedures followed by the Monetary Policy Committee under review.

(2)   In particular, the court's function under subsection (1) shall include determining whether the Committee has collected the regional, sectoral and other information necessary for the purposes of formulating monetary policy.

(3)   The court's function under subsection (1) shall stand delegated to the sub-committee constituted by section 3.

Information and reports

17.   Power to obtain information

(1)   The Bank may by notice in writing require an undertaking to which this section applies to provide the Bank with such information as may be specified in the notice, being information about the relevant financial affairs of the undertaking which the Bank considers it necessary or expedient to have for the purposes of its functions under this Part.

(2)   A notice under subsection (1) may require information to be provided—

(a)   in such form or manner as may be specified in the notice;

(b)   at such time or times as may be so specified;

(c)   in relation to such period or periods as may be so specified.

(3)   An undertaking is one to which this section applies if it has a place of business in the United Kingdom and—

(a)   is an authorised institution, or a former authorised institution, within the meaning of the Banking Act 1987,

(b)   is a European institution within the meaning of the Banking Coordination (Second Council Directive) Regulations 1992 which has lawfully established a branch in the United Kingdom for the purpose of accepting deposits or other repayable funds from the public,

(c)   is a building society within the meaning of the Building Societies Act 1986,

(d)   falls within the subsector 'other monetary financial institutions', as defined by paragraph 2.48 of Annex A to Council Regulation (EC) No. 2223/96, and is not a credit institution,

(e)   carries on a business of granting credits secured on land used for residential purposes, and is not a credit institution,

(f)   is a financial holding company as defined by Article 1 of Council Directive 92/30/EEC,

(g)   has issued a relevant debt security, and is not a credit institution, or

(h)   has acted as an agent in connection with arranging or managing the issue of a relevant debt security, and is not a credit institution.

(4)   The Treasury may by order provide which financial affairs of an undertaking are relevant for the purposes of this section, and may make different provision for different undertakings or classes of undertaking.

(5)   The Treasury may by order amend subsection (3).

(6)   Before making an order under this section, the Treasury shall consult—

(a)   the Bank,

(b)   the Office for National Statistics,

(c)   such persons as appear to them to be representative of persons likely to be materially affected by the order, and

(d)   such other persons as they consider appropriate.

(7)   In this section—

'credit institution' has the same meaning as in the Banking Coordination (Second Council Directive) Regulations 1992;

'relevant debt security' has the same meaning as in the Banking Act 1987 (Exempt Transactions) Regulations 1997 (or any regulations replacing them); and

'undertaking' has the meaning given by section 259 of the Companies Act 1985.

18.   Reports

(1)   The Bank shall prepare and publish reports in accordance with the provisions of this section.

(2)   A report under this section shall contain—

(a)   a review of the monetary policy decisions published by the Bank in the period to which the report relates,

(b)   an assessment of the developments in inflation in the economy of the United Kingdom in the period to which the report relates, and

(c)   an indication of the expected approach to meeting the Bank's objectives under section 11.

(3)   A report under this section shall relate to—

(a)   a period of 3 months, or

(b)   such other period as the Treasury and the Monetary Policy Committee may agree.

(4)   Periods to which reports under this section relate shall be successive, the first such period commencing on such day within the period of 3 months ending with the day on which this Act comes into force as the Treasury shall, after consultation with the Bank, specify in writing to it.

(5)   No report under this section shall be published without the approval of the Monetary Policy Committee.

(6)   A report under this section shall be published as soon as practicable after the end of the period to which it relates and in such manner as the Bank thinks fit.

Treasury's reserve powers

19.   Reserve powers

(1)   The Treasury, after consultation with the Governor of the Bank, may by order give the Bank directions with respect to monetary policy if they are satisfied that the directions are required in the public interest and by extreme economic circumstances.

(2)   An order under this section may include such consequential modifications of the provisions of this Part relating to the Monetary Policy Committee as the Treasury think fit.

(3)   A statutory instrument containing an order under this section shall be laid before Parliament after being made.

(4)   Unless an order under this section is approved by resolution of each House of Parliament before the end of the period of 28 days beginning with the day on which it is made, it shall cease to have effect at the end of that period.

(5)   In reckoning the period of 28 days for the purposes of subsection (4), no account shall be taken of any time during which Parliament is dissolved or prorogued or during which either House is adjourned for more than 4 days.

(6)   An order under this section which does not cease to have effect before the end of the period of 3 months beginning with the day on which it is made shall cease to have effect at the end of that period.

(7)   While an order under this section has effect, section 11 shall not have effect.

Supplementary

20.   Interpretation of Part II

In this Part, 'Monetary Policy Committee' means the Monetary Policy Committee of the Bank of England.

PART III
TRANSFER OF SUPERVISORY FUNCTIONS OF THE BANK TO THE FINANCIAL SERVICES AUTHORITY

Transfer of functions to the Authority

21.   Transfer

The following functions of the Bank are hereby transferred to the Authority—

    (a)   its functions under—

        (i)   the Banking Act 1987,

(ii)   the Banking Coordination (Second Council Directive) Regulations 1992, and

(iii)   section 101(4) of the Building Societies Act 1986,

(banking supervision functions),

(b)   its functions under—

(i)   section 43 of the Financial Services Act 1986, and

(ii)   the Investment Services Regulations 1995,

(functions relating to the listing of money market institutions), and

(c)   its functions under section 171 of the Companies Act 1989 (functions relating to the listing of persons providing settlement arrangements).

22.   Supplementary provisions

Schedule 4 (transfer of functions: supplementary provisions) shall have effect.

23.   Consequential amendments

(1)   Schedule 5 (amendments of primary, and other principal, legislation consequential on the transfer of functions by section 21) shall have effect.

(2)   The Treasury may by order make such amendments or revocation of any instrument made under an Act as they think necessary or expedient in consequence of the transfer of functions by this Part.

(3)   If a reference in a relevant provision to the Bank is predicated on the continuing exercise by the Bank of any of the transferred functions, it shall, in relation to any time after the coming into force of this Act, have effect as a reference to the Authority.

(4)   In subsection (3), 'relevant provision' means a provision which—

(a)   has effect before, as well as after, the coming into force of this Act, and

(b)   is contained in a document other than an Act or an instrument made under an Act.

Authority's position in relation to transferred functions

24.   Status

In relation to the carrying out of any of the transferred functions—

(a)   the Authority shall not be regarded as acting on behalf of the Crown, and

(b)   its members, officers and servants shall not be regarded as Crown servants.

25.   Liability

(1)   In section 43 of the Financial Services Act 1986, at the end there is inserted—

'(5)   Neither the Authority nor any person who is, or is acting as, an officer or servant of the Authority shall be liable in damages for anything done or omitted in the discharge or purported discharge of any of the Authority's functions under this section, unless it is shown that the act or omission was in bad faith.'

(2)   In regulation 26 of the Investment Services Regulations 1995, at the end there is inserted—

'(6)   That section shall also have effect as if the reference in subsection (5) to the Authority's functions under the section included a reference to—

(a)   any function under these Regulations which is a function of the Authority by virtue of the Bank of England Act 1998, and

(b)   so much of any function of the authority under these Regulations as is exercisable by virtue of that Act.'

(3)   In section 171 of the Companies Act 1989, after subsection (6) there is inserted—

'(6A)   Neither the Authority nor any person who is, or is acting as, an officer or servant of the Authority shall be liable in damages for anything done or omitted in the discharge or purported discharge of any of the Authority's functions under this section, unless it is shown that the act or omission was in bad faith.'

26.   Power to charge fees

(1)   Schedule 6 (banking supervision fees) shall have effect.

(2)   In section 43 of the Financial Services Act 1986, after subsection (2) there is inserted—

'(2A)   Without prejudice to the generality of the Authority's power to impose conditions for admission to the list, the conditions for admission may include—

(a)   a condition having the effect of requiring the payment of an application fee, and

(b)   a condition having the effect of requiring the payment of periodic fees.

(2B)   A condition of the kind referred to in subsection (2A)(a) or (b) above—

(a)   may provide for the amount payable to be such as is specified in, or determined under, the condition, and

(b)   may make different provision for different cases.'

(3)   In section 171 of the Companies Act 1989, after subsection (3) there is inserted—

'(3A)   Without prejudice to the generality of the Authority's power to impose conditions for admission to the list, the conditions for admission may include—

(a)   a condition having the effect of requiring the payment of an application fee, and

(b)   a condition having the effect of requiring the payment of periodic fees.

(3B)   A condition of the kind referred to in subsection (3A)(a) or (b)—

(a)   may provide for the amount payable to be such as is specified in, or determined under, the condition, and

(b)   may make different provision for different cases.'

27.   Power to channel information through agent

In section 39(1)(a) of the Banking Act 1987 (power to require the provision of information)—

(a)   after 'provide the Bank,' there is inserted 'or such person acting on behalf of the Authority as may be specified in the notice,', and

(b)   for 'specified in the notice' there is substituted 'so specified'.

Consequential changes to banking bodies

28.   Board of Banking Supervision

(1)   In section 2 of the Banking Act 1987 (Board of Banking Supervision), for subsections (1) and (2) there is substituted—

'(1)   There shall continue to be a committee known as the Board of Banking Supervision.

(2)   The Board shall consist of—

(a)   two ex officio members, namely, the Chairman of the Authority and the holder of such other office within the Authority as the Chairman of the Authority may designate for the purposes of this provision; and

(b)   six independent members, that is to say, members appointed jointly by the Chancellor of the Exchequer and the chairman of the Authority, being persons having no executive responsibility in the Authority.

(2A)   The independent members shall elect one of their number to chair the Board.'

(2)   In that section, in subsections (3), (4), (6) and (7), for 'Bank', wherever occurring, there is substituted 'Authority'.

(3)   In Schedule 1 to that Act (Board of Banking Supervision), for 'Bank', wherever occurring, there is substituted 'Authority'.

29.   Deposit Protection Board

(1)   Schedule 4 to the Banking Act 1987 (Deposit Protection Board) paragraph 1 (constitution) is amended as follows.

(2)   In sub-paragraph (1), for paragraphs (a) to (c) (ex officio members of the Board) there is substituted—

'(a)   the Chairman of the authority, who shall chair the Board;

(b)   the holder of such other office within the Authority as the chairman of the Authority may designate for the purposes of this provision; and

(c)   the Deputy Governor of the Bank of England responsible for financial stability;'.

(3)   For sub-paragraph (2) there is substituted—

'(2)   The Chairman of the Authority shall appoint as ordinary members of the Board—

(a)   three persons who are directors, controllers or managers of contributory institutions; and

(b)   persons who are officers or employees of the Authority.'

(4)   For sub-paragraph (3) there is substituted—

'(3)   An ex officio member of the Board may appoint an alternate member to perform his duties as a member in his absence as follows—

(a)   The chairman of the Authority or the holder of a designated office within the Authority may appoint an officer or employee of the Authority, and

(b)   the Deputy Governor of the Bank of England may appoint an officer or employee of the Bank.'

(5) In sub-paragraph (4) (appointment of alternates for ordinary members), in paragraph (b), for 'Bank' there is substituted 'Authority'.

Supplementary

30. Interpretation of Part III
In this Part—
    'the Authority' means the Financial Services Authority;
    'transferred functions' means the functions transferred to the Authority by this Part.

PART IV
MISCELLANEOUS AND GENERAL

Miscellaneous

31. Qualifications of a designated agency
In paragraph 1 of Schedule 7 to the Financial Services Act 1986 (constitution of a designated agency), in sub-paragraph (2) (members of the governing body to be appointed etc. by the Treasury and Governor of the Bank acting jointly), the words 'and the Governor of the Bank of England acting jointly' are omitted.

32. Listed institutions: exemption of transactions with Treasury
In Schedule 5 to the Financial Services Act 1986 (transactions in relation to which institutions listed under section 43 are exempt from authorisation)—
    (a) in paragraph 1, after 'with another listed institution', there is inserted ', the Treasury',
    (b) in paragraph 4(1)(b) and (2), after 'listed institution' there is inserted ', the Treasury', and
    (c) in paragraph 9(a), after 'with another listed institution' there is inserted ', the Treasury'.

33. Closure of National Savings Stock Register to gilts
(1) The Treasury may by order—
    (a) make provision excluding gilts from registration in the Register on and after a day specified in the order,
    (b) make provision for the transfer to the books of the Bank of the entries in the Register at the beginning of the day specified under paragraph (a) which relate to gilts, and
    (c) make provision for the transfer to the Bank of rights and liabilities of the Director of Savings in relation to the registration of gilts in the Register or any transaction associated therewith.

(2) The power conferred by paragraph (b) of subsection (1) includes power to make provision in relation to gilts which were not registered in the Register at the beginning of the day specified under paragraph (a) of that subsection, but which should have been.

(3)   An order under subsection (1) may contain such consequential, incidental, supplementary and transitional provisions as appear to the Treasury to be necessary or expedient.

(4)   Without prejudice to subsection (3), an order under subsection (1) may contain—

(a)   provision requiring things done by, or in relation to, the Director of Savings to be treated as done by, or in relation to, the Bank,

(b)   provision requiring references in documents to the Register to be construed as references to the books of the Bank, and

(c)   provision requiring certificates issued by the Director of Savings in relation to registration in the Register to be treated as issued by the Bank in relation to registration in the books of the Bank.

(5)   An order under subsection (1) may—

(a)   make different provision for different cases, and

(b)   contain provision amending, or repealing or revoking, an enactment contained in—

(i)   an Act, whenever passed, or

(ii)   an instrument, whenever made, under an Act, whenever passed.

(6)   In this section—

'gilts' means stock or bonds of any of the descriptions included in Part I of Schedule 11 to the Finance Act 1942 (whether on or after the passing of this Act); and

'the Register' means the National Savings Stock Register.

34.   Provision of brokerage service in connection with gilt registration

In section 47 of the Finance Act 1942 (transfer and registration of Government stock), after subsection (1) there is inserted—

'(IZA) Regulations under subsection (1) of this section may make provision with respect to the purchase and sale of such stock and bonds by any person, or any description of person, through the Bank of England and, in relation to purchase or sale under the regulations, may—

(a)   make provision with respect to the commission and fees payable, and

(b)   make provision limiting the amount which any person, or any description of person, may purchase or sell on any day.'

35.   Section 207 of the Companies Act 1989: bearer securities

In section 207 of the Companies Act 1989 (power to make regulations enabling title to securities to be evidenced and transferred without a written instrument), there is inserted at the end—

'(10)   In subsection (1), the reference to transfer without a written instrument includes, in relation to bearer securities, transfer without delivery.'

36.   Disclosure of information: minor amendments

(1)   In the Banking Act 1987, in section 86(2)(a), after 'functions' there is inserted 'or any functions in its capacity as a designated agency within the meaning of the Financial Services Act 1986'.

(2)   Section 86(5) of that Act as applied by paragraph 57(1) of Schedule 5 shall have effect with the following modifications—

(a)   in the definition of 'relevant functions', at the end there is inserted 'and its functions as a supervisor of systems for the transfer of funds between credit institutions and their customers', and

(b)   in the definition of 'relevant recipient', for '1 to 8' there is substituted '1 to 9'.

(3)   Section 87(3A) of that Act as applied by paragraph 59(1) of Schedule 5 shall have effect with the following modifications—

(a)   in the definition of 'relevant functions', at the end there is inserted 'and its functions as a supervisor of systems for the transfer of funds between credit institutions and their customers', and

(b)   in the definition of 'relevant recipient', for '1 to 8' there is substituted '1 to 9'.

(4)   Part V of that Act shall have effect, in relation to information relating to the business or other affairs of institutions which are authorised institutions, but not credit institutions, within the meaning of that Act, with the amendments made by the following regulations—

(a)   regulations 38, 39(2) to (4) and 40 to 42 of the Banking Coordination (Second Council Directive) Regulations 1992, and

(b)   regulation 5 of the Financial Institutions (Prudential Supervision) Regulations 1996.

General

37.   Restriction on disclosure of information

Schedule 7 (which restricts the disclosure of information obtained for monetary policy or cash ratio deposit purposes) shall have effect.

38.   Offences in relation to supplying information to the Bank

(1)   A person who fails without reasonable excuse to comply with any requirement imposed on him under section 17(1) or paragraph 9 of Schedule 2 shall be guilty of an offence and liable on summary conviction to a fine not exceeding level 4 on the standard scale.

(2)   If after conviction of an offence under subsection (1) a person continues the failure for which he was convicted, he shall be guilty of a further offence under that subsection and liable on summary conviction to be punished accordingly.

(3)   A person who in purported compliance with a requirement imposed on him under section 17(1) or paragraph 9 of Schedule 2 provides information which he knows to be false or misleading in a material particular, or recklessly provides information which is false or misleading in a material particular, shall be guilty of an offence and liable—

(a)   on conviction on indictment, to imprisonment for a term not exceeding 2 years, or to a fine, or to both, or

(b)   on summary conviction, to imprisonment for a term not exceeding 3 months, or to a fine not exceeding the statutory maximum, or to both.

39.   Offences by bodies corporate

(1)   Where an offence under this Part committed by a body corporate is proved to have been committed with the consent or connivance of, or to be attributable to any neglect on the part of, any director, manager, secretary or other similar officer of the body corporate, or any person who was purporting to act in any such capacity, he, as well as the body corporate, shall be guilty of that offence and be liable to be proceeded against and punished accordingly.

(2)   Where the affairs of a body corporate are managed by its members, subsection (1) shall apply in relation to the acts and defaults of a member in connection with his functions of management as if he were a director of the body corporate.

40.   Orders

(1)   Any power of the Treasury to make an order under this Act shall be exercisable by statutory instrument.

(2)   An order under—

section 17(4) or (5),

paragraph 1(2) or 5 of Schedule 2, or

paragraph 3(2) of Schedule 7,

shall not be made unless a draft of the order has been laid before and approved by resolution of each House of Parliament.

(3)   A statutory instrument containing an order under—

section 23(2),

paragraph 2(2) or 8 of Schedule 2,

paragraph 1(5) of Schedule 4, or

paragraph 3(3) of Schedule 7,

shall be subject to annulment in pursuance of a resolution of either House of Parliament.

(4)   A statutory instrument containing an order under section 33 shall be subject to annulment in pursuance of a resolution of the House of Commons.

(5)   Section 19 contains its own provisions about parliamentary procedure in relation to an order under that section.

41.   General interpretation

In this Act, 'the Bank' means the Bank of England.

42.   Transitional provisions and savings

Schedule 8 (transitional provisions and savings) shall have effect.

43.   Repeals

The enactments and instruments specified in Schedule 9 are hereby repealed or revoked to the extent specified in the final column of that Schedule.

Final provisions

44. Extent

(1)   This Act extends to Northern Ireland.

(2)   Section 33 extends to the Channel Islands and the Isle of Man.

(3)   The extent of any amendment, repeal or revocation by this Act is the same as that of the enactment amended, repealed or revoked.

45. Commencement

This Act shall come into force on such day as the Treasury may by order appoint. [The Act was brought into force on 1 June 1998 by the Bank of England Act 1998 (Commencement) Order 1998 (SI 1998/1120).]

46. Short title

This Act may be cited as the Bank of England Act 1998.

SCHEDULES

Section 1   SCHEDULE 1
COURT OF DIRECTORS

Terms of office

1.—(1)   Appointment as Governor or Deputy Governor of the Bank shall be for a period of 5 years.

(2)   A person appointed as Governor or Deputy Governor of the Bank shall work exclusively for the Bank.

2.   Appointment as director of the Bank shall be for a period of 3 years, except that initially some appointments may be for shorter and different periods so as to secure that appointments expire at different times.

3.   A person appointed as director of the Bank in place of a person who ceased to hold office before the end of the term for which he was appointed shall be appointed for the remainder of that person's term of office.

4.   A person appointed as Governor, Deputy Governor or director of the Bank may resign his office by written notice to the Bank.

Qualification for appointment

5.—(1)   A person is disqualified for appointment as Governor, Deputy Governor or director of the Bank if he is a Minister of the Crown or a person serving in a government department in employment in respect of which remuneration is payable out of money provided by Parliament.

(2)   A person is disqualified for appointment as director of the Bank if he is a servant of the Bank.

6.   The fact that a person has held office as Governor, Deputy Governor or director of the Bank does not disqualify him for re-appointment to that office or for appointment to any other of those offices.

Removal from office

7.—(1)   A person appointed as Governor or Deputy Governor of the Bank shall vacate office if he becomes a person to whom paragraph 5(1) applies.

(2)   A person appointed as director of the Bank shall vacate office if he becomes a person to whom paragraph 5(1) or (2) applies.

8.   The Bank may, with the consent of the Chancellor of the Exchequer, remove a person from office as Governor, Deputy Governor or director of the Ban' if it is satisfied—

(a)   that he has been absent from meetings of the court for more than 3 months without the consent of the court,

(b)   that he has become bankrupt, that his estate has been sequestrated or that he has made an arrangement with or granted a trust deed for his creditors, or

(c)   that he is unable or unfit to discharge his functions as a member.

Powers

9.   The court may act notwithstanding the existence of one or more vacancies among its members.

10.   The court may appoint such sub-committees as it thinks fit.

11.   The court may delegate such duties and powers as it thinks fit to—

(a)   a member of the court,

(b)   any officer, servant or agent of the Bank,

(c)   a sub-committee consisting of—

(i)   members of the court, or

(ii)   one or more members of the court and one or more of the officers, servants and agents of the Bank.

Meetings

12.—(1)   The court shall meet at least one a month.

(2)   The Governor of the Bank (or in his absence a Deputy Governor of the Bank) may summon a meeting at any time on giving such notice as in his judgment the circumstances may require.

Proceedings

13.—(1)   At a meeting of the court, the proceedings shall be regulated as follows.

(2)   The quorum shall be 9.

(3)   The chair shall be taken by the Governor of the Bank or, if he is not present, by the director of the Bank who is for the time being designated under subsection (4) of section 3 to chair the sub-committee constituted by that section.

(4)   If a member of the court has any direct or indirect interest in any dealing or business with the Bank—

(a)   he shall disclose his interest to the court at the time of the dealing or business being negotiated or transacted, and

(b)   he shall have no vote in relation to the dealing or business, unless the court has resolved that the interest does not give rise to a conflict of interest.

(5)   A member of the court shall have no vote in relation to any question arising which touches or concerns him but shall withdraw and be absent during the debate of any matter in which he is concerned.

(6)   Subject to sub-paragraphs (2) to (5), the court shall determine its own procedure.

Remuneration

14.—(1)   A person appointed as Governor or Deputy Governor of the Bank shall be entitled to be paid by the Bank such remuneration as it may determine.

(2)   The Bank may pay, or create and maintain a fund for the payment of, pensions or capital grants to members, or former members, of the court who have rendered exclusive services to the Bank.

15.   A director of the Bank shall be entitled to be paid by the Bank such remuneration as the Bank may determine with the approval of the Chancellor of the Exchequer.

Section 6   SCHEDULE 2
                     CASH RATIO DEPOSITS

Eligible institutions

1.—(1)   The following are eligible institutions for the purposes of this Schedule—

(a)   an institution authorised under the Banking Act 1987,

(b)   a European authorised institution within the meaning of the Banking Coordination (Second Council Directive) Regulations 1992 which has lawfully established a branch in the United Kingdom for the purpose of accepting deposits or other repayable funds from the public, and

(c)   a building society authorised under the Building Societies Act 1986.

(2)   The Treasury may by order amend sub-paragraph (1) as they think fit.

Liablity base

2.—(1)   For the purposes of this Schedule, the liability base of an eligible institution at any time is the aggregate of those sterling and foreign currency liabilities of the institution which are eligible liabilities.

(2)   The Treasury may by order define eligible liabilities for the purposes of this paragraph and make provision about the calculation of any description of eligible liability, including provision for the amount of a liability of any description to be treated as reduced by the amount of an asset of any description.

Call notices

3.—(1)   The Bank may give an eligible institution notice under this paragraph.

(2)   Notice under this paragraph ('a call notice') shall be in writing and shall specify—

(a)   the period to which it relates, and

(b)   the amount which, in relation to that period, is the institution's depositable amount.

(3)   The period to be specified under sub-paragraph (2)(a)—

(a)   shall be a period of 6 months beginning at least 4 working days after the date of the notice, and

(b)   shall not include any part of a period specified in a previous call notice given to the institution concerned.

Calculation of depositable amount

4.—(1)   In the case of any call notice, the amount to be specified under paragraph 3(2)(b) is the amount, or, as the case may be, the sum of the amounts, produced by multiplying so much of the institution's average liability base for the reference period as falls into each value band by the ratio applicable to that band.

(2)   The Bank may use such method to calculate an institution's average liability base for the purposes of this paragraph as it thinks fit, and may use different methods for different institutions.

(3)   For the purposes of this paragraph, value bands and the ratios applicable to them are such as may be specified under paragraph 5.

Value bands and applicable ratios

5.   The Treasury may by order specify for the purposes of paragraph 4 value bands and the ratios applicable to them.

Effect of call notice

6.—(1)   Where the Bank has given an eligible institution a call notice, then, if at any time in the period to which the notice relates the following conditions are met, namely—

(a)   the institution is an eligible institution, and

(b)   the institution does not have on deposit in the appropriate account with the Bank the amount specified in the notice as its depositable amount in relation to that period,

the Bank may by notice in writing require the institution to make a payment in lieu of deposit.

(2)   A notice under sub-paragraph (1) shall specify what period it covers, and the period specified must—

(a)   fall within the period to which the call notice relates, and

(b)   be a period throughout which the conditions mentioned in sub-paragraph (1) have been met.

(3)   The amount which the Bank may by a notice under sub-paragraph (1) require an institution to pay is an amount equal to interest for the period covered by the notice, at 4% over the benchmark rate, on the average shortfall during that period.

(4)   The Bank may use such method to calculate the average shortfall as it thinks fit.

(5)   In sub-paragraph (1)(b), the reference to the appropriate account, in relation to an eligible institution, is to such account of the institution with the Bank as is designated by the Bank for the purposes of this Schedule.

(6)   For the purposes of sub-paragraph (3), the shortfall, at any time, is the amount which the institution needs to deposit to prevent the condition mentioned in sub-paragraph (1)(b) applying.

Benchmark rate of interest

7.—(1)   The benchmark rate of interest for the purposes of paragraph 6(3) shall be determined as follows.

(2)   First, determine a rate of interest for each working day of the period covered by the notice under paragraph 6(1) by taking the average of the rates at which 3 month deposits in sterling are bid at 11.00 am on the day by the 5 eligible institutions having in the opinion of the Bank the largest eligible liabilities at the end of the reference period for the relevant call notice.

(3)   Second, determine an average rate of interest by reference to the rates determined in accordance with sub-paragraph (2), the average rate so determined being the benchmark rate.

(4)   In sub-paragraph (2), the reference to the relevant call notice is to the call notice by virtue of which the Bank is entitled to give the notice under paragraph 6(1).

8.   The Treasury may by order amend or replace paragraph 7.

Power to obtain information

9.—(1)   The Bank may by notice in writing require an eligible institution to provide the Bank with such information as may be specified in the notice, being information which the Bank considers it necessary or expedient to have for the purposes of its functions under this Schedule.

(2)   A notice under sub-paragraph (1) may require information to be provided—
  (a)   in such form or manner as may be specified in the notice;
  (b)   at such time or times as may be so specified;
  (c)   in relation to such period or periods as may be so specified.

Orders

10.   Before making an order under this Schedule, the Treasury shall consult—
  (a)   the Bank,
  (b)   such persons as appear to them to be representative of persons likely to be materially affected by the order, and
  (c)   such other persons as they think fit.

11.   In exercising the power to make orders under paragraph 2(2) or 5, the Treasury shall have regard to the financial needs of the Bank.

Interpretation

12.   In this Schedule—
'reference period', in relation to a call notice, means the period of 6 months ending immediately before the month in which the notice is given; and
'working day' means any day other than a Saturday, a Sunday, Christmas Day, Good Friday or a day which is a bank holiday under the Banking and Financial Dealings Act 1971 in any part of the United Kingdom.

Modifications for new entrants

13.—(1)　In its application to the first call notice to be given to an institution or society after it becomes an eligible institution, this Schedule shall have effect with the following modifications.

(2)　In paragraph 3(3)(a), after 'period of' there is inserted 'not more than'.

(3)　In paragraph 7(2), for 'the end of the reference period for the relevant call notice' there is substituted 'such time before the beginning of the period to which the relevant call notice relates as the Bank thinks fit'.

(4)　In paragraph 12, in the definition of 'reference period', for the words from 'the period' to the end there is substituted 'such period prior to the notice as the Bank thinks fit'.

Section 13　　　　　　　　　SCHEDULE 3
　　　　　　　MONETARY POLICY COMMITTEE

Terms of office of appointed members

1.　Appointment as a member of the Committee under section 13(2)(b) or (c) shall be for a period of 3 years, except that initially some appointments may be for shorter and different periods so as to secure that appointments expire at different times.

2.　A person appointed under section 13(2)(b) or (c) in place of a person who ceased to hold office before the end of the term for which he was appointed shall be appointed for the remainder of that person's term of office.

3.　A person appointed under section 13(2)(b) or (c) may resign his office by written notice to the Bank.

4.—(1)　A person who holds office as a member of the Committee under section 13(2)(c) shall be a servant of the Bank.

(2)　The terms and conditions of service under sub-paragraph (1) shall be such as the Bank may determine.

(3)　The function of determining terms and conditions of service under sub-paragraph (2) shall stand delegated to the sub-committee constituted by section 3.

Qualification for appointment

5.　A person is disqualified for appointment under section 13(2)(b) or (c) if—

(a)　he is a Minister of the Crown, or a person serving in a government department in employment in respect of which remuneration is payable out of money provided by Parliament, or

(b)　he is a member of the court of directors of the Bank.

6.　The fact that a person has held office under section 13(2)(b) or (c) does not disqualify him for further appointment to such office.

Removal of appointed members

7.　A person appointed under section 13(2)(b) or (c) shall vacate office if he becomes a person to whom paragraph 5(a) or (b) applies.

8.   A person appointed under section 13(2)(b) shall vacate office if he ceases to have executive responsibility within the Bank for monetary policy analysis or, as the case may be, monetary policy operations.

9.—(1)   The Bank may, with the consent of the Chancellor of the Exchequer, remove a member appointed under section 13(2)(b) or (c) if it is satisfied—

(a)   that he has been absent from the Committee's meetings for more than 3 months without the Committee's consent,

(b)   that he has become bankrupt, that his estate has been sequestrated or that he has made an arrangement with or granted a trust deed for his creditors, or

(c)   that he is unable or unfit to discharge his functions as a member.

(2)   The function of removing a member under sub-paragraph (1) shall stand delegated to the sub-committee constituted by section 3.

Meetings

10.—(1)   The Committee shall meet at least once a month.

(2)   The Governor of the Bank (or in his absence the Deputy Governor of the Bank with executive responsibility for monetary policy) may summon a meeting at any time on giving such notice as in his judgment the circumstances may require.

Proceedings

11.—(1)   At a meeting of the Committee, the proceedings shall be regulated as follows.

(2)   The quorum shall be 6, of whom 2 must hold office as Governor or Deputy Governor of the Bank.

(3)   The chair shall be taken by the Governor of the Bank or, if he is not present, the Deputy Governor of the Bank with executive responsibility for monetary policy.

(4)   Decisions shall be taken by a vote of all those members present at the meeting.

(5)   In the event of a tie, the chairman shall have a second casting vote.

(6)   Subject to sub-paragraphs (2) to (5), the Committee shall determine its own procedure.

12.   The Committee may, in relation to sub-paragraph (2), (3) or (4) of paragraph 11, determine circumstances in which a member who is not present at, but is in communication with, a meeting, is to be treated for the purposes of that sub-paragraph at present at it.

13.   A representative of the Treasury may attend, and speak at, any meeting of the Committee.

Report to court of directors of the Bank

14.   The Committee shall submit a monthly report on its activities to the court of directors of the Bank.

Parliamentary disqualification

15.   In Part III of Schedule 1 to the House of Commons Disqualification Act 1975 (other disqualifying offices), there is inserted at the appropriate place—

'Member of the Monetary Policy Committee of the Bank of England appointed under section 13(2)(b) or (c) of the Bank of England Act 1998.';
and a corresponding amendment is made in Part III of Schedule 1 to the Northern Ireland Assembly Disqualification Act 1975.

Section 22   SCHEDULE 4
TRANSFER OF FUNCTIONS: SUPPLEMENTARY PROVISIONS

Continuity of exercise of functions

1.—(1)   The transfer of functions by this Part shall not affect the validity of anything done (or having effect as if done) by or in relation to the Bank before the day on which this Act comes into force ('the transfer day').

(2)   Anything which, immediately before the transfer day, is in the process of being done by or in relation to the Bank may, if it relates to any of the transferred functions, be continued by or in relation to the Authority.

(3)   Anything done (or having effect as if done) by, or in relation to, the Bank before the transfer day for the purpose of, or in connection with, any of the transferred functions, shall, so far as is required for continuing its effect on and after that day, have effect as if done by, or in relation to, the Authority.

(4)   Any reference to the Bank in any document constituting or relating to anything to which the foregoing provisions of this paragraph apply shall, so far as is required for giving effect to those provisions, be construed as a reference to the Authority.

(5)   The Treasury may, in relation to any of the transferred functions, by order exclude, modify or supplement any of the foregoing provisions of this paragraph or make such other transitional provisions as they think necessary or expedient.

Transfer of staff

2.   The transfer of functions by this Part shall be regarded for the purposes of the Transfer of Undertakings (Protection of Employment) Regulations 1981 as the transfer of part of an undertaking, whether or not it would be so regarded apart from this provision.

Transfer of property, rights and liabilities

3.—(1)   The Bank shall make a scheme under this paragraph for the transfer to the Authority of such of the Bank's property, rights and liabilities as appear to the Bank appropriate to be so transferred in consequence of the transfer of functions by this Part.

(2)   A scheme under this paragraph made by the Bank shall not be capable of coming into force unless it is approved by the Treasury.

(3)   The Bank may not submit a scheme under this paragraph to the Treasury for their approval without the consent of the Authority.

(4)   Where a scheme under this paragraph is submitted to the Treasury for their approval, they may, before approving it, make such modifications to it as appear to them to be appropriate.

(5)   Where this sub-paragraph applies, the Treasury may, after consultation with the Bank and the Authority, make a scheme under this paragraph for the transfer to the Authority of such of the Bank's property, rights and liabilities as appear to them appropriate to be so transferred in consequence of the transfer of functions by this Part.

(6)   Sub-paragraph (5) applies if—

(a)   the Bank fails, before such time as may be notified to it by the Treasury as the latest time for submission of a scheme under this paragraph, to submit such a scheme to them for their approval, or

(b)   the Treasury decide not to approve a scheme that has been submitted to them by the Bank (either with or without modifications).

(7)   A scheme under this paragraph shall come into force on such day as the Treasury may by order appoint.

(8)   When a scheme under this paragraph comes into force, the property, rights and liabilities of the Bank to which the scheme relates shall, by virtue of this paragraph and without further assurance, be transferred to and vested in the Authority in accordance with the provisions of the scheme.

(9)   The Bank shall provide the Treasury with all such information and other assistance as they may reasonably require for the purposes of, or otherwise in connection with, the exercise of any power conferred on them by this paragraph.

4.—(1)   The property, rights and liabilities capable of being transferred in accordance with a scheme under paragraph 3 shall include property, rights and liabilities that would not otherwise be capable of being transferred or assigned by the Bank.

(2)   The transfers authorised by sub-paragraph (1) include transfers which are to take effect as if there were—

(a)   no such requirement to obtain any person's consent or concurrence,

(b)   no such liability in respect of a contravention of any other requirement, and

(c)   no such interference with any interest or right,

as there would be, in the case of any transaction apart from this Act, by reason of provisions having effect (whether under any enactment or agreement or otherwise) in relation to the terms on which the Bank is entitled or subject in relation to any property, right or liability.

5.—(1)   A scheme under paragraph 3 may also contain provision—

(a)   for rights and liabilities to be transferred so as to be enforceable by or against both the Bank and the Authority,

(b)   for the creation in favour of the Bank of an interest or right in or in relation to property transferred in accordance with the scheme,

(c)   for giving effect to a transfer to the Authority in accordance with the scheme by the creation in favour of the Authority of an interest or right in or in relation to property retained by the Bank,

(d)   for imposing on the Bank and the Authority obligations to enter into such written agreements with each other as may be specified in the scheme, and

(e)   for imposing on either one of them obligations to execute such instruments in favour of the other as may be so specified.

(2)   An obligation imposed by a provision included in a scheme by virtue of sub-paragraph (1)(d) or (e) shall be enforceable by civil proceedings by the Bank or the Authority for an injunction or for any other appropriate relief.

(3)   A transaction of any description effected in pursuance of a provision included in a scheme by virtue of sub-paragraph (1)(d) or (e)—

(a)   shall have effect subject to the provisions of any enactment which provides for transactions of that description to be registered in any statutory register, but

(b)   subject to that, shall be binding on all other persons, notwithstanding that it would, apart from this provision, have required the consent or concurrence of any other person.

6.—(1)   A scheme under paragraph 3 may make such supplemental, consequential and transitional provision for the purpose of, or in connection with, any transfer of property, rights or liabilities for which the scheme provides or in connection with any other provisions contained in the scheme as the Bank may consider appropriate.

(2)   In particular, such a scheme may provide—

(a)   that for purposes connected with any transfer made in accordance with the scheme (including the transfer of rights and liabilities under an enactment) the Authority is to be treated as the same person in law as the Bank,

(b)   that, so far as may be necessary for the purposes of or in connection with any such transfer, agreements made, transactions effected and other things done by or in relation to the Bank are to be treated as made, effected or done by or in relation to the Authority,

(c)   that, so far as may be necessary for the purposes of or in connection with any such transfer, references to the Bank in any agreement (whether or not in writing), deed, bond, instrument or other document are to have effect with such modifications as are specified in the scheme,

(d)   that proceedings commenced by or against the Bank are to be continued by or against the Authority, and

(e)   that the Bank and the Authority are to co-operate with each other for the purposes of and in connection with the scheme.

Section 23   SCHEDULE 5
TRANSFER OF FUNCTIONS: CONSEQUENTIAL AMENDMENTS

PART I
BANKING SUPERVISION

CHAPTER I
BANKING ACT 1987

1.   The Banking Act 1987 is amended as follows.

2.   In section 1—

(a)   in subsection (1), for the words from the beginning to 'Bank')' there is substituted 'The Financial Services Authority (in this Act referred to as 'the Authority')',

(b)   in subsections (2) and (3), for 'Bank' there is substituted 'Authority', and

(c) in subsection (4)—

(i)   for the words from the beginning to 'Bank', in the second place where it occurs, there is substituted 'Neither the Authority nor any person who is, or is acting as, an officer or servant of the Authority', and

(ii)   for 'Bank', in the third place where it occurs, there is substitued 'Authority'.

3. In sections 3(1) and 4(3), for 'Bank' there is substituted 'Authority'.

4. In sections 7 to 10, for 'Bank', wherever occurring, there is substituted 'Authority'.

5. In section 11—

(a) for 'Bank', wherever occurring, except subsection (1A)(c), there is substituted 'Authority', and

(b) in subsection (1A)(c)—

(i)   for 'the Bank is informed by The Securities and Investments Board, or' there is substituted 'it appears to the Authority, or the Authority is informed by', and

(ii)   in paragraph (ii), for 'that Board or' there is substituted 'the Authority or that'.

6. In section 12—

(a) for 'Bank', wherever occurring, there is substituted 'Authority', and

(b) in subsection (1)(a), for 'Bank's' there is substituted 'Authority's'.

7. In sections 12A to 17, for 'Bank', wherever occurring, there is substituted 'Authority'.

8. In section 19—

(a) for 'Bank', wherever occurring, there is substituted 'Authority', and

(b) in subsection (3), for 'Bank's' there is substituted 'Authority's'.

9. In sections 20 to 27, for 'Bank', wherever occurring, there is substituted 'Authority'.

10. In section 29—

(a) for 'Bank', wherever occurring, there is substituted 'Authority', and

(b) in subsection (3), for 'Bank's' there is substituted 'Authority's'.

11. In sections 30 to 34 and 36 to 42 for 'Bank', wherever occurring, there is substituted 'Authority'.

12. In section 43(1)—

(a) for 'Bank', there is substituted 'Authority', and

(b) for 'Bank's' there is substituted 'Authority's'.

13. In sections 46 to 49, for 'Bank', wherever occurring, there is substituted 'Authority'.

14. In sections 52(2A), 58(2A)(b), 59(1)(a) and (4), 65(1), 67(6), 68(7) and 69(7), for 'Bank' there is substituted 'Authority'.

15. In sections 70 to 72 and 75, for 'Bank', wherever occurring, there is substituted 'Authority'.

16. In section 76—

(a) for 'Bank', wherever occurring, there is substituted 'Authority', and

(b) in subsection (3)(b), for 'Bank's' there is substituted 'Authority's'.

17.   In sections 77 to 18, for 'Bank', wherever occurring, there is substituted 'Authority'.

18.   In sections 92 to 96, 99 to 101 and 105, for 'Bank', wherever occurring, there is substituted 'Authority'.

19.   In section 106(1)—

(a)   in the definition of 'Authorisation', for 'Bank' there is substituted 'Authority',

(b)   after that definition there is inserted—

'"The authority" means the Financial Services authority;', and

(c)   in the definition of 'relevant supervisory authority', in paragraph (b), for 'Bank' there is substituted 'Authority'.

20.   In Schedule 3, for 'Bank', wherever occurring, there is substituted 'Authority'.

CHAPTER II
BANKING COORDINATION (SECOND COUNCIL DIRECTIVE) REGULATIONS 1992

21.   The Banking Coordination (Second Council Directive) Regulations 1992 are amended as follows.

22.   In regulation 2(1)—

(a)   after the provision about the construction of 'authorised or permitted' there is inserted—

'"the Authority" means the Financial Services Authority (formerly known as the Securities and Investments Board);', and

(b)   in the definition of 'the Board', at the end there is inserted '(now known as the Financial Services Authority)'.

23.   In regulations 8 to 10, for 'Bank', wherever occurring, there is substituted 'Authority'.

24.   In regulation 11—

(a)   for 'Bank', wherever occurring, there is substituted 'Authority', and

(b)   in paragraph (1), for 'Bank's' there is substituted 'Authority's'.

25.   In regulations 12 to 13A for 'Bank', wherever occurring, there is substituted 'Authority'.

26.   For regulation 14 there is substituted—

'14.—(1)   In any case where—

(a)   the Authority receives a notice under paragraph 3 of Schedule 2 to these Regulations; and

(b)   the notice states that the institution concerned intends to establish a branch in the United Kingdom for the purpose of carrying on a home-regulated activity appearing to the Authority to constitute investment business,

the Authority shall, before the expiry of the period of two months beginning with the day on which it received the notice, draw to the attention of the institution such provisions of these Regulations, the Financial Services Act or rules or regulations made under that Act as, having regard to the activities mentioned in the notice, it considers appropriate.

(2)   In any case where—

(a)   the Authority receives a notice under paragraph 4 of Schedule 2 to these Regulations; and

(b)   the institution concerned is, or as a result of the proposed change mentioned in the notice will be, carrying on in the United Kingdom a home-regulated activity appearing to the Authority to constitute investment business,

the Authority shall, before the expiry of the period of one month beginning with the day on which it received the notice, draw to the attention of the institution such provisions of these Regulations, the Financial Services Act or rules or regulations made under that Act as, having regard to the proposed change mentioned in the notice, it considers appropriate.'

27.   In regulations 2, 23, 48 and 58, for 'Bank', wherever occurring, there is substituted 'Authority'.

28.   In regulation 62(a), for 'Bank's' there is substituted 'Authority's'.

29.   In Schedules 2 and 3, for 'Bank', wherever occurring, there is substituted 'Authority'.

30.   In Schedule 4, paragraph 1(6)(a) is omitted.

31.   In Schedules 5 to 7, for 'Bank', wherever occurring, there is substituted 'Authority'.

32.   In Schedule 8—

(a)   for 'Bank', wherever occurring, there is substituted 'Authority', and

(b)   for 'Bank's', wherever occurring, there is substituted 'Authority's'.

33.   In Schedule 9, in paragraph 19(c), for 'Bank' there is substituted 'Authority'.

34.   In Schedule 10—

(a)   in paragraph 33, for 'Bank' there is substituted 'Authority', and

(b)   in paragraph 40(2), for 'Bank of England' there is substituted 'Financial Services Authority'.

35.   In Schedule 11, in paragraphs 4(6) and 5(2), for 'Bank' there is substituted 'Authority'.

CHAPTER III
OTHER ENACTMENTS

Consumer Credit Act 1974 (c. 39)

36.   In the Consumer Credit Act 1974, in section 16(3)(f), for 'Bank of England' there is substituted 'Financial Services Authority'.

Insolvency Act 1986 (c. 45)

37.   In the Insolvency Act 1986, in section 422(1), for 'Bank of England' there is substituted 'Financial Services Authority'.

Building Societies Act 1986 (c. 53)

38.—(1)   Section 101 of the Building Societies Act 1986 is amended as follows.

(2)   In subsection (4), for 'Bank', in both places, there is substituted 'Authority'.

(3)   In subsection (6)—

(a)   for the definition of 'the Bank' there is substituted—

' "the Authority" means the Financial Services Authority', and

(b)   In paragraph (c) of the definition of 'financial institution', for 'Bank' there is substituted 'Authority'.

Financial Services Act 1986 (c. 60)

39.   In the Financial Services Act 1986, in sections 128C(3)(a)(iii), 185(4) and 186(7), for 'Bank of England' there is substituted 'Financial Services Authority'.

Insolvency (Northern Ireland) Order 1989 SI 1989/2405 (N.I. 19)

40.   In the Insolvency (Northern Ireland) Order 1989, in Article 366, for 'Bank of England' there is substituted 'Financial Services Authority'.

Courts and Legal Services Act 1990 (c. 41)

41.—(1)   The Courts and Legal Services Act 1990 is amended as follows.

(2)   In sections 37(8)(a) and 48(4)(a), the words 'by the Bank of England' are omitted.

(3)   In section 52(6)—

(a)   in paragraph (a), the words 'by the Bank of England' are omitted, and

(b)   for 'with the Bank of England' there is substituted 'with the Financial Services Authority'.

(4)   In section 54(1), in the inserted subsection (2)(e)(i), the words 'by the Bank of England', are omitted.

Charities Act 1993 (c. 10)

42.   In the Charities Act 1993, in section 28(8)(b)(ii), for 'Bank of England' there is substituted 'Financial Services Authority'.

Building Societies Act 1997 (c. 32)

43.—(1)   Section 32 of the Building Societies Act 1997 is amended as follows.

(2)   In subsection (1), for 'Bank' there is substituted 'Authority'.

(3)   In subsection (3)(a), for 'Governor of the Bank' there is substituted 'Chairman of the Authority'.

(4)   In subsection (7), for the definition of 'the Bank' there is substituted—

' "the Authority" means the Financial Services Authority.'

PART II
SUPERVISION UNDER SECTION 43 OF THE FINANCIAL SERVICES ACT 1986

Financial Services Act 1986 (c. 60)

44.—(1)   Section 43 of the Financial Services Act 1986 is amended as follows.

(2)   In subsection (1), for 'Bank of England' there is substituted 'Financial Services Authority ('the Authority')'.

(3)   In subsections (2) and (3), for 'Bank of England' there is substituted 'Authority'.

(4)   In subsection (4), for 'Bank' there is substituted 'Authority'.

Investment Services Regulations 1995 (SI 1995/3275)

45.—(1)   The Investment Services Regulations 1995 are amended as follows.

(2)   In regulation 2(1)—

(a)   after the definition of 'authorised person' there is inserted—

'"the Authority" means the Financial Services Authority (formerly known as the Securities and Investments Board);', and

(b)   in the definition of 'the Board', at the end there is inserted '(now known as the Financial Services Authority)'.

(3)   In regulations 17(4) and 18(2), for 'Bank' there is substituted 'Authority'.

(4)   In regulation 26—

(a)   in paragraph (2)—

(i)   in sub-paragraph (b), for 'Bank', in the first place where it occurs, there is substituted 'Authority', and the words 'by the Bank' are omitted, and

(ii)   in sub-paragraph (c), for 'Bank' there is substituted 'Authority' and for 'Bank's' there is substituted 'Authority's', and

(b)   in paragraphs (3) and (4), for 'Bank', wherever occurring, there is substituted 'Authority'.

(5)   In regulation 42(10), at the end there is inserted 'in a case in which it is the relevant regulator by virtue of regulation 46(5)(b)(i) below'.

(6)   In regulation 44(2), for the words from the beginning to 'person, the Bank,' there is substituted 'The Authority'.

(7)   In regulation 46(5), for paragraphs (b) and (c) there is substituted 'and

(b)   the Authority, in a case in which the firm in question—

(i)   is subject, in providing core services, to rules made by the Authority, or

(ii)   is not an authorised person and is an exempted person by virtue of being admitted to the list maintained for the purposes of section 43 of the Financial Services Act.'

(8)   In regulation 54(1), for 'Bank', wherever occurring, there is substituted 'Authority'.

(9)   In regulation 56, at the end there is inserted—

'(3)   Paragraph (1) above does not have effect in relation to—

(a)   any function acquired by virtue of the Bank of England Act 1998, or

(b)   so much of any function as is exercisable by virtue of that Act.'

(10)   In Schedule 6, in paragraphs 4(6)(b) and 7(5)(b), for 'the Bank' there is substituted 'it'.

(11)   In that Schedule, in paragraph 8, the existing provision becomes sub-paragraph (1) and after that sub-paragraph there is inserted—

'(2) Sub-paragraph (1) above shall not apply where the decision is in relation to a UK authorised investment firm which is an exempted person by virtue of its inclusion in the list maintained for the purposes of section 43 of the Financial Services Act and which is not an authorised person.'

PART III
SUPERVISION UNDER SECTION 171 OF THE COMPANIES ACT 1989

Companies Act 1989 (c. 40)

46.   The Companies Act 1989 is amended as follows.

47.—(1)   Section 171 is amended as follows.

(2)   In subsection (1), for 'Bank of England' there is substituted 'Financial Services Authority ('the Authority')'.

(3)   In subsection (2), for 'Bank of England', in both places, there is substituted 'Authority'.

(4)   After that subsection there is inserted—

'(2A)   In subsection (2), references to supervision by the Authority are to supervision otherwise than in its capacity as a designated agency within the meaning of the Financial Services Act 1986.'

(5)   In subsection (3)(a), for 'Bank of England' there is substituted 'Authority'.

(6)   After that subsection there is inserted—

'(3C)   The Authority shall consult the Bank of England before it submits to the Treasury for approval under subsection (3) its proposals for conditions or arrangements of the kind referred to in that subsection.'

(7)   In subsection (4), for 'Bank of England' and 'Bank' there is substituted 'Authority'.

(8)   In subsection (6), after 'Bank of England' there is inserted 'and the Authority'.

48.—(1)   Section 176 is amended as follows.

(2)   In subsection (2)(b), for 'Bank of England' there is substituted 'Financial Services Authority'.

(3)   For subsection (6) there is substituted—

'(6)   Before making regulations under this section relating to a description of charges defined by reference to their being granted in favour of a person included in the list maintained by the Financial Services Authority for the purposes of section 171, or in connection with exchange facilities or clearing services provided by a person included in that list, the Secretary of State and the Treasury shall consult the Authority and the Bank of England.

(6A)   Before making regulations under this section relating to a description of charges defined by reference to their being granted in favour of the Bank of England, or in connection with settlement arrangements provided by the Bank, the Secretary of State and the Treasury shall consult the Bank.'

Companies (No. 2) (Northern Ireland) Order 1990 (SI 1990/1504 (N.I. 10))

49.—(1)   The Companies (No. 2) (Northern Ireland) Order 1990 is amended as follows.

50.   In article 93(3), for 'and the Bank of England' there is substituted ', the Bank of England and the Financial Services Authority'.

51.—(1)   Article 98 is amended as follows.

(2)   In paragraph (2)(b), for 'Bank of England' there is substituted 'Financial Services Authority'.

(3)   For paragraph (6) there is substitued—

'(6)   Before making regulations under this Article relating to a description of charges defined by reference to their being granted in favour of a person included in the list maintained by the Financial Services Authority for the purposes of section 171 of the Companies Act 1989, or in connection with exchange facilities or clearing services provided by a person included in that list, the Department shall consult the Treasury, the Authority and the Bank of England.

(6A)   Before making regulations under this Article relating to a description of charges defined by reference to their being granted in favour of the Bank of England, or in connection with settlement arrangements provided by the Bank, the Department shall consult the Treasury and the Bank.'

PART IV
GENERAL: DISCLOSURE OF INFORMATION

CHAPTER I
BANKING ACT 1987

52.   The Banking Act 1987 is amended as follows.

53.—(1)   Section 83 is amended as follows.

(2)   In subsection (1)—

(a)   for 'Bank' there is substituted 'Authority',

(b)   after paragraph (a) there is inserted—

'(aa)   its functions in its capacity as a designated agency within the meaning of the Financial Services Act 1986; or',

(c)   paragraph (b) is omitted,

(d)   in paragraph (c), the words 'and gilt market' are omitted, and

(e)   paragraph (d), and the word 'or' immediately preceding it, are omitted.

(3)   In subsections (2) and (3), for 'Bank', wherever occurring, there is substituted 'Authority'.

54.—(1)   Section 84 is amended as follows.

(2)   In subsection (1), for 'Bank', in both places, there is substituted 'Authority'.

(3)   In the Table in that subsection, after entry 4 there is inserted—

'4A The Bank of England   Functions in its capacity as a monetary authority or supervisor of systems for the transfer of funds between credit institutions and their customers.'

(4)   In that Table, in entry 18, for 'Bank' there is substituted 'Authority'.

(5)   In subsections (2), (4), (5), (5A), (6) and (7), for 'Bank', wherever occurring, there is substituted 'Authority'.

55.   In section 85(1) and (2), for 'Bank', wherever occurring, there is substituted 'Authority'.

56.—(1)   Section 86 is amended as follows.

(2)   In subsections (1), (2)(a), (3) and (4A), for 'Bank', wherever occurring, there is substituted 'Authority'.

(3)   In subsection (5), for the definition of 'relevant functions' there is substituted—

> ' "relevant functions", in relation to the Authority, means its functions under this Act and its functions as a supervisor of money market institutions;'

57.—(1)   Section 86 shall also have effect without the amendments made by paragraph 56 above or section 36(1) above, but with the substitution of the following for the definition of 'relevant functions' in subsection (5)—

> ' "relevant functions", in relation to the Bank, means its functions as a monetary authority;'

(2)   In its application by virtue of sub-paragraph (1), section 86 shall have effect as if the provisions of Part V of the Banking Act 1987 were not amended by the preceding paragraphs of this Part of this Schedule, but were amended as follows.

(3)   In section 84, in subsection (1), in the Table, after entry 1 there is inserted—

'1A The Authority.	Functions under the Financial Services Act 1986 (other than as a designated agency within the meaning of that Act), the Banking Act 1987 or section 171 of the Companies Act 1989.'

(4)   In that section, for subsections (5) and (5A) there is substituted—

> '(5)   Section 82 above does not preclude the disclosure by the Bank of information to the Treasury if disclosure appears to the Bank to be in the public interest and in accordance with article 12(7) of the First Council Directive.
>
> (5A)   Section 82 above does not preclude the disclosure by the Bank of information to the Secretary of State for purposes other than those specified in relation to him in subsection (1) above if—
>
> (a)   the disclosure is made with the consent of the Treasury,
>
> (b)   the information relates to an authorised institution or former authorised institution and does not enable the financial affairs of any other identifiable person to be ascertained, and
>
> (c)   disclosure appears to the Bank to be—
>
> (i)   in the public interest, and
>
> (ii)   in accordance with article 12(7) of the First Council Directive.'

58.—(1)   Section 87 is amended as follows.

(2)   In subsection (2)—

(a)   for 'Bank' there is substituted 'Authority', and

(b)   for 'subsection (3)' there is substituted 'subsection (3)(ha)'.

(3)   In subsection (3)—

(a)   for 'Bank' there is substituted 'Authority, and

(b)   for 'paragraph (3)' there is substituted 'paragraph (3)(ha)'.

(4)   In subsections (3A) and (4), for 'Bank' there is substituted 'Authority'.

59.—(1)   Section 87(2), (3) and (3A) shall also have effect without the amendments made by paragraph 58, but with the following modifications.

(2)   In subsections (2) and (3), the words 'for the purpose of enabling or assisting it to discharge its functions under this Act or' are omitted.

(3)   In subsection (3A)—

(a)   in paragraph (b), for 'section 84(5)(a) or (5A)' there is substituted 'section 84(5A)', and

(b)   for ' ''relevant functions'' has the same meaning as in section 86 above' there is substituted ' ''relevant functions'', in relation to the Bank, means its functions as a monetary authority;'

(4)   In their application by virtue of sub-paragraph (1), section 87(2), (3) and (3A) shall have effect as if the provisions of Part V of the Banking Act 1987 were not amended by the preceding paragraphs of this Part of this Schedule, but were amended as follows.

(5)   In section 84, in subsection (1), in the Table, after entry 1 there is inserted—

'1A The Authority.'   Functions under the Financial
                                             Services Act 1986 (other than as a
                                             designated agency within the
                                             meaning of that Act), the Banking Act
                                             1987 or section 171 of the Companies
                                             Act 1989.'

(6)   In that section, for subsection (5A) there is substituted—

'(5A)   Section 82 above does not preclude the disclosure by the Bank of information to the Secretary of State for purposes other than those specified in relation to him in subsection (1) above if—

(a)   the disclosure is made with the consent of the Treasury, and

(b)   the information relates to an authorised institution or former authorised institution and does not enable the financial affairs of any other identifiable person to be ascertained, and

(c)   disclosure appears to the Bank to be—

(i)   in the public interest and

(ii)   in accordance with article 12(7) of the First Council Directive.'

CHAPTER II
OTHER ENACTMENTS

Consumer Credit Act 1974 (c. 39)

60.   In section 174(3A) of the Consumer Credit Act 1974—

(a)   for 'Bank of England' there is substituted 'Financial Services Authority', and

(b)   for 'Bank' there is substituted 'Authority'.

Insurance Companies Act 1982 (c. 50)

61.—(1)   Paragraph 3 of Schedule 2B to the Insurance Companies Act 1982 is amended as follows.

(2)   In sub-paragraph (1), in the Table, after entry 1 there is inserted—

| '1A The Financial Services Authority. | Functions under the Financial Services Act 1986 (other than as a designated agency within the meaning of that Act), the Banking Act 1987 or section 171 of the Companies Act 1989.' |

(3)   In sub-paragraph (5), at the end there is inserted ', or

(e)   the Financial Services Authority under that Act (other than in its capacity as a designated agency) or the Banking Act 1987;'.

Companies Act 1985 (c. 6)

62.—(1)   Section 449 of the Companies Act 1985 is amended as follows.

(2)   In subsection (1), for paragraph (f) there is substituted—

'(f)   for the purpose of enabling or assisting the Bank of England to discharge its functions,

(fa)   for the purpose of enabling or assisting the Financial Services Authority to discharge—

(i)   any functions under the Financial Services Act 1986, other than as a designated agency within the meaning of that Act,

(ii)   its functions under the Banking Act 1987, or

(iii)   its functions under section 171 of the Companies Act 1989,'.

(3)   In subsection (3), after paragraph (h) there is inserted—

'(ha)   the Financial Services Authority, other than in its capacity as a designated agency within the meaning of the Financial Services Act 1986,'.

Companies (Northern Ireland) Order 1986 (SI 1986/1032 (N.I. 6))

63.—(1)   Article 442 of the Companies (Northern Ireland) Order 1986 is amended as follows.

(2)   In paragraph (1), for sub-paragraph (f) there is substituted—

'(f)   for the purpose of enabling or assisting the Bank of England to discharge its functions;

(fa)   for the purpose of enabling or assisting the Financial Services Authority to discharge—

(i)   any functions under the Financial Services Act 1986, other than as a designated agency within the meaning of that Act,

(ii)   its functions under the Banking Act 1987, or

(iii)   its functions under section 171 of the Companies Act 1989;'.

(3)   In subsection (3), after paragraph (h) there is inserted—

'(ha)   the Financial Services Authority, other than in its capacity as a designated agency within the meaning of the Financial Services Act 1986,'.

Building Societies Act 1986 (c. 53)

64.—(1)   The Building Societies Act 1986 is amended as follows.

(2)   In section 53, in subsection (5)—

(a)   for 'Bank of England', in the first place where it occurs, there is substituted 'Financial Services Authority',

(b)   for paragraph (b) there is substituted—

'(b)   by the Authority of any of its functions under the Banking Act 1987 or as a supervisor of money market institutions;', and

(c)   for 'Bank of England', in the second place where it occurs, there is substituted 'Authority'.

(3)   In that section, after subsection (5) there is inserted—

'(5A)   Nothing in subsection (1) above prohibits the disclosure of information to the Bank of England where, in the opinion of the Commission, it is desirable or expedient that the information should be disclosed with a view to facilitating the discharge—

(a)   by the Commission of any of its functions under this Act; or

(b)   by the Bank of any of its functions;

nor does subsection (1) above prohibit further disclosure of the information by the Bank of England with the consent of the Commission.'

(4)   In section 54(3A)—

(a)   for 'Bank of England', in the first place where it occurs, there is substituted 'Financial Services Authority, other than in its capacity as a designated agency within the meaning of the Financial Services Act 1986,', and

(b)   for 'Bank of England', in the second place where it occurs, there is substituted 'Financial Services Authority'.

Financial Services Act 1986 (c. 60)

65.—(1)   The Financial Services Act 1986 is amended as follows.

(2)   In section 179(3)—

(a)   after paragraph (b) there is inserted—

'(ba)   the Financial Services Authority, other than in its capacity as a designated agency;' and

(b)   paragraph (f) is omitted.

(3)   In section 180(1)—

(a)   after paragraph (e) there is inserted—

(ea)   for the purpose of enabling or assisting the Financial Services Authority to discharge—

(i)   its functions under this Act, other than as a designated agency,

(ii)   its functions under the Banking Act 1987, or

(iii)   its functions under section 171 of the Companies Act 1989;' and

(b)   in paragraph (f), for the words from 'its' to the end there is substituted 'any of its functions'.

Companies Act 1989 (c. 40)

66.—(1)   The Companies Act 1989 is amended as follows.

(2)   In section 82—

(a)   in subsection (2)(a)(iii) for 'Bank of England' there is substituted 'Financial Services Authority', and

(b)   in subsection (5)—

(i)   for 'Bank of England', in both places, there is substituted 'Financial Services Authority', and

(ii)   for 'Bank' there is substituted 'Authority'.

(3)   In section 87(4), in the Table, in the entry relating to the Bank of England, for the words in the second column there is substituted 'Any of its functions', and after that entry there is inserted—

'The Financial Services Authority.	Functions under the Financial Services Act 1986 (other than as a designated agency within the meaning of that Act), the Banking Act 1987 or section 171 of the Companies Act 1989.'

Courts and Legal Services Act 1990 (c. 41)

67.   In section 50(2) of the Courts and Legal Services Act 1990—

(a)   after paragraph (f) there is inserted—

'(fa)   the Financial Services Authority to discharge any of its functions under the Financial Services Act 1986 (other than as a designated agency within the meaning of that Act), the Banking Act 1987 or section 171 of the Companies Act 1989;', and

(b)   in paragraph (p)(i), for 'Bank of England' there is substituted 'Financial Services Authority'.

Friendly Societies Act 1992 (c. 40)

68.   In section 64(5) of the Friendly Societies Act 1992, in the Table, in the entry relating to the Bank of England, for the words in the second column there is substituted 'Any of its functions', and after that entry there is inserted—

'The Financial Services Authority.	Functions under the Financial Services Act 1986 (other than as a designated agency within the meaning of that Act), the Banking Act 1987 or section 171 of the Companies Act 1989.'

Pension Schemes Act 1993 (c. 48)

69.—(1)   The Pension Schemes Act 1993 is amended as follows.

(2)   In section 149(6)(e), for 'Bank of England' there is substituted 'Financial Services Authority'.

(3)   In section 158A(1), in the Table, in the entry relating to the Bank of England, for the words in the second column there is substituted 'Any of its functions', and after that entry there is inserted—

| 'The Financial Services Authority. | Functions under the Financial Services Act 1986 (other than as a designated agency within the meaning of that Act), the Banking Act 1987 or section 171 of the Companies Act 1989.' |

Pension Schemes (Northern Ireland) Act 1993 (c. 49)

70.—(1)   The Pension Schemes (Northern Ireland) Act 1993 is amended as follows.

(2)   In section 145(6)(e), for 'Bank of England' there is substituted 'Financial Services Authority'.

(3)   In section 154A(1), in the Table, in the entry relating to the Bank of England, for the words in the second column there is substituted 'Any of its functions', and after that entry there is inserted—

| 'The Financial Services Authority. | Functions under the Financial Services Act 1986 (other than as a designated agency within the meaning of that Act), the Banking Act 1987 or section 171 of the Companies Act 1989.' |

Pensions Act 1995 (c. 26)

71.   In section 107(1) of the Pensions Act 1995, in the Table, in the entry relating to the Bank of England, for the words in the second column there is substituted 'Any of its functions', and after that entry there is inserted—

| 'The Financial Services Authority. | Functions under the Financial Services Act 1986 (other than as a designated agency within the meaning of that Act), the Banking Act 1987 or section 171 of the Companies Act 1989.' |

Pensions (Northern Ireland) Order 1995 (SI 1995/3213 (N.I. 22))

72.   In Article 105(1) of the Pensions (Northern Ireland) Order 1995, in the Table, in the entry relating to the Bank of England, for the words in the second column there is substituted 'Any of its functions', and after that entry there is inserted—

| 'The Financial Services Authority. | Functions under the Financial Services Act 1986 (other than as a designated agency within the meaning of that Act), the Banking Act 1987 or section 171 of the Companies Act 1989.' |

SCHEDULE 6
BANKING SUPERVISION FEES

Powers

1.—(1)   Every application for authorisation under the Banking Act 1987 and every notice given to the Authority under section 75 of that Act (notice by overseas institution of establishment of representative office in the United Kingdom) shall be accompanied by such fee as the Authority may by regulations prescribe; and no such application or notice shall be regarded as duly made or given unless this subparagraph is complied with.

(2)   Every authorised institution and every European authorised institution which has lawfully established a branch in the United Kingdom for the purpose of accepting deposits or other repayable funds from the public shall pay such periodical fees to the Authority as it may by regulations prescribe.

(3)   The powers conferred by this paragraph may be used to prescribe such fees as will enable the Authority—

(a)   to meet the expenses which it incurs in carrying out the transferred functions or for any incidental purposes, and

(b)   to repay the principal of, and pay any interest on, any money which it has borrowed and which has been used for the purpose of meeting expenses which it has incurred in relation to the transfer to it of the transferred functions.

(4)   Regulations under this paragraph shall specify the time when the fees are to be paid and may—

(a)   provide for the determination of the fees in accordance with a specified scale or other specified factors,

(b)   provide for the return or abatement of any fees, and

(c)   make different provision for different cases.

(5)   In this paragraph—

'authorised' has the same meaning as in the Banking Act 1987;

'European authorised institution' has the same meaning as in the Banking Coordination (Second Council Directive) Regulations 1992;

'institution' has the same meaning as in the Banking Act 1987.

Consultation

2.—(1)   Before making regulations under paragraph 1, the Authority shall—

(a)   publish the proposed regulations in such manner as appears to it best calculated to bring the proposals to the attention of those likely to be affected by them, together with a statement that representations about the proposals can be made to the Authority within a specified time, and

(b)   have regard to any representations duly made in accordance with the statement.

(2)   Sub-paragraph (1) does not apply where the Authority considers that the delay involved in complying with it would be prejudicial to the interests of depositors.

Mode of exercise

3.   Power to make regulations under paragraph 1 is exercisable by instrument in writing which shall state that it is made under that paragraph.

Publication

4.—(1)   Immediately after regulations under paragraph 1 are made they shall be printed and made available to the public with or without payment.

(2)   A person shall not be liable to pay a fee under regulations under paragraph 1 if he shows that, at the time the fee became payable, the regulations had not been made available as required by this paragraph.

Proof of regulations

5.—(1)   The production of a printed copy of regulations purporting to be made by the Authority under paragraph 1 on which is endorsed a certificate signed by an officer of the authority authorised by it for that purpose and stating—

(a)   that the regulations were made by the Authority,

(b)   that the copy is a true copy of the regulations, and

(c)   that on a specified date the regulations were made available to the public as required by paragraph 4,

shall be prima facie evidence or, in Scotland, sufficient evidence of the facts stated in the certificate.

(2)   Any certificate purporting to be signed as mentioned in sub-paragraph (1) shall be deemed to have been duly signed unless the contrary is shown.

(3)   Any person wishing in any legal proceedings to cite regulations under paragraph 1 may require the Authority to cause a copy of them to be endorsed with such a certificate as is mentioned in this paragraph.

Section 37   SCHEDULE 7
              RESTRICTION ON DISCLOSURE OF INFORMATION

Restricted information

1.—(1)   Subject to sub-paragraph (2), information is restricted information for the purposes of this paragraph if—

(a)   it is obtained by the Bank by virtue of the power conferred by section 17(1) or paragraph 9 of Schedule 2 (whether or not it was obtained pursuant to a notice under that provision), and

(b)   it relates to the business or other affairs of any person.

(2)   Information is not restricted information for the purposes of this paragraph if—

(a)   it has been made available to the public from the sources, or

(b)   it is in the form of a summary or collection of information so framed as not to enable information relating to any particular person to be ascertained from it.

(3)   Except as permitted by the following provisions of this Schedule, restricted information shall not be disclosed by—

(a) the Bank or any officer or servant of the Bank, or

(b) any person obtaining the information directly or indirectly from the Bank, without the consent of the person from whom the Bank obtained the information and, if different, the person to whom the information relates.

(4) Any person who discloses information in contravention of this paragraph shall be guilty of an offence and liable—

(a) on conviction on indictment to imprisonment for a term not exceeding 2 years, or to a fine, or to both;

(b) on summary conviction, to imprisonment for a term not exceeding 3 months, or to a fine not exceeding the statutory maximum, or to both.

Disclosure for the purposes of the Bank's functions

2.—(1) Paragraph 1 does not preclude the disclosure of information in any case in which disclosure is for the purpose of enabling or assisting the Bank to discharge—

(a) its functions as a monetary authority,

(b) its functions as a supervisor of systems for the transfer of funds between credit institutions and their customers, or

(c) its functions under Schedule 2.

(2) In sub-paragraph (1)(b), 'credit institution' has the same meaning as in the Banking Coordination (Second Council Directive) Regulations 1992.

Disclosure by the Bank to other authorities

3.—(1) Paragraph 1 does not preclude the disclosure by the Bank of information to any authority specified in the first column of the following Table if the Bank considers that the disclosure would enable or assist that authority to discharge any of the functions specified in relation to it in the second column of that Table.

TABLE

Authority	Functions
The Treasury.	Functions under the Insurance Companies Act 1982 or the Financial Services Act 1986.
An inspector appointed under Part XIV of the Companies Act 1985, section 94 or 177 of the Financial Services Act 1986 or Part XV of the Companies (Northern Ireland) Order 1986.	Functions under that Part or section.
A person authorised to exercise powers or appointed under section 43A or 44 of the Insurance Companies Act 1982, section 447 of the Companies Act 1985, section 106 of the Financial Services Act 1986, article 440 of the Companies	Functions under that section or article.

(Northern Ireland) Order 1986 or section
84 of the Companies Act 1989.

A designated agency within the meaning of the Financial Services Act 1986.	Functions under that Act or Part VII of the Companies Act 1989.
The Financial Services Authority.	Functions under the Financial Services Act 1986 (other than as a designated agency within the meaning of that Act), the Banking Act 1987 or section 171 of the Companies Act 1989.
The Office for National Statistics.	Functions under the Statistics of Trade Act 1947.
The Friendly Societies Commission.	Functions under the enactments relating to friendly societies or under the Financial Services Act 1986.
The Building Societies Commission.	Functions under the Building Societies Act 1986 and protecting the interests of the shareholders and depositors of building societies.
The Occupational Pensions Regulatory Authority.	Functions under the Pension Schemes Act 1993 or the Pensions Act 1995 or any enactment in force in Northern Ireland corresponding to either of them.

(2)   The Treasury may by order amend the Table in sub-paragraph (1) by—

(a)   adding any public or other authority and specifying functions in relation to it,

(b)   removing any authority for the time being specified in the Table, or

(c)   altering the functions for the time being specified in the Table in relation to any authority.

(3)   The Treasury may by order restrict the circumstances in which, or impose conditions subject to which, disclosure is permitted in the case of any authority for the time being specified in the Table.

(4)   Before making an order under this Paragraph, the Treasury shall consult the Bank.

Onward disclosure

4.—(1)   Paragraph 1 does not preclude the disclosure by any authority specified in the first column of the Table in paragraph 3(1) of information obtained by it by virtue of that provision if it makes the disclosure—

(a)   with the consent of the Bank, and

(b)   for the purpose of enabling or assisting it to discharge any functions specified in relation to it in the second column of that Table.

(2)   Before deciding whether to give its consent to disclosure under this paragraph, the Bank shall take account of such representations as the authority proposing to make the disclosure may make about the desirability of or necessity for the disclosure.

Other permitted disclosures

5.   Paragraph 1 does not preclude the disclosure of information—

(a)   with a view to the institution of, or otherwise for the purposes of, any proceedings in connection with a payment due under Schedule 2 (payment in lieu of cash ratio deposit),

(b)   with a view to the institution of, or otherwise for the purposes of, any criminal proceedings, whether under this Act or otherwise, or

(c)   in pursuance of any Community obligation.

Section 42   SCHEDULE 8
                TRANSITIONAL PROVISIONS AND SAVINGS

Bank's immunity from suit

1.   Section 1(4) of the Banking Act 1987 (immunity in relation to things done or omitted in discharge of functions under the Act) shall continue to have effect without the amendments made by paragraph 2(c) of Schedule 5—

(a)   in relation to things done or omitted before the day on which this Act comes into force, and

(b)   in relation to anything done on or after that day for the purposes of, or in connection with, any proceedings arising from anything done or omitted before that day.

Disclosure of information

2.   Sections 83 to 85 of the Banking Act 1987 (exceptions to restriction on disclosure of information received under or for the purposes of the Act) shall, in relation to information received before the day on which this Act comes into force, continue to have effect without the amendments made by paragraphs 53 to 55 of Schedule 5, but with the modifications mentioned in paragraphs 3 to 5 below.

3.—(1)   Section 83 is amended as follows.

(2)   In subsection (1), paragraphs (a) and (c) are omitted.

(3)   Subsections (2) and (3) are omitted.

4.—(1)   Section 84 is amended as follows.

(2)   In subsection (1), in the Table, after entry 1 there is inserted—

'1A The Financial Services   Functions under the Financial
Authority.   Services Act 1986 (other than as a
                                    designated agency within the
                                    meaning of that Act), the Banking Act
                                    1987 or section 171 of the Companies
                                    Act 1989.';

and in entry 18, for 'Bank' there is substituted 'Financial Services Authority'.

(3)   Subsections (2) and (3) are omitted.

(4)   In subsection (6)(a)(i), for 'Bank' there is substituted 'Financial Services Authority'.

5.   In section 85(1)(f), for 'Bank' there is substituted 'Financial Services Authority'.

Pre-commencement consultation

6.   If, before the day on which this Act comes into force, anything is done which, had it been done after that day, would to any extent have satisfied—

(a)   any requirement to consult before making an order under this Act, or

(b)   any requirement of paragraph 2(1) of Schedule 6,

that requirement shall to that extent be taken to have been satisfied.

Membership of the Deposit Protection Board

7.   The terms of a person's appointment as an ordinary member of the Deposit Protection Board shall, if he holds office as such immediately before the coming into force of this Act, have effect after the coming into force of this Act as if any reference to the Bank were a reference to the Financial Services Authority and any reference to the Governor of the Bank were a reference to the Chairman of the Financial Services Authority.

Section 43   SCHEDULE 9
                        REPEALS AND REVOCATIONS

PART I
REPEALS

Chapter	Short title	Extent of repeal
1946 c. 27	The Bank of England Act 1946	Sections 2 and 4(2). Schedule 2.
1986 c. 60.	The Financial Services Act 1986.	Section 179(3)(f). In Schedule 7, in paragraph 1(2), the words 'and the Governor of the Bank of England acting jointly'.
1987 c. 22.	The Banking Act 1987.	In section 83(1), paragraph (b), in paragraph (c), the words 'and gilt market', and paragraph (d) and the word 'or' immediately preceding it.
1990 c. 41	The Courts and Legal Services Act 1990.	In sections 37(8)(a), 48(4)(a) and 52(6), the words 'by the Bank of England'. In section 54(1), in the inserted subsection (2)(e)(i), the words 'by the Bank of England,'.

PART II
REVOCATIONS

Number	Title	Extent of revocation
SI 1992/3218	The Banking Coordination (Second Council Directive) Regulations 1992.	Regulation 76(4). In Schedule 4, paragraph 1(6)(a). In Schedule 10, in paragraphs 8(1) and 31, the words 'by the Bank,'.
1995/3275.	The Investment Services Regulations 1995.	Regulations 8(3), 13 and 14. In regulation 26(2)(b), the words 'by the Bank'. In Schedule 3, in paragraph 1, in sub-paragraph (1)(b), the words ', or in the case of a listed firm, the Bank,', in sub-paragraph (2), in paragraph (b), the words ', or in the case of a listed firm, the Bank,' and, in paragraph (c), in both places, the words 'or, as the case may be, the Bank', in paragraph 3(2), the words 'or, as the case may be, the Bank', in paragraph 4, in sub-paragraph (1), the words ', or, in the case of a listed firm, to the Bank,', in sub-paragraph (2), the words 'or, as the case may be, to the Bank', and, in sub-paragraph (3), the words 'or, as the case may be, the Bank', in paragraph 5, in sub-paragraph (1), in paragraph (a), the words ', or, in the case of a listed firm, to the Bank,' and, in

Number	Title	Extent of revocation
		paragraphs (b) and (c), the words 'or, as the case may be, the Bank', wherever occurring, in sub-paragraph (2), the words 'or, as the case may be, to the Bank', in sub-paragraph (3), the words 'or, as the case may be, the Bank', and paragraph 6.
		In Schedule 6, in paragraph 1, in sub-paragraph (1), the words ', or in the case of a listed person, to the Bank,' and, in sub-paragraph (2), in paragraph (a), the words ', or, in the case of a listed firm, to the Bank,', and, in paragraphs (b) and (c)(ii), the words 'or, as the case may be, the Bank', in paragraph 2, the words 'or, as the case may be, to the Bank', in paragraphs 3 and 4, the words 'or, as the case may be, the Bank', wherever occurring, in paragraph 5, in sub-paragraph (1), the words 'or, in a case in which a firm is a listed person, to the Bank' and, in sub-paragraph (2), the words 'or, in the case of a firm which is a listed person, the Bank', in paragraph 6, in sub-paragraph (1), in paragraph (a), the words 'or, in the case of a firm

Number	Title	Extent of revocation
		which is a listed person, to the Bank' and, in paragraph (b), the words 'or, as the case may be, the Bank', and in sub-paragraph (2), the words 'or, in the case of a firm which is a listed person, to the Bank', in paragraph 7, the words 'or, as the case may be, the Bank', wherever occurring, and paragraph 9.

Appendix 2
Banking Act 1987

Apart from headings, *words in italics* will be repealed and **words in bold** will be inserted when the relevant provisions of the Bank of England Act 1998 are brought into force (1 June 1998).

1987 CHAPTER 22

An Act to make new provision for regulating the acceptance of deposits in the course of a business, for protecting depositors and for regulating the use of banking names and descriptions; to amend section 187 of the Consumer Credit Act 1974 in relation to arrangements for the electronic transfer of funds; to clarify the powers conferred by section 183 of the Financial Services Act 1986; and for purposes connected with those matters.   [15 May 1987]

BE IT ENACTED by the Queen's most Excellent Majesty, by and with the advice and consent of the Lords Spiritual and Temporal, and Commons, in this present Parliament assembled, and by the authority of the same, as follows:—

PART I
REGULATION OF DEPOSIT-TAKING BUSINESS

The Bank of England and the Board of Banking Supervision

1. Functions and duties of the Bank of England

(1) *The Bank of England (in this Act referred to as 'the Bank')* **The Financial Services Authority (in this Act referred to as 'the Authority')** shall have the powers conferred on it by this Act and the duty generally to supervise the institutions authorised by it in the exercise of those powers.

(2) It shall also be the duty of the *Bank* **Authority** to keep under review the operation of this Act and developments in the field of banking which appear to it to be relevant to the exercise of its powers and the discharge of its duties.

(3) The *Bank* **Authority** shall, as soon as practicable after the end of each of its financial years, make to the Chancellor of the Exchequer and publish in such manner

as it thinks appropriate a report on its activities under this Act in that year; and the Chancellor of the Exchequer shall lay copies of every such report before Parliament.

(4)   *Neither the Bank nor any person who is a member of its Court of Directors or who is, or is acting as, an officer or servant of the Bank* **Neither the Authority nor any person who is, or is acting as, an officer or servant of the Authority** shall be liable in damages for anything done or omitted in the discharge or purported discharge of the functions of the *Bank* **Authority** under this Act unless it is shown that the act or omission was in bad faith.

2.   The Board of Banking Supervision

(1)   As soon as practicable after the coming into force of this section the Bank shall establish a committee to be known as the Board of Banking Supervision.

(2)   The Board shall consist of—

(a)   three ex officio members, namely, the Governor of the Bank for the time being, who shall be the chairman of the Board, the Deputy Governor of the Ban¹ for the time being and the executive director of the Bank for the time being responsible for the supervision of institutions authorised under this Act; and

(b)   six independent members, that is to say, members appointed jointly by the Chancellor of the Exchequer and the Governu ., being persons having no executive responsiblity in the Bank.

(1)   There shall continue to be a committee known as the Board of Banking Supervision.

(2)   The Board shall consist of—

(a)   two ex officio members, namely, the Chairman of the Authority, who shall chair the Board, and the holder of such other office within the Authority as the chairman of the Authority may designate for the purposes of this provision; and

(b)   six independent members, that is to say, members appointed jointly by the Chancellor of the Exchequer and the Chairman of the Authority, being persons having no executive responsibiity in the authority.

(3)   It shall be the duty of the independent members to give such advice as they think fit to the ex officio members—

(a)   on the exercise by the *Bank* **Authority** of its functions under this Act, either generally or in any particular respect or in relation to a particular institution or institutions; and

(b)   on any matter relating to or arising out of the exercise of those functions.

(4)   The *Bank* **Authority** shall make regular reports to the Board on matters which the *Bank* **Authority** considers relevant to the discharge by the independent members of their duty under subsection (3) above and shall provide them with such other information as they may reasonably require.

(5)   The ex officio members shall give written notice to the Chancellor of the Exchequer in any case in which it is decided that the advice of the independent members should not be followed and the independent members shall be entitled to place before the Chancellor the reasons for their advice.

(6)   The Board shall prepare an annual report on its activities and that report shall be included in the report made by the *Bank* **Authority** under section 1(3) above for the financial year in question.

(7)   Section 1(4) above shall apply to an act or omission by a member of the Board in the discharge or purported discharge of his functions under this section as it applies to an act or omission of a person there mentioned in the discharge or purported discharge of the functions of the *Bank* **Authority**.

(8)   Schedule 1 to this Act shall have effect with respect of the Board.

Restriction on acceptance of deposits

3.   Restriction on acceptance of deposits

(1)   Subject to section 4 below, no person shall in the United Kingdom accept a deposit in the course of carrying on (whether there or elsewhere) a business which for the purposes of this Act is a deposit-taking business unless that person is an institution for the time being authorised by the *Bank* **Authority** under the following provisions of this Part of this Act.

(2)   Any person who contravenes this section shall be guilty of an offence and liable—

(a)   on conviction on indictment, to imprisonment for a term not exceeding two years or to a fine or to both;

(b)   on summary conviction, to imprisonment for a term not exceeding six months or to a fine not exceeding the statutory maximum or to both.

(3)   The fact that a deposit has been taken in contravention of this section shall not affect any civil liability arising in respect of the deposit or the money deposited.

4.   Exempted persons and exempted transactions

(1)   Section 3 above shall not apply to the acceptance of a deposit by the Bank or by a person for the time being specified in Schedule 2 to this Act.

(2)   The exemption of a person specified in that Schedule shall be subject to any restriction there specified in the case of that person.

(3)   The Treasury may after consultation with the *Bank* **Authority** by order amend that Schedule—

(a)   by adding any person or relaxing any restriction; or

(b)   by removing any person for the time being specified in it or imposing or extending any restriction.

(4)   Section 3 above shall not apply to any transaction prescribed for the purposes of this subsection by regulations made by the Treasury.

(5)   Regulations under subsection (4) above may prescribe transactions by reference to any factors appearing to the Treasury to be appropriate and, in particular, by reference to all or any of the following—

(a)   the amount of the deposit;

(b)   the total liability of the person accepting the deposit to his depositors or to any other creditors;

(c)   the circumstances in which or the purpose for which the deposit is made;

(d)   the identity of the person by whom the deposit is made or accepted, including his membership of a class whose membership is determined otherwise than by the Treasury;

(e)   the number of, or the amount involved in, transactions of any particular description carried out by the person accepting the deposit or the frequency with which he carries out transactions of any particular description.

(6)   Regulations under subsection (4) above may make any exemption for which they provide subject to compliance with specified conditions or requirements.

(7)   Any order under subsection (3)(a) above and any regulations under subsection (4) above shall be subject to annulment in pursuance of a resolution of either House of Parliament, and no order shall be made under subsection (3)(b) above unless a draft of it has been laid before and approved by a resolution of each House of Parliament.

5.   Meaning of 'deposit'

(1)   Subject to the provisions of this section, in this Act 'deposit' means a sum of money (whether denominated in a currency or in ecus) paid on terms—

(a)   under which it will be repaid, with or without interest or a premium, and either on demand or at a time or in circumstances agreed by or on behalf of the person making the payment and the person receiving it; and

(b)   which are not referable to the provision of property or services or the giving of security;

and references in this Act to money deposited and to the making of a deposit shall be construed accordingly.

(1A)   In subsection (1) above 'ecu' means—

(a)   the European currency unit as defined in Article 1 of Council Regulation No. 3320/94/EC; or

(b)   any other unit of account which is defined by reference to the European currency unit as so defined.

(2)   For the purposes of subsection (1)(b) above, money is paid on terms which are referable to the provision of property or services or to the giving of security if, and only if—

(a)   it is paid by way of advance or part payment under a contract for the sale, hire or other provision of property or services, and is repayable only in the event that the property or services is not or are not in fact sold, hired or otherwise provided;

(b)   it is paid by way of security for the performance of a contract or by way of security in respect of loss which may result from the non-performance of a contract; or

(c)   without prejudice to paragraph (b) above, it is paid by way of security for the delivery up or return of any property, whether in a particular state of repair or otherwise.

(3)   Except so far as any provision of this Act otherwise provides, in this Act 'deposit' does not include—

(a)   a sum paid by the Bank or an authorised institution;

(b)   a sum paid by a person for the time being specified in Schedule 2 to this Act;

(c)   a sum paid by a person, other than a person within paragraph (a) or (b) above, in the course of carrying on a business consisting wholly or mainly of lending money;

(d)   a sum which is paid by one company to another at a time when one is a subsidiary of the other or both are subsidiaries or another company or the same individual is a majority or principal shareholder controller of both of them; or

(e)   a sum which is paid by a person who, at the time when it is paid, is a close relative of, a director, controller or manager of that person.

(4)   In the application of paragraph (e) of subsection (3) above to a sum paid by a partnership that paragraph shall have effect as if for the reference to the person paying the sum there were substituted a reference to each of the partners.

(5)   In subsection (3)(e) above 'close relative', in relation to any person, means—

(a)   his spouse;

(b)   his children and step-children, his parents and step-parents, his brothers and sisters and step-brothers and step-sisters; and

(c)   the spouse of any person within paragraph (b) above.

6.   Meaning of 'deposit-taking business'

(1)   Subject to the provisions of this section, a business is a deposit-taking business for the purposes of this Act if—

(a)   in the course of the business money received by way of deposit is lent to others; or

(b)   any other activity of the business is financed wholly or to any material extent, out of the capital of or the interest on money received by way of deposit.

(2)   Notwithstanding that paragraph (a) or (b) of subsection (1) above applies to a business, it is not a deposit-taking business for the purposes of this Act if—

(a)   the person carrying it on does not hold himself out as accepting deposits on a day to day basis; and

(b)   any deposits which are accepted are accepted only on particular occasions, whether or not involving the issue of debentures or other securities.

(3)   For the purposes of subsection (1) above all the activities which a person carries on by way of business shall be regarded as a single business carried on by him.

(4)   In determining for the purposes of subsection (2)(b) above whether deposits are accepted only on particular occasions regard shall be had to the frequency of those occasions and to any characteristics distinguishing them from each other.

(5)   For the purposes of subsection (2) above there shall be disregarded any deposit in respect of the acceptance of which the person in question is exempt from the prohibition in section 3 above and any money received by way of deposit which is not used in the manner described in subsection (1) above.

7.   Power to amend definitions

(1)   The Treasury may after consultation with the *Bank* **Authority** by order amend the meaning of deposit or deposit-taking business for the purposes of all or any provisions of this Act.

(2)   Without prejudice to the generality of the power conferred by subsection (1) above, an order under that subsection amending the meaning of deposit-taking business may provide for taking into account as activities of an institution the activities of any person who is connected with it in such manner as is specified in the order.

(3)   Any order under this section shall be subject to annulment in pursuance of a resolution of either House of Parliament.

(4)   An order under this section may contain such transitional provisions as the Treasury think necessary or expedient and may exclude or modify the effect of the order on any other enactment which is expressed to have effect in relation to a deposit or a deposit-taking business within the meaning of this Act.

Authorisations

8.   Applications for authorisation

(1)   Any institution may make an application for authorisation to the *Bank* **Authority** other than—

(a)   a credit institution incorporated in or formed under the law of any part of the United Kingdom whose principal place of business is outside the United Kingdom; and

(b)   a credit institution incorporated in or formed under the law of another member State.

(2)   Any such application—

(a)   shall be made in such manner as the *Bank* **Authority** may direct; and

(b)   shall be accompanied by—

(i)   a statement setting out the nature and scale of the deposit-taking business which the applicant intends to carry on, any plans of the applicant for the future development of that business and particulars of the applicant's arrangements for the management of that business; and

(ii)   such other information or documents as the *Bank* **Authority** may reasonably require for the purpose of determining the application.

(3)   At any time after receiving an application and before determining it the *Bank* **Authority** may by written notice require the applicant or any person who is or is to be a director, controller or manager of the applicant to provide additional information or documents.

(4)   The directions and requirements given or imposed under subsections (2) and (3) above may differ as between different applications.

(5)   Any information or statement to be provided to the *Bank* **Authority** under this section shall be in such form as the *Bank* **Authority** may specify; and the *Bank* **Authority** may by written notice require the applicant or any such person as is mentioned in subsection (3) above to provide a report by an accountant or other qualified person approved by the *Bank* **Authority** on such aspects of that information as may be specified by the *Bank* **Authority**.

(6)   An application may be withdrawn by written notice to the *Bank* **Authority** at any time before it is granted or refused.

9. Grant and refusal of authorisation

(1) The *Bank* **Authority** may, on an application duly made in accordance with section 8 above and after being provided with all such information, documents and reports as it may require under that section, grant or refuse the application.

(2) The *Bank* **Authority** shall not grant an application unless satisfied that the criteria specified in Schedule 3 to this Act are fulfilled with respect to the applicant.

(3) In the case of an application by an applicant whose principal place of business is in a country or territory outside the United Kingdom the *Bank* **Authority** may regard itself as satisfied that the criteria specified in paragraphs 1, 4 and 5 of that Schedule are fulfilled if—

  (a) the relevant supervisory authority in that country or territory informs the *Bank* **Authority** that it is satisfied with respect to the prudent management and overall financial soundness of the applicant; and

  (b) the *Bank* **Authority** is satisfied as to the nature and scope of the supervision exercised by that authority.

(3A) The *Bank* **Authority** shall refuse an application made by a credit institution if it appears to the *Bank* **Authority** that—

  (a) the institution is an undertaking which is closely linked with any person; and

  (b) the institution's close links with that person, or any matters relating to any non-EEA laws or administrative provisions to which that person is subject, are such as would prevent the effective exercise by the *Bank* **Authority** of its supervisory functions in relation to the institution;

and in this subsection and subsection (1B) of section 11 below 'non-EEA laws' means laws of a country or territory which is not a contracting party to the agreement on the European Economic Area signed at Oporto on 2nd May 1992 as adjusted by the Protocol signed at Brussels on 17th May 1993, and 'non-EEA administrative provisions' shall be construed accordingly.

(4) In determining whether to grant or refuse an application the *Bank* **Authority** may take into account any matters relating—

  (a) to any person who is or will be employed by or associated with the applicant for the purposes of the applicant's deposit-taking business; and

  (b) if the applicant is a body corporate, to any other body corporate in the same group or to any director or controller of any such other body.

(5) No authorisation shall be granted to a partnership or unincorporated association if the whole of the assets available to it are owned by a single individual.

(6) An authorisation granted to a partnership shall be granted in the partnership name and, without prejudice to sections 11 and 12 below, shall not be affected by any change in the partners.

(7) Before granting an authorisation to a credit institution incorporated in or formed under the law of any part of the United Kingdom which is—

  (a) a subsidiary undertaking;

  (b) a subsidiary undertaking of the parent undertaking; or

  (c) controlled by the parent controller,

of a credit institution which is for the time being authorised to act as such an institution by the relevant supervisory authority in another member State, the *Bank* **Authority** shall consult that authority,

10.   Notice of grant or refusal

(1)   Where the *Bank* **Authority** grants an application for authorisation it shall give written notice of that fact to the applicant.

(2)   Where the *Bank* **Authority** proposes to refuse an application for authorisation it shall give the applicant written notice of its intention to do so, stating the grounds on which it proposes to act and giving particulars of the applicant's rights under subsection (4) below.

(3)   Where the ground or a ground for the proposed refusal is that the *Bank* **Authority** is not satisfied that the criterion in paragraph 1 of Schedule 3 to this Act is fulfilled in the case of any such person as is there mentioned, the *Bank* **Authority** shall give that person a copy of the notice mentioned in subsection (2) above, together with a statement of his rights under subsection (4) below.

(4)   An applicant who is given a notice under subsection (2) above and a person who is given a copy of it under subsection (3) above may within such period (not being less than twenty-eight days) as is specified in the notice make written representations to the *Bank* **Authority**; and where such representations are made the *Bank* **Authority** shall take them into account before reaching a decision on the application.

(5)   Where the *Bank* **Authority** refuses an application it shall give written notice of that fact that the applicant and to any such person as is mentioned in subsection (3) above, stating the reasons for the refusal and (except in the case of a refusal in pursuance of a direction under section 26A below) giving particulars of the rights conferred by section 27 below.

(6)   Any notice under subsection (5) above shall be given before the end of the period of six months beginning with the day on which the application was received by the *Bank* **Authority** or, where the *Bank* **Authority** has under section 8 above required additional information or documents in connection with the application, before the end of whichever of the following first expires—

(a)   the period of six months beginning with the day on which the additional information or documents are provided;

(b)   the period of twelve months beginning with the day on which the application was received.

(7)   The *Bank* **Authority** may omit from the copy given to a person under subsection (3) above and from a notice given to him under subsection (5) above any matter which does not relate to him.

11.   Revocation of authorisation

(1)   The *Bank* **Authority** may revoke the authorisation of an institution if it appears to the *Bank* **Authority** that—

(a)   any of the criteria specified in Schedule 3 to this Act is not or has not been fulfilled, or may not be or may not have been fulfilled, in respect of the institution;

(b)   the institution has failed to comply with any obligation imposed on it by or under this Act;

(c)   a person has become a controller of the institution in contravention of section 21 below or has become or remains a controller after being given a notice of objection under section 22, 23 or 24 below;

(d)   the *Bank* **Authority** has been provided with false, misleading or inaccurate information by or on behalf of the institution or, in connection with an application for authorisation, by or on behalf of a person who is or is to be a director, controller or manager of the institution; or

(e)   the interests of depositors or potential depositors of the institution are in any other way threatened, whether by the manner in which the institution is conducting or proposes to conduct its affairs or for any other reason.

(1A)   The *Bank* **Authority** may revoke the authorisation of a credit institution incorporated in or formed under the law of any part of the United Kingdom if—

(a)   it appears to the *Bank* **Authority** that the institution's principal place of business is or may be outside the United Kingdom;

(b)   it appears to the *Bank* **Authority** that the institution has carried on in the United Kingdom or elsewhere a listed activity (other than the acceptance of deposits from the public) without having given prior notice to the *Bank* **Authority** of its intention to do so;

(c)   *the Bank is informed by The Securities and Investments Board, or* **it appears to the Authority, or the Authority is informed by** a connected UK authority having regulatory functions in relation to the provision of financial services, that the institution—

(i)   has contravened any provision of the Financial Services Act 1986 or any rules or regulations made under it;

(ii)   in purported compliance with any such provisions, has furnished *that Board or* **the Authority or that** authority with false, misleading or inaccurate information;

(iii)   has contravened any prohibition or requirement imposed under that Act; or

(iv)   has failed to comply with any statement of principle issued under that Act;

(d)   the *Bank* **Authority** is informed by the Director General of Fair Trading that the institution, or any of the institution's employees agents or associates (whether past or present) or, where the institution is a body corporate, any controller of the institution or an associate of any such controller, has done any of the things specified in paragraphs (a) to (d) of section 25(2) of the Consumer Credit Act 1974;

(e)   it appears to the *Bank* **Authority** that the institution has failed to comply with any obligation imposed on it by the Banking Coordination (Second Council Directive) Regulations 1992; or

(f)   the *Bank* **Authority** is informed by a supervisory authority in another member State that the institution has failed to comply with any obligation imposed on it by or under any rule of law in force in that State for purposes connected with the implementation of the Second Council Directive.

(1B)   The *Bank* **Authority** may revoke the authorisation of a credit institution if it appears to the *Bank* **Authority** that—

    (a)   the institution is an undertaking which is closely linked with any person; and

    (b)   the institution's close links with that person, or any matters relating to any non-EEA laws or administrative provisions to which that person is subject, are such as to prevent the effective exercise by the *Bank* **Authority** of its supervisory functions in relation to the institution.

(2)   The *Bank* **Authority** may revoke the authorisation of an institution if it appears to the *Bank* **Authority** that the institution—

    (a)   has not accepted a deposit in the United Kingdom in the course of carrying on a deposit-taking business (whether there or elsewhere) within the period of twelve months beginning with the day on which it was authorised; or

    (b)   having accepted a deposit or deposits as aforesaid, has subsequently not done so for any period of more than six months.

(3)   If in the case of an authorised institution whose principal place of business is in a country or territory outside the United Kingdom it appears to the *Bank* **Authority** that the relevant supervisory authority in that country or territory has withdrawn from the institution an authorisation corresponding to that conferred by the *Bank* **Authority** under this Part of this Act, the *Bank* **Authority** may revoke the authorisation and shall do so if that country or territory is a member State.

(3A)   In relation to a credit institution incorporated in or formed under the law of any part of the United Kingdom, subsection (3) above shall have effect as if the words 'and shall do so if that country or territory is a member State' were omitted.

(4)   In the case of an authorised institution which is an authorised person under the Financial Services Act 1986 or holds a consumer credit licence under the Consumer Credit Act 1974 the *Bank* **Authority** may revoke the authorisation if it appears to the *Bank* **Authority** that the institution has ceased to be an authorised person under the said Act of 1986 (otherwise than at the request or with the consent of the institution) or that the licence under the said Act of 1974 has been revoked.

(5)   The Treasury may after consultation with the *Bank* **Authority** by order make provision corresponding to subsection (4) above in relation to any authorisation or licence granted under such other enactments as may appear to the Treasury to be appropriate; but any such order shall be subject to annulment in pursuance of a resolution of either House of Parliament.

(6)   If in the case of an authorised institution wherever incorporated it appears to the *Bank* **Authority** that—

    (a)   a winding-up order has been made against it in the United Kingdom; or

    (b)   a resolution for its voluntary winding up in the United Kingdom has been passed,

the *Bank* **Authority** shall revoke the authorisation; and the *Bank* **Authority** may revoke the authorisation of any authorised institution incorporated outside the United Kingdom if it appears to the *Bank* **Authority** that an event has occurred in respect of it outside the United Kingdom which corresponds as nearly as may be to either of those mentioned in paragraphs (a) and (b) above.

(7) The *Bank* **Authority** may revoke the authorisation of an authorised institution incorporated in the United Kingdom if it appears to the *Bank* **Authority** that—

(a) a composition or arrangement with creditors has been made in respect of the institution;

(b) a receiver or manager of the institution's undertaking has been appointed; or

(c) possession has been taken, by or on behalf of the holders of any debenture secured by a charge, of any property of the institution comprised in or subject to the charge;

or, in the case of an authorised institution incorporated elsewhere, that an event has occurred in respect of it which corresponds as nearly as may be to any of those mentioned in paragraphs (a), (b) and (c) above.

(8) The *Bank* **Authority** may revoke the authorisation of an authorised institution if it appears to the *Bank* **Authority** that an administration order has been made in relation to the institution under section 8 of the Insolvency Act 1986 or under Article 21 of the Insolvency (Northern Ireland) Order 1989.

(9) The *Bank* **Authority** shall revoke the authorisation of an unincorporated institution if it appears to the *Bank* **Authority** that a winding-up order has been made against it in the United Kingdom and may revoke the authorisation of such an institution if it appears to the *Bank* **Authority** that—

(a) the institution has been dissolved; or

(b) a bankruptcy order, an award of sequestration, an order of adjudication of bankruptcy or a composition or arrangement with creditors has been made or a trust deed for creditors granted in respect of that institution or any of its members; or

(c) any event corresponding as nearly as may be to any of those mentioned in paragraph (b) above or in subsection (6)(a) or (b) or (7)(b) or (c) above has occurred in respect of that institution or any of its members; or

(d) the whole of the assets available to the institution have passed into the ownership of a single individual.

(10) The rules and prohibitions referred to in subsection (1A)(c) above include the rules of any recognised self-regulating organisation of which the institution is a member and any prohibition imposed by virtue of those rules; and in subsection (1A)(d) above—

'Associate' has the same meaning as in section 25(2) of the Consumer Credit Act 1974;

'conroller' has the meaning given by section 189(1) of that Act.

12. Restriction of authorisation

(1) Where it appears to the *Bank* **Authority**—

(a) that there are grounds on which the *Bank's* **Authority's** power to revoke an institution's authorisation are exercisable; but

(b) that the circumstances are not such as to justify revocation, the *Bank* **Authority** may restrict the authorisation instead of revoking it.

(2)   An authorisation may be restricted—

    (a)   by imposing such limit on its duration as the *Bank* **Authority** thinks fit;

    (b)   by imposing such conditions as it thinks desirable for the protection of the institution's depositors or potential depositors; or

    (c)   by the imposition both of such a limit and of such conditions.

(3)   A limit on the duration of an authorisation shall not be such as to allow the authorisation to continue in force for more than three years from the date on which it is imposed; and such a limit may, in particular, be imposed in a case in which the *Bank* **Authority** considers that an institution should be allowed time to repay its depositors in an orderly manner.

(4)   The conditions imposed under this section may in particular—

    (a)   require the institution to take certain steps or to refrain from adopting or pursuing a particular course of action or to restrict the scope of its business in a particular way;

    (b)   impose limitations on the acceptance of deposits, the granting of credit or the making of investments;

    (c)   prohibit the institution from soliciting deposits, either generally or from persons who are not already depositors;

    (d)   prohibit it from entering into any other transaction or class of transactions;

    (e)   require the removal of any director, controller or manager;

    (f)   specify requirements to be fulfilled otherwise than by action taken by the institution.

(5)   Any condition imposed under this section may be varied or withdrawn by the *Bank* **Authority**; and any limit imposed under this section on the duration of an authorisation may be varied but not so as to allow the authorisation to continue in force for longer than the period mentioned in subsection (3) above from the date on which the limit was first imposed.

(6)   An institution which fails to comply with any requirement or contravenes any prohibition imposed on it by a condition under this section shall be guilty of an offence and liable—

    (a)   on conviction on indictment, to a fine;

    (b)   on summary conviction, to a fine not exceeding the statutory maximum.

(7)   The fact that a condition imposed under this section has not been complied with (whether or not constituting an offence under subsection (6) above) shall be a ground for the revocation of the authorisation in question but shall not invalidate any transaction.

(8)   An institution whose authorisation is restricted by the imposition of a limit on its duration may apply under section 8 above for a new authorisation and, if that authorisation is granted, the restricted authorisation shall cease to have effect.

12A.   Revocation or restriction on information from supervisory authority

(1)   The section applies where, in the case of an authorised institution which is a credit institution incorporated in or formed under the law of any part of the United Kingdom, the *Bank* **Authority** is informed by a supervisory authority in another

member State that the institution is failing to comply with an obligation imposed by or under any rule of law in force in that State for purposes connected with the implementation of the Second Council Directive.

(2)   The *Bank* **Authority** shall as soon as practicable send a copy of the information received by it to every other authority which it knows is a connected UK authority.

(3)   The *Bank* **Authority** shall also—

(a)   consider whether to exercise its powers under section 11 or 12 above; and

(b)   notify its decision, and any action which it has taken or intends to take, to the supervisory authority and to every other authority which it knows is a connected UK authority.

13.   Notice of revocation or restriction

(1)   Subject to section 14 below where the *Bank* **Authority** proposes—

(a)   to revoke an authorisation; or

(b)   to restrict an authorisation; or

(c)   to vary the restrictions imposed on an authorisation otherwise than with the agreement of the institution concerned,

the *Bank* **Authority** shall give to the institution concerned written notice of its intention to do so.

(2)   If the proposed action is within paragraph (b) or (c) of subsection (1) above the notice under that subsection shall specify the proposed restrictions or, as the case may be, the proposed variation.

(3)   A notice under subsection (1) above shall state the grounds on which the *Bank* **Authority** proposes to act and give particulars of the institution's rights under subsection (5) below.

(3A)   Where the *Bank* **Authority** gives a notice under subsection (1) above to a credit institution incorporated in or formed under the law of any part of the United Kingdom, it shall give a copy of that notice to every other authority which the *Bank* **Authority** knows is—

(a)   a connected UK authority; or

(b)   a supervisory authority in another member State in which the institution is carrying on a listed activity.

(4)   Where—

(a)   the ground or a ground for a proposed revocation or for a proposal to impose or vary a restriction is that it appears to the *Bank* **Authority** that the criterion in paragraph 1 of Schedule 3 to this Act is not or has not been fulfilled, or may not be or may not have been fulfilled, in the case of any person; or

(b)   a proposed restriction consists of or includes a condition requiring the removal of any person as director, controller or manager,

the *Bank* **Authority** shall give that person a copy of the notice mentioned in subsection (1) above, together with a statement of his rights under subsection (5) below.

(5)   An institution which is given a notice under subsection (1) above and a person who is given a copy of it under subsection (4) above may within the period of fourteen

days beginning with the day on which the notice was given make representations to the *Bank* **Authority**.

(6)   After giving a notice under subsection (1) above and taking into account any representations made under subsection (5) above the *Bank* **Authority** shall decide whether—

(a)   to proceed with the action proposed in the notice;

(b)   to take no further action;

(c)   if the proposed action was to revoke the institution's authorisation, to restrict its authorisation instead;

(d)   if the proposed action was to restrict the institution's authorisation or to vary the restrictions on an authorisation, to restrict it or to vary the restrictions in a different manner.

(7)   The *Bank* **Authority** shall give the institution and any such person as is mentioned in subsection (4) above written notice of its decision and, except where the decision is to take no further action, the notice shall state the reasons for the decision and give particulars of the rights conferred by subsection (9) and section 27 below.

(8)   A notice under subsection (7) above of a decision to revoke or restrict an authorisation or to vary the restrictions on an authorisation shall, subject to section 27(4) below, have the effect of revoking the authorisation or, as the case may be, restricting the authorisation or varying the restrictions in the manner specified in the notice.

(9)   Where the decision notified under subsection (7) above is to restrict the authorisation or to vary the restrictions on an authorisation otherwise than as stated in the notice given under subsection (1) above the institution may within the period of seven days beginning with the day on which the notice was given under subsection (7) above make written representations to the *Bank* **Authority** with respect to the restrictions and the *Bank* **Authority** may, after taking those representations into account, alter the restrictions.

(10)   A notice under subsection (7) above shall be given within the period of twenty-eight days beginning with the day on which the notice under subsection (1) above was given; and if no notice under subsection (7) is given within that period the *Bank* **Authority** shall be treated as having at the end of that period given a notice under that subsection to the effect that no further action is to be taken.

(11)   Where the *Bank* **Authority** varies a restriction on an institution's authorisation with its agreement or withdraws a restriction consisting of a condition the variation or withdrawal shall be effected by written notice to the institution.

(12)   The *Bank* **Authority** may omit from the copy given to a person under subsection (4) above and from a notice given to him under subsection (7) above any matter which does not relate to him.

14.   Mandatory revocation and restriction in cases of urgency

(1)   No notice need be given under section 13 above in respect of—

(a)   the revocation of an institution's authorisation in any case in which revocation is mandatory under section 11 above; or

(b)   the imposition or variation of a restriction on an institution's authorisation in any case in which the *Bank* **Authority** considers that the restriction should be imposed or varied as a matter of urgency.

(2)   In any such case the *Bank* **Authority** may by written notice to the institution revoke the authorisation or impose or vary the restriction.

(3)   Any such notice shall state the reasons for which the *Bank* **Authority** has acted and, in the case of a notice imposing or varying a restriction, particulars of the rights conferred by subsection (5) and by section 27 below.

(4)   Subsection (4) of section 13 above shall apply to a notice under subsection (2) above imposing or varying a restriction as it applies to a notice under subsection (1) of that section in respect of a proposal to impose or vary a restriction; but the *Bank* **Authority** may omit from a copy given to a person by virtue of this subsection any matter which does not relate to him.

(5)   An institution to which a notice is given under this section of the imposition or variation of a restriction and a person who is given a copy of it by virtue of subsection (4) above may within the period of fourteen days beginning with the day on which the notice was given make representations to the *Bank* **Authority**.

(6)   After giving a notice under subsection (2) above imposing or varying a restriction and taking into account any representations made in accordance with subsection (5) above the *Bank* **Authority** shall decide whether—

(a)   to confirm or rescind its original decision; or

(b)   to impose a different restriction or to vary the restriction in a different manner.

(7)   The *Bank* **Authority** shall within the period of twenty-eight days beginning with the day on which the notice was given under subsection (2) above give the institution concerned written notice of its decision under subsection (6) above and, except where the decision is to rescind the original decision, the notice shall state the reasons for the decision.

(8)   Where the notice under subsection (7) above is of a decision to take the action specified in subsection (6)(b) above the notice under subsection (7) shall have the effect of imposing the restriction or making the variation specified in the notice and with effect from the date on which it is given.

(9)   Where a notice of the proposed revocation of an institution's authorisation under section 13 above is followed by a notice revoking its authorisation under this section the latter notice shall have the effect of terminating any right to make representations in respect of the proposed revocation and any pending appeal proceedings in respect of a decision implementing that proposal.

15.   Surrender of authorisation

(1)   An authorised institution may surrender its authorisation by written notice to the *Bank* **Authority**.

(2)   A surrender shall take effect on the giving of the notice or, if a later date is specified in it, on that date; and where a later date is specified in the notice the institution may by a further written notice to the *Bank* **Authority** substitute an earlier date, not being earlier than that on which the first notice was given.

(3)   The surrender of an authorisation shall be irrevocable unless it is expressed to take effect on a later date and before that date the *Bank* **Authority** by notice in writing to the institution allows it to be withdrawn.

(4)   Where the *Bank* **Authority** receives a notice of surrender under subsection (1) above from a credit institution incorporated in or formed under the law of any part of the United Kingdom, it shall give a copy of that notice to every other authority which the *Bank* **Authority** knows is—

(a)   a connected UK authority; or

(b)   a supervisory authority in another member State in which the institution is carrying on a listed activity.

16.   Statement of principles

(1)   The *Bank* **Authority** shall, as soon as practicable after the coming into force of this section, publish in such manner as it thinks appropriate a statement of the principles in accordance with which it is acting or proposing to act—

(a)   in interpreting the criteria specified in Schedule 3 to this Act and the grounds for revocation specified in section 11 above; and

(b)   in exercising its power to grant, revoke or restrict an authorisation.

(2)   If in the course of a financial year of the *Bank* **Authority** it makes a material change in the principles in accordance with which it is acting or proposing to act as mentioned in subsection (1) above it shall include a statement of the change in the report made by it for that year under section 1(3) above; and the *Bank* **Authority** may, at any time, publish in such manner as it thinks appropriate a statement of the principles in accordance with which it is acting or proposing to act as mentioned in that subsection.

17.   Information as to authorised institutions

(1)   Every report made by the *Bank* **Authority** under section 1(3) above shall contain a list of the institutions which are authorised under this Act at the end of the financial year to which the report relates.

(2)   The *Bank* **Authority** shall make available to any person on request and on payment of such fee, if any, as the *Bank* **Authority** may reasonably require a list of the institutions which are authorised either at the date of the request or at such earlier date, being not more than one month earlier, as may be specified in the list.

(3)   The *Bank* **Authority** may give public notice of the fact that an institution has ceased to be authorised.

18.   False statements as to authorised status

(1)   No person other than an authorised institution shall—

(a)   describe himself as an authorised institution; or

(b)   so hold himself out as to indicate or be reasonably understood to indicate that he is an authorised institution.

(2)   No person shall falsely state, or do anything which falsely indicates, that he is entitled although not an authorised institution to accept a deposit in the course of carrying on a business which for the purposes of this Act is a deposit-taking business.

(3)   Any person who contravenes this section shall be guilty of an offence and liable—

(a)   on conviction on indictment, to imprisonment for a term not exceeding two years or to a fine or to both;

(b)   on summary conviction, to imprisonment for a term not exceeding six months or to a fine not exceeding the statutory maximum or to both.

Directions

19.   Directions to institutions

(1)   The *Bank* **Authority** may give an institution directions under this section—

(a)   when giving it notice that the *Bank* **Authority** proposes to revoke its authorisation;

(b)   at any time after such a notice has been given to the institution (whether before or after its authorisation is revoked);

(c)   when giving the institution a notice of revocation under section 14(2) above by virtue of section 11(6)(b) above in the case of a members' voluntary winding up;

(d)   at any time after the institution has served a notice surrendering its authorisation, whether with immediate effect or with effect from a later date specified in the notice;

(e)   at or at any time after the expiry (otherwise than by virtue of section 12(8) above) of a restricted authorisation of the institution;

(f)   at any time after a disqualification notice has been served on the institution under section 183 of the Financial Services Act 1986.

(2)   Dirctions under this section shall be such as appear to the *Bank* **Authority** to be desirable in the interests of the institution's depositors or potential depositors, whether for the purpose of safeguarding its assets or otherwise, and may in particular—

(a)   require the institution to take certain steps or to refrain from adopting or pursuing a particular course of action or to restrict the scope of its business in a particular way;

(b)   impose limitations on the acceptance of deposits, the granting of credit or the making of investments;

(c)   prohibit the institution from soliciting deposits either generally or from persons who are not already depositors;

(d)   prohibit it from entering into any other transaction or class of transactions;

(e)   require the removal of any director, controller or manager.

(3)   No direction shall be given by virtue of paragraph (a) or (b) of subsection (1) above, and any direction given by virtue of either of those paragraphs shall cease to have effect, if the *Bank* **Authority** gives the institution notice that it is not proposing to take any further action pursuant to the notice mentioned in that paragraph or if the *Bank's* **Authority's** decision to revoke the institution's authorisation is reversed on appeal.

(4)   No direction shall be given by virtue of paragraph (d) of subsection (1) above, and any direction given by virtue of that paragraph shall cease to have effect, if the *Bank* **Authority** allows the institution to withdraw the surrender of its authorisation.

(5)   No direction shall be given to an institution under this section after it has ceased to have any liability in respect of deposits for which it had a liability at a time when it was authorised; and any such direction which is in force with respect to an institution shall cease to have effect when the institution ceases to have any such liability.

(6)   An institution which fails to comply with any requirement or contravenes any prohibition imposed on it by a direction under this section shall be guilty of an offence and liable—

(a)   on conviction on indictment, to a fine;

(b)   on summary conviction, to a fine not exceeding the statutory maximum.

(7)   A contravention of a prohibition imposed under this section shall not invalidate any transaction.

20.   Notification and confirmation of directions

(1)   A direction under section 19 above shall be given by notice in writing and may be varied by a further direction; and a direction may be revoked by the *Bank* **Authority** by a notice in writing to the institution concerned.

(2)   A direction under that section, except one varying a previous direction with the agreement of the institution concerned—

(a)   shall state the reasons for which it is given and give particulars of the institution's rights under subsection (4) and section 27 below; and

(b)   without prejudice to section 19(3), (4) and (5) above, shall cease to have effect at the end of the period of twenty-eight days beginning with the day in which it is given unless before the end of that period it is confirmed by a further written notice given by the *Bank* **Authority** to the institution concerned.

(3)   Where a direction requires the removal of a person as director, controller or manager of an institution the *Bank* **Authority** shall give that person a copy of the direction (together with a statement of his rights under subsection (4) below) and, if the direction is confirmed, a copy of the notice mentioned in subsection (2)(b) above.

(4)   An institution to which a direction is given which requires confirmation under subsection (2) above and a person who is given a copy of it under subsection (3) above may, within the period of fourteen days beginning with the day on which the direction is given, make written representations to the *Bank* **Authority**; and the *Bank* **Authority** shall take any such representations into account in deciding whether to confirm the direction.

(5)   The *Bank* **Authority** may omit from the copies given to a person under subsection (3) above any matter which does not relate to him.

Objections to controllers

21.   Notification of new or increased control

(1)   No person shall become a minority, 10 per cent, 20 per cent, 33 per cent, majority or principal shareholder controller, a parent controller or an indirect controller of an authorised institution unless—

(a)   he has served on the *Bank* **Authority** a written notice stating that he intends to become such a controller of the institution; and

(b)   either the *Bank* **Authority** has, before the end of the period of three months beginning with the date of service of that notice, notified him in writing that there is no objection to his becoming such a controller of the institution or that period has elapsed without the *Bank* **Authority** having served on him under section 22 or 23 below a written notice of objection to his becoming such a controller of the institution.

(2)   Subsection (1) above applies also in relation to a person becoming a partner in an authorised institution which is a partnership formed under the law of any part of the United Kingdom.

(3)   A notice under paragraph (a) of subsection (1) above shall contain such information as the *Bank* **Authority** may direct and the *Bank* **Authority** may, after receiving such a notice from any person, by notice in writing require him to provide such additional information or documents as the *Bank* **Authority** may reasonably require for deciding whether to serve a notice of objection.

(4)   Where additional information or documents are required from any person by a notice under subsection (3) above the time between the giving of the notice and the receipt of the information or documents shall be added to the period mentioned in subsection (1)(b) above.

(5)   A notice served by a person under paragraph (a) of subsection (1) above shall not be regarded as a compliance with that paragraph except as respects his becoming a controller of the institution in question within the period of one year beginning—

(a)   in a case where the *Bank* **Authority** has notified him that there is no objection to his becoming such a controller, with the date of that notification;

(b)   in a case where the period mentioned in paragraph (b) of that subsection has elapsed without any such notification and without his having been served with a written notice of objection, with the expiration of that period;

(c)   in a case in which he has been served with a notice of objection which has been quashed on appeal, with the date on which it is quashed.

22.   Objection to new or increased control

(1)   The *Bank* **Authority** may serve a notice of objection under this section on a person who has given a notice under section 21 above unless it is satisfied—

(a)   that the person concerned is a fit and proper person to become a controller of the description in question of the institution;

(b)   that the interests of depositors and potential depositors of the institution would not be in any other manner threatened by that person becoming a controller of that description of the institution; and

(c)   without prejudice to paragraphs (a) and (b) above, that, having regard to that person's likely influence on the institution as a controller of the description in question the criteria in Schedule 3 to this Act would continue to be fulfilled in the case of the institution or, if any of those criteria is not fulfilled, that that person is likely to undertake adequate remedial action.

(1A)   Before deciding whether or not to serve a notice of objection under this section in any case where—

(a) the person concerned is, or is a parent controller of, a credit institution which is for the time being authorised to act as such an institution by the relevant supervisory authority in another member State; and

(b) the notice under section 21 above stated an intention to become a parent controller,
the *Bank* **Authority** shall consult that authority.

(2) Before serving a notice of objection under this section the *Bank* **Authority** shall serve the person concerned with a preliminary written notice stating that the *Bank* **Authority** is considering the service on that person of a notice of objection; and that notice—

(a) shall specify which the matters mentioned in subsection (1) above the *Bank* **Authority** is not satisfied about and, subject to subsection (5) below, the reasons for which it is not satisfied; and

(b) shall give particulars of the rights conferred by subsection (3) below.

(3) A person served with a notice under subsection (2) above may, within the period of one month beginning with the day on which the notice is served, make written representations to the *Bank* **Authority**; and where such representations are made the *Bank* **Authority** shall take them into account in deciding whether to serve a notice of objection.

(4) A notice of objection under this section shall—

(a) specify which of the matters mentioned in subsection (1) above the *Bank* **Authority** is not satisfied about and, subject to subsection (5) below, the reasons for which it is not satisfied; and

(b) give particulars of the rights conferred by section 27 below.

(5) Subsections (2)(a) and (4)(a) above shall not require the *Bank* **Authority** to specify any reason which would in its opinion involve the disclosure of confidential information the disclosure of which would be prejudicial to a third party.

(6) Where a person required to give a notice under section 21 above in relation to his becoming a controller of any description becomes a controller of that description without having given the notice the *Bank* **Authority** may serve him with a notice of objection under this section at any time within three months after becoming aware of his having done so and may, for the purpose of deciding whether to serve him with such a notice, require him by notice in writing to provide such information or documents as the *Bank* **Authority** may reasonably require.

(7) The period mentioned in section 21(1)(b) above (with any extension under subsection (4) of that section) and the period mentioned in subsection (6) above shall not expire if it would otherwise do so, until fourteen days after the end of the period within which representations can be made under subsection (3) above.

23. Objection by direction of the Treasury

(1) The Treasury may direct the *Bank* **Authority** to serve a notice of objection under this section on a person—

(a) who has given notice under section 21 above of his intention to become a shareholder controller of any description of an institution which is not a credit institution; or

(b)   who has become such a controller without giving the required notice under that section,
if it appears to the Treasury that, in the event of his becoming or, as the case may be, as a result of his having become such a controller, a notice could be served on the institution by the Treasury under section 183 of the Financial Services Act 1986 (disqualification or restriction of persons connected with overseas countries which do not afford reciprocal facilities for financial business).

(2)   No direction shall be given in a case within subsection (1)(b) above more than three months after the Treasury becomes aware of the fact that the person concerned has become a controller of the relevant description.

(3)   Any notice of objection served by virtue of a direction under this section shall state the grounds on which it is served.

24.   Objection to existing shareholder controller

(1)   Where it appears to the *Bank* **Authority** that a person who is a shareholder controller of any description of an authorised institution incorporated in the United Kingdom is not or is not longer a fit and proper person to be such a controller of the institution it may serve him with a written notice of objection to his being such a controller of the institution.

(2)   Before serving a notice of objection under this section the *Bank* **Authority** shall serve the person concerned with a preliminary written notice stating that the *Bank* **Authority** is considering the service on that person of a notice of objection; and that notice shall—

(a)   subject to subsection (5) below, specify the reasons for which it appears to the *Bank* **Authority** that the person in question is not or is no longer a fit and proper person as mentioned in subsection (1) above, and

(b)   give particulars of the rights conferred by subsection (3) below.

(3)   A person served with a notice under subsection (2) above may, within the period of one month beginning with the day on which the notice is served, make written representations to the *Bank* **Authority**; and where such representations are made the *Bank* **Authority** shall take them into account in deciding whether to serve a notice of objection.

(4)   A notice of objection under this section shall—

(a)   subject to subsection (5) below, specify the reasons for which it appears to the *Bank* **Authority** that the person in question is not or is no longer a fit and proper person as mentioned in subsection (1) above; and

(b)   give particulars of the rights conferred by section 27 below.

(5)   Subsections (2)(a) and (4)(a) above shall not require the *Bank* **Authority** to specify any reason which would in its opinion involve the disclosure of confidential information the disclosure of which would be prejudicial to a third party.

25.   Contraventions by controller

(1)   Subject to subsection (2) below, any person who contravenes section 21 above by—

(a)   failing to give the notice required by paragraph (a) of subsection (1) of that section; or

(b)   becoming a controller of any description to which that section applies before the end of the period mentioned in paragraph (b) of that subsection in a case where the *Bank* **Authority** has not served him with a preliminary notice under section 23(2) above,

shall be guilty of an offence.

(2)   A person shall not be guilty of an offence under subsection (1) above if he shows that he did not know of the acts or circumstances by virtue of which he became a controller of the relevant description; but where any person becomes a controller of any such description without such knowledge and subsequently becomes aware of the fact that he has become such a controller he shall be guilty of an offence unless he gives the *Bank* **Authority** written notice of the fact that he has become such a controller within fourteen days of becoming aware of that fact.

(3)   Any person who—

(a)   before the end of the period mentioned in paragraph (b) of subsection (1) of section 21 above becomes a controller of any description to which that subsection applies after being served with a preliminary notice under section 22(2) above;

(b)   contravenes section 21 above by becoming a controller of any description after being served with a notice of objection to his becoming a controller of that description; or

(c)   having become a controller of any description in contravention of that section (whether before or after being served with such a notice of objection) continues to be such a controller after such a notice has been served on him,

shall be guilty of an offence.

(4)   A person guilty of an offence under subsection (1) or (2) above shall be liable on summary conviction to a fine not exceeding the fifth level on the standard scale.

(5)   A person guilty of an offence under subsection (3) above shall be liable—

(a)   on conviction on indictment, to imprisonment for a term not exceeding two years or to a fine or to both;

(b)   on summary conviction, to a fine not exceeding the statutory maximum and, in respect of an offence under paragraph (c) of that subsection, to a fine not exceeding one tenth of the statutory maximum for each day on which the offence has continued.

26.   Restrictions on and sale of shares

(1)   The powers conferred by this section shall be exercisable where a person—

(a)   has contravened section 21 above by becoming a shareholder controller of any description after being served with a notice of objection to his becoming a controller of that description; or

(b)   having become a shareholder controller of any description in contravention of that section continues to be one after such a notice has been served on him; or

(c)   continues to be a shareholder controller of any description after being served under section 24 above with a notice of objection to his being a controller of that description.

(2)   The *Bank* **Authority** may by notice in writing served on the person concerned direct that any specified shares to which this section applies shall, until further notice, be subject to one or more of the following restrictions—

(a)   any transfer of, or agreement to transfer, those shares or, in the case of unissued shares, any transfer of or agreement to transfer the right to be issued with them shall be void;

(b)   no voting rights shall be exercisable in respect of the shares;

(c)   no further shares shall be issued in right of them or in pursuance of any offer made to their holder;

(d)   except in a liquidation, no payment shall be made of any sums due from the institution on the shares, whether in respect of capital or otherwise.

(3)   The court may, on the application of the *Bank* **Authority**, order the sale of any specified shares to which this section applies and, if they are for the time being subject to any restrictions under subsection (2) above, that they shall cease to be subject to those restrictions.

(4)   No order shall be made under subsection (3) above in a case where the notice of objection was served under section 22 or 24 above—

(a)   until the end of the period within which an appeal can be brought against the notice of objection; and

(b)   if such an appeal is brought, until it has been determined or withdrawn.

(5)   Where an order has been made under subsection (3) above the court may, on the application of the *Bank* **Authority**, make such further order relating to the sale or transfer of the shares as it thinks fit.

(6)   Where shares are sold in pursuance of an order under this section the proceeds of sale, less the costs of the sale, shall be paid into court for the benefit of the persons beneficially interested in them; and any such person may apply to the court for the whole or part of the proceeds to be paid to him.

(7)   This section applies—

(a)   to all the shares in the institution of which the person in question is a controller of the relevant description which are held by him or any associate of his and were not so held immediately before he became such a controller of the institution; and

(b)   where the person in question became a controller of the relevant description of an institution as a result of the acquisition by him or any associate of his or shares in another company, to all the shares in that company which are held by him or any associate of his and were not so held before he became such a controller of that institution.

(8)   A copy of the notice served on the person concerned under subsection (2) above shall be served on the institution or company to whose shares it relates and, if it relates to shares held by an associate of that person, on that associate.

(9)   The jurisdiction conferred by this section shall be exercisable by the High Court and the Court of Session.

Implementation of certain EC decisions

26A. Treasury directions for implementing decisions

(1)   In this section 'relevant decision' means any decision of the Council or Commission of the Communities under article 9(4) of the Second Council Directive (relations with third countries: limitation or suspension of decisions regarding application for authorisations).

(2)   For the purpose of implementing a relevant decision, the Treasury may direct the *Bank* **Authority**—

(a)   to refuse an application for authorisation made by a credit institution incorporated in or formed under the law of any part of the United Kingdom;

(b)   to defer its decision on such an application either indefinitely or for such period as may be specified in the direction; or

(c)   to serve a notice of objection on a person—

(i)   who has given notice under section 21 above of his intention to become a parent controller of any description of such an institution; or

(ii)   who has become such a controller without giving the required notice under that section.

(3)   A direction to the *Bank* **Authority** may relate to a particular institution or a class of institution and may be given before the application in question or, as the case may be, any notice under section 21 above is received.

(4)   Any notice of objection served by virtue of a direction falling within subsection (2)(c) above shall state the grounds on which it is served.

(5)   A direction under this section may be revoked at any time by the Treasury, but such revocation shall not affect anything done in accordance with the direction before it was revoked.

Appeals

27. Rights of appeal

(1)   An institution which is aggrieved by a decision of the *Bank* **Authority**—

(a)   to refuse an application by the institution for authorisation otherwise than in a case in which the refusal is in pursuance of a direction under section 26A above;

(b)   to revoke its authorisation otherwise than in a case in which revocation is mandatory under section 11 above;

(c)   to restrict its authorisation, to restrict it in a particular manner or to vary any restrictions of its authorisation; or

(d)   to give it a direction under section 19 above or to vary a direction given to it under that section,

may appeal against the decision to a tribunal constituted in accordance with section 28 below.

(2)   Where—

(a)   the ground or a ground for a decision within paragraph (a), (b) or (c) of subsection (1) above is that mentioned in section 10(3) or 13(4)(a) above; or

(b)   the effect of a decision within paragraph (c) or (d) of that subsection is to require the removal of a person as director, controller or manager of an institution, the person to whom the ground relates or whose removal is required may appeal to a tribunal constituted as aforesaid against the finding that there is such a ground for the decision or, as the case may be, against the decision to require his removal.

(3)   Any person on whom a notice of objection is served under section 22 or 24 above may appeal to a tribunal constituted as aforesaid against the decision of the *Bank* **Authority** to serve the notice; but this subsection does not apply to a person in any case in which he has failed to give a notice or become or continued to be a controller in circumstances in which his doing so constitutes an offence under section 25(1), (2) or (3) above.

(4)   The revocation of an institution's authorisation pursuant to a decision against which there is a right of appeal under this section shall not have effect—

(a)   until the end of the period within which an appeal can be brought; and

(b)   if such an appeal is brought, until it is determined or withdrawn.

(5)   The Tribunal may suspend the operation of a restriction or direction or a variation of a restriction or direction pending the determination of an appeal in respect of the decision imposing or varying the restriction or giving or varying the direction.

28.   Constitution of tribunals

(1)   Where an appeal is brought under section 27 above a tribunal to determine the appeal shall be constituted in accordance with subsection (2) below.

(2)   The tribunal shall consist of—

(a)   a chairman appointed by the Lord Chancellor or, in a case where the institution concerned is a company registered in Scotland or has its principal or prospective principal place of business in the United Kingdom in Scotland, by the Lord Chancellor in consultation with the Lord Advocate; and

(b)   two other members appointed by the Chancellor of the Exchequer.

(3)   The chairman shall be—

(a)   a person who has a 7 year general qualification, within the meaning of section 71 of the Courts and Legal Services Act 1990;

(b)   an advocate or solicitor in Scotland of at least 7 years' standing; or

(c)   a member of the Bar of Northern Ireland or solicitor of the Supreme Court of Northern Ireland of at least 7 years' standing;

and the other two members shall be persons appearing to the Chancellor of the Exchequer to have respectively experience of accountancy and experience of banking.

(3A)   A person shall not be appointed after the day on which he attains the age of 70 to be the chairman of a tribunal under this section.

(4)   The Treasury may out of money provided by Parliament pay to the persons appointed as members of a tribunal under this section such fees and allowances in respect of expenses as the Treasury may determine and may also out of such money defray any other expenses of a tribunal.

29.   Determination of appeals

(1)   On an appeal under section 27(1) or (3) above the question for the determination of the tribunal shall be whether, for the reasons adduced by the

appellant, the decision was unlawful or not justified by the evidence on which it was based.

(2)   On any such appeal the tribunal may confirm or reverse the decision which is the subject of the appeal but shall not have power to vary it except that—

(a)   where the decision was to revoke an authorisation the tribunal may direct the *Bank* **Authority** to restrict it instead;

(b)   where the decision was to impose or vary any restrictions the tribunal may direct the *Bank* **Authority** to impose different restrictions or to vary them in a different way; or

(c)   where the decision was to give or vary a direction the tribunal may direct the *Bank* **Authority** to give a different direction or to vary it in a different way.

(3)   Where the tribunal gives a direction to the *Bank* **Authority** under subsection (2)(a), (b) or (c) above it shall be for the *Bank* **Authority** to decide what restrictions should be imposed or how they should be varied or, as the case may be, what direction should be given or how a direction should be varied; and—

(a)   the *Bank* **Authority** shall by notice in writing to the institution concerned impose the restrictions, give the direction or make the variation on which it has decided;

(b)   the institution may appeal to the tribunal against the *Bank's* **Authority's** decision,

and on any such appeal the tribunal may confirm the decision or give a further direction under paragraph (b) or (c) of subsection (2) above and, if it gives such a further direction, this subsection shall continue to apply until the *Bank's* **Authority's** decision is confirmed by the tribunal or accepted by the institution.

(4)   Where the tribunal reverses a decision of the *Bank* **Authority** to refuse an application for authorisation it shall direct the *Bank* **Authority** to grant it.

(5)   On an appeal under section 27(2)(a) above the question for the determination of the tribunal shall be whether, for the reasons adduced by the appellant, the finding of the *Bank* **Authority** was not justified by the evidence on which it was based; and on an appeal under section 27(2)(b) above the question for the determination of the tribunal shall be whether, for the reasons adduced by the appellant, the decision requiring the appellant's removal was unlawful or not justified by the evidence on which it was based.

(6)   A decision by the tribunal on an appeal under section 27(2)(a) above that a finding in respect of the appellant was not justified shall not affect any refusal, revocation or restriction wholly or partly based on that finding; but on an appeal under section 27(2)(b) above the tribunal may confirm or reverse the decision to require the removal of the appellant.

(7)   Notice of a tribunal's determination, together with a statement of its reasons, shall be given to the appellant and to the *Bank* **Authority**; and, unless the tribunal otherwise directs, the determination shall come into operation when the notice is given to the appellant and to the *Bank* **Authority**.

(8)   Notice of a tribunal's determination of an appeal under section 27(2) above shall also be given to the institution concerned and, where the determination is to

reverse a decision to require the removal of the appellant as director, controller or manager of an institution, the determination shall not come into operation until notice of the determination has been given to that institution.

30. Costs, procedure and evidence

(1) A tribunal may give such directions as it thinks fit for the payment of costs or expenses by any party to the appeal.

(2) On an appeal under section 27(2) above the institution concerned shall be entitled to be heard.

(3) Subject to subsection (4) below, the Treasury may make regulations with respect to appeals under this Part of this Act; and those regulations may in particular make provision—

(a) as to the period within which and the manner in which such appeals are to be brought;

(b) as to the manner in which such appeals are to be conducted, including provision for any hearing to be held in private, as to the persons entitled to appear on behalf of the parties and for enabling appeals to be heard notwithstanding the absence of a member of the tribunal other than the chairman;

(c) as to the procedure to be adopted where appeals are brought both by an institution and a person who is or is to be a director, controller or manager of the institution, including provision for hearing the appeals together and for the mutual disclosure of information;

(d) for requiring an appellant or the *Bank* **Authority** to disclose or allow the inspection of documents in his or its custody or under his or its control;

(e) for requiring any person, on tender of the necessary expenses of his attendance, to attend and give evidence or produce documents in his custody or under his control and for authorising the administration of oaths to witnesses;

(f) for enabling an appellant to withdraw an appeal or the *Bank* **Authority** to withdraw its opposition to an appeal and for the consequences of any such withdrawal;

(g) for taxing or otherwise settling any costs or expenses which the tribunal directs to be paid and for the enforcement of any such direction;

(h) for enabling any preliminary or incidental functions in relation to an appeal to be discharged by the chairman of a tribunal; and

(j) as to any other matter connected with such appeals.

(4) Regulations under this section with respect to appeals where the institution concerned—

(a) is a company registered in Scotland; or

(b) has its principal or prospective principal place of business in the United Kingdom in Scotland,

shall be made by the Lord Advocate.

(5) A person who, having been required in accordance with regulations under this section to attend and give evidence, fails without reasonable excuse to attend or give evidence, shall be liable on summary conviction to a fine not exceeding the fifth level on the standard scale.

(6) A person who without reasonable excuse alters, suppresses, conceals, destroys or refuses to produce any document which he has been required to produce in accordance with regulations under this section, or which he is liable to be so required to produce, shall be guilty of an offence and liable—

(a) on conviction on indictment, to imprisonment for a term not exceeding two years or to a fine or to both;

(b) on summary conviction, to a fine not exceeding the statutory maximum.

(7) Any regulations made under this section shall be subject to annulment in pursuance of a resolution of either House of Parliament.

31. Further appeals on points of law

(1) An institution or other person who has appealed to a tribunal may appeal to the court on any question of law arising from the decision of the appeal by the tribunal and an appeal on any such question shall also lie at the instance of the *Bank* **Authority**; and if the court is of opinion that the decision was erroneous in point of law, it shall remit the matter to the tribunal for re-hearing and determination by it.

(2) In subsection (1) above 'the court' means the High Court, the Court of Session or the High Court in Northern Ireland according to whether—

(a) if the institution concerned is a company registered in the United Kingdom, it is registered in England and Wales, Scotland or Northern Ireland;

(b) in the case of any other institution, its principal or prospective principal place of business in the United Kingdom is situated in England and Wales, Scotland or Northern Ireland.

(3) No appeal to the Court of Appeal or to the Court of Appeal in Northern Ireland shall be brought from a decision under subsection (1) above except with the leave of that court or of the court or judge from whose decision the appeal is brought.

(4) An appeal shall lie, with the leave of the Court of Session or the House of Lords, from any decision of the Court of Session under this section, and such leave may be given on such terms as to costs, expenses or otherwise as the Court of Session or the House of Lords may determine.

Invitations to make deposits

32. Advertisement regulations

(1) The Treasury may after consultation with the *Bank* **Authority** and the Building Societies Commission make regulations for regulating the issue, form and content of deposit advertisements.

(2) Regulations under this section may make different provision for different cases and, without prejudice to the generality of subsection (1) above, may in particular—

(a) prohibit the issue of advertisements of any description (whether by reference to their contents, to the persons by whom they are issued or otherwise);

(b) make provision with respect to matters which must be, as well as matters which may not be, included in advertisements;

(c)   provide for exemptions from any prohibition or requirement imposed by the regulations, including exemptions by reference to a person's membership of a class whose membership is determined otherwise than by the Treasury.

(3)   Subject to subsection (4) below, any person who issues or causes to be issued in the United Kingdom an advertisement the issue of which is prohibited by regulations under this section or which does not comply with any requirements imposed by those regulations shall be guilty of an offence and liable—

(a)   on conviction on indictment, to imprisonment for a term not exceeding two years or to a fine or to both;

(b)   on summary conviction, to imprisonment for a term not exceeding six months or to a fine not exceeding the statutory maximum or to both.

(4)   A person whose business it is to publish or arrange for the publication of advertisements shall not be guilty of an offence under this section if he proves that he received the advertisement for publication in the ordinary course of his business, that the matters contained in the advertisement were not (wholly or in part) devised or selected by him or by any person under his direction or control and that he did not know and had no reason for believing that publication of the advertisement would constitute an offence.

(5)   In this section 'a deposit advertisement' means any advertisement containing—

(a)   an invitation to make a deposit; or

(b)   information which is intended or might reasonably be presumed to be intended to lead directly or indirectly to the making of a deposit;
and for the purposes of this section an advertisement includes any means of bringing such an invitation or such information to the notice of the person or persons to whom it is addressed and references to the issue of an advertisement shall be construed accordingly.

(6)   For the purposes of this section—

(a)   an advertisement issued or caused to be issued by any person by way of display or exhibition in a public place shall be treated as issued or caused to be issued by him on every day on which he causes or permits it to be displayed or exhibited;

(b)   an advertisement inviting deposits with a person specified in the advertisement shall be presumed, unless the contrary is proved, to have been issued to the order of that person.

(7)   For the purposes of this section an advertisement issued outside the United Kingdom shall be treated as issued in the United Kingdom if it is directed to persons in the United Kingdom or is made available to them otherwise than in a newspaper, journal, magazine or other periodical publication published and circulating principally outside the United Kingdom or in a sound or television broadcast transmitted principally for reception outside the United Kingdom.

(8)   Regulations under this section shall be subject to annulment in pursuance of a resolution of either House of Parliament.

33.   Advertisement directions

(1)   If the *Bank* **Authority** considers that any deposit advertisement issued or proposed to be issued by or on behalf of an authorised institution is misleading, the *Bank* **Authority** may by notice in writing give the institution a direction under this section.

(2)   A direction under this section may contain all or any of the following prohibitions or requirements—

(a)   a prohibition on the issue of advertisements of a specified kind;

(b)   a requirement that advertisements of a particular description shall be modified in a specified manner;

(c)   a prohibition on the issue of any advertisements which are, wholly or subsantially, repetitions of an advertisement which has been issued and which is identified in the direction;

(d)   a requirement to take all practical steps to withdraw from display in any place any advertisements or any advertisements of a particular description specified in the direction.

(3)   Not less than seven days before giving a direction under this section the *Bank* **Authority** shall give the institution concerned notice in writing of its intention to give the direction stating the reasons for the proposed direction and giving particulars of the rights conferred by subsection (4) below.

(4)   An institution to which a notice is given under subsection (3) above may within the period of seven days beginning with the day on which the notice was given make written representations to the *Bank* **Authority**; and the *Bank* **Authority** shall take any such representation into account in deciding whether to give the direction.

(5)   A direction under this section may be varied by a further direction; and a direction may be revoked by the *Bank* **Authority** by a notice in writing to the institution concerned.

(6)   Any person who issues or causes to be issued an advertisement the issue of which is prohibited by a direction under this section or which does not comply with any requirements imposed by such a direction shall be guilty of an offence and liable—

(a)   on conviction on indictment, to imprisonment for a term not exceeding two years or to a fine or to both;

(b)   on summary conviction, to imprisonment for a term not exceeding six months or to a fine not exceeding the statutory maximum or to both.

(7)   In this section 'deposit advertisement' has the same meaning as in section 32 above and subsections (4) and (6) of that section shall apply also for the purposes of this section.

34.   Unsolicited calls

(1)   The Treasury may after consultation with the *Bank* **Authority** and the Building Societies Commission make regulations for regulating the making of unsolicited calls—

(a)   on persons in the United Kingdom; or

(b)   from the United Kingdom on persons elsewhere,
with a view to procuring the making of deposits.

(2)   Regulations under this section may make different provision for different cases and, without prejudice to the generality of subsection (1) above, may in particular—

(a)   prohibit the soliciting of deposits from, and the making of agreements with a view to the acceptance of deposits from, persons on whom unsolicited calls are made and prohibit the procuring of such persons to make deposits or to enter into such agreements;

(b)   specify persons by whom or circumstances in which unsolicited calls may be made;

(c)   require specified information to be disclosed to persons on whom unsolicited calls are made.

(3)   Any person who contravenes regulations made under this section shall be guilty of an offence and liable—

(a)   on conviction on indictment, to imprisonment for a term not exceeding two years or to a fine or to both;

(b)   on summary conviction, to imprisonment for a term not exceeding six months or to a fine not exceeding the statutory maximum or to both.

(4)   In this section 'unsolicited call' means a personal visit or oral communication made without express invitation.

(5)   Regulations under this section shall be subject to annulment in pursuance of a resolution of either House of Parliament.

35.   Fraudulent inducement to make a deposit

(1)   Any person who—

(a)   makes a statement, promise or forecast which he knows to be misleading, false or deceptive, or dishonestly conceals any material facts; or

(b)   recklessly makes (dishonestly or otherwise) a statement, promise or forecast which is misleading, false or deceptive,

is guilty of an offence if he makes the statement, promise or forecast or conceals the facts for the purpose of inducing, or is reckless as to whether it may induce, another person (whether or not the person to whom the statement, promise or forecast is made or from whom the facts are concealed)—

(i)   to make, or refrain from making, a deposit with him or any other person; or

(ii)   to enter, or refrain from entering, into an agreement for the purpose of making such a deposit.

(2)   This section does not apply unless—

(a)   the statement, promise or forecast is made in or from, or the facts are concealed in or from, the United Kingdom or arrangements are made in or from the United Kingdom for the statement, promise or forecast to be made or the facts to be concealed;

(b)   the person on whom the inducement is intended to or may have effect is in the United Kingdom; or

(c)   the deposit is or would be made, or the agreement is or would be entered into, in the United Kingdom.

(3)   A person guilty of an offence under this section shall be liable—

(a)   on conviction on indictment, to imprisonment for a term not exceeding seven years or to a fine or to both;

(b)   on summary conviction, to imprisonment for a term not exceeding six months or to a fine not exceeding the statutory maximum or to both.

(4)   For the purposes of this section the definition of deposit in section 5 above shall be treated as including any sum that would be otherwise excluded by subsection (3) of that section.

Information

36.   Notification of change of director, controller or manager

(1)   Subject to subsection (3) below, an authorised institution shall give written notice to the *Bank* **Authority** of the fact that any person has become or ceased to be a director, controller or manager of the institution.

(2)   A notice required to be given under subsection (1) above shall be given before the end of the period of fourteen days beginning with the day on which the institution becomes aware of the relevant facts.

(3)   The *Bank* **Authority** may by a notice in writing wholly or partly dispense from the obligation imposed by subsection (1) above any authorised institution whose principal place of business is outside the United Kingdom.

(4)   An institution which fails to give a notice required by this section shall be guilty of an offence and liable on summary conviction to a fine not exceeding the fifth level on the standard scale.

36A.   Annual notification of shareholder controllers

(1)   An authorised institution which is a credit institution incorporated in or formed under the law of any part of the United Kingdom shall at least once in each year give to the *Bank* **Authority** written notice of the name of each person who, to the institution's knowledge, is a shareholder controller of the institution at the date of the notice.

(2)   A notice under subsection (1) above shall also, in relation to each such person, state to best of the institution's knowledge—

(a)   whether he is a minority, 10 per cent, 20 per cent, 33 per cent or 50 per cent shareholder controller;

(b)   what percentage of the shares of the institution he holds either alone or with any associate or associates; and

(c)   what percentage of the voting power at a general meeting of the institution he is entitled to exercise, or control the exercise of, either alone or with any associate or associates;

and in this subsection 'share' has the same meaning as in Part VII of the Companies Act 1985 or Part VIII of the Companies (Northern Ireland) Order 1986.

(3)   An institution which fails to give a notice required by this section shall be guilty of an offence and liable on summary conviction to a fine not exceeding the fifth level on the standard scale.

37.   Notification of acquisition of significant shareholding

(1)   A person who becomes a significant shareholder in relation to an authorised institution incorporated in the United Kingdom shall within seven days give written notice of that fact to the *Bank* **Authority**.

(2)   For the purposes of this section 'a significant shareholder', in relation to an institution, means a person who is not a shareholder controller but who, either alone or with any associate or associates—

(a)   holds 5 per cent or more of the shares in the institution or another institution of which it is a subsidiary undertaking; or

(b)   is entitled to exercise, or control the exercise of, 5 per cent or more of the voting power at any general meeting of the institution or of another institution of which it is such an undertaking;

and in this subsection 'share' has the same meaning as in Part VII of the Companies Act 1985 or Part VIII of the Companies (Northern Ireland) Order 1986.

(3)   Subject to subsection (4) below, any person who contravenes subsection (1) above shall be guilty of an offence.

(4)   A person shall not be guilty of an offence under subsection (3) above if he shows that he did not know of the acts or circumstances by virtue of which he became a significant shareholder in relation to the institution; but where any person becomes such a shareholder without such knowledge and subsequently becomes aware of the fact that he has become such a shareholder he shall be guilty of an offence unless he gives the *Bank* **Authority** written notice of the fact that he has become such a shareholder within fourteen days of becoming aware of that fact.

(5)   A person guilty of an offence under this section shall be liable on summary conviction to a fine not exceeding the fifth level on the standard scale.

37A.   Prior notification of ceasing to be a relevant controller

(1)   A person shall not cease to be a minority, 10 per cent, 20 per cent, 33 per cent or 50 per cent shareholder controller or a parent controller of an authorised institution whch is a credit institution incorporated in or formed under the law of any part of the United Kingdom unless he has first given to the *Bank* **Authority** written notice of his intention to cease to be such a controller of the institution.

(2)   If, after ceasing to be such a controller of such an institution, a person will, either alone or with any associate or associates—

(a)   still hold 10 per cent or more of the shares in the institution or another institution of which it is a subsidiary undertaking;

(b)   still be entitled to exercise or control the exercise of 10 per cent or more of the voting power at any general meeting of the institution or of another institution of which it is such an undertaking; or

(c)   still be able to exercise a significant influence over the management of the institution or another institution of which it is s'ich an undertaking by virtue of—

(i)   a holding of share in; or

(ii)   an entitlement to exercise, or control the exercise of, the voting power at any general meeting of,

the institution or, as the case may be, the other institution concerned,

his notice under subsection (1) above shall state the percentage of the shares or voting power which he will (alone or with any associate or associates) hold or be entitled to exercise or control; and in this subsection 'share' has the same meaning as in Part VII of the Companies Act 1985 or Part VIII of the Companies (Northern Ireland) Order 1986.

(3)   Subject to subsection (4) below, any person who contravenes subsection (1) or (2) above shall be guilty of an offence.

(4)   Subject to subsection (5) below, a person shall not be guilty of an offence under subsection (3) above if he shows that he did not know of the acts or circumstances by virtue of which he ceased to be a controller of the relevant description in sufficient time to enable him to comply with subsection (1) above.

(5)   Notwithstanding anything in subsection (4) above, a person who ceases to be a controller of a relevant description without having complied with subsection (1) above shall be guilty of an offence if, within fourteen days of becoming aware of the fact that he has ceased to be such a controller—

(a)   he fails to give the *Bank* **Authority** written notice of that fact; or

(b)   he gives the *Bank* **Authority** such a notice but the notice fails to comply with subsection (2) above.

(6)   A person guilty of an offence under this section shall be liable on summary conviction to a fine not exceeding the fifth level on the standard scale.

38.   Reports of large exposures

(1)   An authorised institution, other than one whose principal place of business is outside the United Kingdom, shall make a report to the *Bank* **Authority** if—

(a)   it has entered into a transaction or transactions relating to any one person as a result of which it is exposed to the risk of incurring losses in excess of 10 per cent of its available capital resources; or

(b)   it proposes to enter into a transaction or transactions relating to any one person which, either alone or together with a previous transaction or previous transactions entered into by it in relation to that person, would result in its being exposed to the risk of incurring losses in excess of 25 per cent of those resources.

(2)   Subsection (1) above applies also where the transaction or transactions relate to different persons if they are connected in such a way that the financial soundness of any of them may affect the financial soundness of the other or others or the same factors may affect the financial soundness of both or all of them.

(3)   If an authorised institution to which subsection (1) above applies has one or more subsidiaries which are not authorised institutions the *Bank* **Authority** may by notice in writing to that institution direct that that subsection shall apply to it as if the transactions and available capital resources of the subsidiary or subsidiaries, or such of them as are specified in the notice, were included in those of the institution.

(4)   The reports required to be made by an institution under subsection (1) above shall be made, in a case within paragraph (a) of that subsection, in respect of such period or periods and, in a case within paragraph (b) of that subsection, at such time before the transaction or transactions are entered into, as may be specified by notice in writing given to the institution by the *Bank* **Authority**; and those reports shall be in such form and contain such particulars as the *Bank* **Authority** may reasonably require.

(5)   For the purposes of this section a transaction entered into by an institution relates to a person if it is—

(a)   a transaction under which that person incurs an obligation to the institution or as a result of which he may incur such an obligation;

(b)   a transaction under which the institution will incur, or as a result of which it may incur, an obligation in the event of that person defaulting on an obligation to a third party; or

(c)   a transaction under which the institution acquires or incurs an obligation to acquire, or as a result of which it may incur an obligation to acquire, an asset the value of which depends wholly or mainly on that person performing his obligations or otherwise on his financial soundness;

and the risk of loss attributable to a transaction is, in a case within paragraph (a) or (b) above, the risk of the person concerned defaulting on the obligation there mentioned and, in a case within paragraph (c) above, the risk of the person concerned defaulting on the obligations there mentioned or of a deterioration in his financial soundness.

(6)   Any question whether an institution is or would be exposed to risk as mentioned in subsection (1) above (or in that subsection as extended by subsection (2)) shall be determined in accordance with principles published by the *Bank* **Authority** or notified by it to the institution concerned; and those principles may in particular make provision for determining the amount at risk in particular circumstances or the extent to which any such amount is to be taken into account for the purposes of this section.

(7)   For the purposes of this section the available capital resources of an institution (or, in a case within subsection (3) above, of an institution and its relevant subsidiary or subsidiaries) and the value of those resources at any time shall be determined by the *Bank* **Authority** and notified by it to the institution by notice in writing; and any such determination, which may be varied from time to time, shall be made by the *Bank* **Authority** after consultation with the institution concerned and in accordance with principles published by the *Bank* **Authority**.

(8)   The principles referred to in subsection (6) and (7) above may make different provision for different cases and those referred to in subsection (6) may, in particular, exclude from consideration, either wholly or in part, risks resulting from transactions of a particular description or entered into in particular circumstances or with persons of particular descriptions.

(9)   An institution which fails to make a report as required by this section shall be guilty of an offence; but where an institution shows that at the time when the report

was required to be made it did not know that the facts were such as to require the making of the report it shall not be guilty of an offence by reason of its failure to make a report at the time but shall be guilty of an offence unless it makes the report within seven days of becoming aware of those facts.

(10)   An institution guilty of an offence under this section shall be liable on summary conviction to a fine not exceeding the fifth level on the standard scale.

(11)   The Treasury may after consultation with the *Bank* **Authority** by order—

(a)   amend subsection (1) above so as to substitute for either of the percentages for the time being specified in that subsection such other percentage as may be specified in the order;

(b)   make provision, whether by amending subsection (5) above or otherwise, with respect to the transactions and risks to be taken into account for the purposes of this section,

but any such order shall be subject to annulment in pursuance of a resolution of either House of Parliament.

(12)   For the avoidance of doubt it is hereby declared that references in this section to 'one person' include references to a partnership.

39.   Power to obtain information and require production of documents

(1)   The *Bank* **Authority** may by notice in writing served on an authorised institution—

(a)   require the institution to provide the *Bank* **Authority, or such person acting on behalf of the Authority as may be specified in the notice,** at such time or times or at such intervals or in respect of such period or periods as may be *specified in the notice* **so specified**, with such information as the *Bank* **Authority** may reasonably require for the performance of its functions under this Act;

(b)   require the institution to provide the *Bank* **Authority** with a report by an accountant or other person with relevant professional skill on, or on any aspect of, any matter about which the *Bank* **Authority** has required or could require the institution to provide information under paragraph (a) above.

(2)   The accountant or other person appointed by an institution to make any report required under subsection (1)(b) above shall be a person nominated or approved by the *Bank* **Authority**; and the *Bank* **Authority** may require his report to be in such form as is specified in the notice.

(3)   The *Bank* **Authority** may—

(a)   by notice in writing served on an authorised institution require it to produce, within such time and at such place as may be specified in the notice, such document or documents of such description as may be so specified;

(b)   authorise an officer, servant or agent of the *Bank* **Authority**, on producing evidence of his authority, to require any such institution to provide him forthwith with such information, or to produce to him forthwith such documents, as he may specify, being such information or documents as the *Bank* **Authority** may reasonably require for the performance of its functions under this Act.

(4)   Where, by virtue of subsection (3) above, the *Bank* **Authority** or any officer, servant or agent of the *Bank* **Authority** has power to require the production of any

documents from an authorised institution, the *Bank* **Authority** or that officer, servant or agent shall have the like power to require the production of those documents from any person who appears to be in possession of them; but where any person from whom such production is required claims a lien on documents produced by him, the production shall be without prejudice to the lien.

(5) The power under this section to require an institution or other person to produce any documents includes power—

(a)   if the documents are produced, to take copies of them or extracts from them and to require that institution or person, or any other person who is a present or past director, controller or manager of, or is or was at any time employed by or acting as an employee of, the institution in question, to provide an explanation of any of them; and

(b)   if the documents are not produced, to require the person who was required to produce them to state, to the best of his knowledge and belief, where they are.

(6) If it appears to the *Bank* **Authority** to be desirable in the interests of the depositors or potential depositors of an authorised institution to do so, it may also exercise the powers conferred by subsections (1) and (3) above in relation to any undertaking which is or has at any relevant time been—

(a)   a parent undertaking, subsidiary undertaking or related company of that institution;

(b)   a subsidiary undertaking of a parent undertaking of that institution;

(c)   a parent undertaking of a subsidiary undertaking of that institution; or

(d)   an undertaking in the case of which a shareholder controller of that institution, either alone or with any associate or associates, holds 50 per cent or more of the shares or is entitled to exercise, or control the exercise of, more than 50 per cent of the voting power at a general meeting;

or in relation to any partnership of which that institution is or has at any relevant time been a member.

(7)   If it appears to the *Bank* **Authority** to be desirable to do so in the interests of the depositors or potential depositors of an authorised institution which is a partnership ('the authorised partnership'), it may also exercise the powers conferred by subsection (1) and (3) above in relation to—

(a)   any other partnership having a member in common with the authorised partnership;

(b)   any undertaking which is or has at any time been a member of the authorised partnership;

(c)   any undertaking in the case of which the partners in the authorised partnership, either alone or with any associate or associates, hold 20 per cent or more of the shares or are entitled to exercise, or control the exercise of, more than 50 per cent of the voting power at a general meeting; or

(d)   any subsidiary undertaking or parent undertaking of any such undertaking as is mentioned in paragraph (b) or (c) above or any parent undertaking of any such subsidiary undertaking.

(7A) In subsections (6) and (7) above 'share' has the same meaning as in Part VII of the Companies Act 1985 or Part VIII of the Companies (Northern Ireland) Order 1986.

(8) The foregoing provisions of this section shall apply to a former authorised institution as they apply to an authorised institution.

(9) The *Bank* **Authority** may by notice in writing served on any person who is or is to be a director, controller or manager of an authorised institution require him to provide the *Bank* **Authority**, within such time as may be specified in the notice, with such information or documents as the *Bank* **Authority** may reasonably require for determining whether he is a fit and proper person to hold the particular position which he holds or is to hold.

(10) The *Bank* **Authority** may exercise the powers conferred by subsections (1) and (3) above in relation to any person who is a significant shareholder of an authorised institution within the meaning of section 37 above if the *Bank* **Authority** considers that the exercise of those powers is desirable in the interests of the depositors or potential depositors of that institution.

(11) Any person who without reasonable excuse fails to comply with a requirement imposed on him under this section shall be guilty of an offence and liable on summary conviction to imprisonment for a term not exceeding six months or to a fine not exceeding the fifth level on the standard scale or to both.

(12) A statement made by a person in compliance with a requirement imposed by virtue of this section may be used in evidence against him.

(13) Nothing in this section shall compel the production by a barrister, advocate or solicitor of a document containing a privileged communication made by him or to him in that capacity.

40. Right of entry to obtain information and documents

(1) Any officer, servant or agent of the *Bank* **Authority** may, on producing if required evidence of his authority, enter any premises occupied by a person on whom a notice has been served under section 39 above for the purpose of obtaining there the information or documents required by that notice and of exercising the powers conferred by subsection (5) of that section.

(2) Any officer, servant or agent of the *Bank* **Authority** may, on producing if required evidence of his authority, enter any premises occupied by any person on whom a notice could be served under section 39 above for the purpose of obtaining there such information or documents as are specified in the authority, being information or documents that could have been required by such a notice; but the *Bank* **Authority** shall not authorise any person to act under this subsection unless it has reasonable cause to believe that if such a notice were served it would not be complied with or that any documents to which it would relate would be removed, tampered with or destroyed.

(3) Any person who intentionally obstructs a person exercising rights conferred by this section shall be guilty of an offence and liable on summary conviction to imprisonment for a term not exceeding six months or to a fine not exceeding the fifth level on the standard scale or to both.

Investigations

41.   Investigations on behalf of the Bank

(1)   If it appears to the *Bank* **Authority** desirable to do so in the interests of the depositors or potential depositors of an authorised institution the *Bank* **Authority** may appoint one or more competent persons to investigate and report to the *Bank* **Authority** on—

(a)   the nature, conduct or state of the institution's business or any particular aspect of it; or

(b)   the ownership or control of the institution;

and the *Bank* **Authority** shall give written notice of any such appointment to the institution concerned.

(2)   If a person appointed under subsection (1) above thinks it necessary for the purposes of his investigation, he may also investigate the business of any undertaking which is or has at any relevant time been—

(a)   a parent undertaking, subsidiary undertaking or related company of the institution under investigation;

(b)   a subsidiary undertaking or related company of a parent undertaking of that institution;

(c)   a parent undertaking of a subsidiary undertaking of that institution; or

(d)   an undertaking in the case of which a shareholder controller of that institution, either alone or with any associate or associates, holds 20 per cent or more of the shares or is entitled to exercise, or control the exercise of, more than 20 per cent of the voting power at a general meeting;

or the business of any partnership of which that institution is or has at any relevant time been a member.

(3)   If a person appointed under subsection (1) above thinks it necessary for the purposes of his investigation in the case of an authorised institution which is a partnership ('the authorised partnership'), he may also investigate the business of—

(a)   any other partnership having a member in common with the authorised partnership;

(b)   any undertaking which is or has at any time been a member of the authorised partnership;

(c)   any undertaking in the case of which the partners in the authorised partnership, either alone or with any associate or associates, hold 20 per cent or more of the shares or are entitled to exercise, or control the exercise of, more than 20 per cent of the voting power at a general meeting; or

(d)   any subsidiary undertaking, related company or parent undertaking of any such undertaking as is mentioned in paragraph (b) or (c) above or any parent undertaking of any such subsidiary undertaking.

(3A)   In subsections (2) and (3) above 'share' has the same meaning as in Part VII of the Companies Act 1985 or Part VIII of the Companies (Northern Ireland) Order 1986.

(4)   Where a person appointed under subsection (1) above decides to investigate the business of any body by virtue of subsection (2) or (3) above he shall give it written notice to that effect.

(5)   It shall be the duty of every person who is or was a director, controller, manager, employee, agent, banker, auditor or solicitor of a body which is under investigation (whether by virtue of subsection (1), (2) or (3) above), any person appointed to make a report in respect of that body under section 8(5) or 39(1)(b) above and anyone who is a significant shareholder in relation to that body within the meaning of section 37 above—

(a)   to produce to the persons appointed under subsection (1) above, within such time and at such place as they may require, all documents relating to the body concerned which are in his custody or power;

(b)   to attend before the persons so appointed at such time and place as they may require; and

(c)   otherwise to give those persons all assistance in connection with the investigation which he is reasonably able to give;

and those persons may take copies of or extracts from any documents produced to them under paragraph (a) above.

(6)   The foregoing provisions of this section shall apply to a former authorised institution as they apply to an authorised institution.

(7)   For the purpose of exercising his powers under this section a person appointed under subsection (1) above may enter any premises occupied by a body which is being investigated by him under this section; but he shall not do so without prior notice in writing unless he has reasonable cause to believe that if such a notice were given any documents whose production could be required under this section would be removed, tampered with or destroyed.

(8)   A person exercising powers by virtue of an appointment under this section shall, if so required, produce evidence of his authority.

(9)   Any person who—

(a)   without reasonable excuse fails to produce any documents which it is his duty to produce under subsection (5) above;

(b)   without reasonable excuse fails to attend before the persons appointed under subsection (1) above when required to do so;

(c)   without reasonable excuse fails to answer any question which is put to him by persons so appointed with respect to an institution which is under investigation or a body which is being investigated by virtue of subsection (2) or (3) above; or

(d)   intentionally obstructs a person in the exercise of the rights conferred by subsection (7) above,

shall be guilty of an offence and liable on summary conviction to imprisonment for a term not exceeding six months or to a fine not exceeding the fifth level on the standard scale or to both.

(10)   A statement made by a person in compliance with a requirement imposed by virtue of this section may be used in evidence against him.

(11)   Nothing in this section shall compel the production by a barrister, advocate or solicitor of a document containing a privileged communication made by him or to him in that capacity.

42.   Investigation of suspected contraventions

(1)   Where the *Bank* **Authority** has reasonable grounds for suspecting that a person is guilty of contravening section 3 or 35 above the *Bank* **Authority** or any duly authorised officer, servant or agent of the *Bank* **Authority** may by notice in writing require that or any other person—

(a)   to provide, at such place as may be specified in the notice and either forthwith or at such time as may be so specified, such information as the *Bank* **Authority** may reasonably require for the purpose of investigating the suspected contravention;

(b)   to produce, at such place as may be specified in the notice and either forthwith or at such time as may be so specified, such documents, or documents of such description, as may be specified, being documents the production of which may be reasonably required by the *Bank* **Authority** for that purpose.

(c)   to attend at such place and time as may be specified in the notice and answer questions relevant for determining whether such a contravention has occurred.

(2)   The *Bank* **Authority** or a duly authorised officer, servant or agent of the *Bank* **Authority** may take copies of or extracts from any documents produced under this section.

(3)   Any officer, servant or agent of the *Bank* **Authority** may, on producing if required evidence of his authority, enter any premises occupied by a person on whom a notice has been served under subsection (1) above for the purpose of obtaining there the information or documents required by the notice, putting the questions referred to in paragraph (c) of that subsection or exercising the powers conferred by subsection (2) above.

(4)   Any person who without reasonable excuse fails to comply with a requirement imposed on him under this section or intentionally obstructs a person in the exercise of the rights conferred by subsection (3) above shall be guilty of an offence and liable on summary conviction to imprisonment for a term not exceeding six months or to a fine not exceeding the fifth level on the standard scale or to both.

(5)   A statement made by a person in compliance with a requirement imposed by virtue of this section may be used in evidence against him.

(6)   Nothing in this section shall compel the production by a barrister, advocate or solicitor of a document containing a privileged communication made by him or to him in that capacity.

43.   Powers of entry in cases of suspected contraventions

(1)   A justice of the peace may issue a warrant under this section if satisfied on information on oath laid by an officer or servant of the *Bank* **Authority** or laid under the *Bank's* **Authority's** authority that there are reasonable grounds for suspecting that a person is guilty of such a contravention as is mentioned in section 42 above and—

(a) that that person has failed to comply with a notice served on him under that section; or

(b) that there are reasonable grounds for suspecting the completeness of any information provided or documents produced by him in response to such a notice; or

(c) that there are reasonable grounds for suspecting that if a notice were served on him under that section it would not be complied with or that any documents to which it would relate would be removed, tampered with or destroyed.

(2) A warrant under this section shall authorise any constable, together with any other person named in the warrant and any other constables—

(a) to enter any premises occupied by the person mentioned in subsection (1) above which are specified in the warrant, using such force as is reasonably necessary for the purpose;

(b) to search the premises and take possession of any documents appearing to be such documents as are mentioned in subsection (1)(c) above or to take, in relation to any such documents, any other steps which may appear to be necessary for preserving them or preventing interference with them;

(c) to take copies of or extracts from any such documents;

(d) to require any person named in the warrant to answer questions relevant for determining whether that person is guilty of any such contravention as is mentioned in section 42 above.

(3) A warrant under this section shall continue in force until the end of the period of one month beginning with the day on which it is issued.

(4) Any documents of which possession is taken under this section may be retained—

(a) for a period of three months; or

(b) if within that period proceedings to which the documents are relevant are commenced against any person for any such contravention as is mentioned in section 42 above, until the conclusion of those proceedings.

(5) Any person who intentionally obstructs the exercise of any right conferred by a warrant issued under this section or fails without reasonable excuse to comply with any requirement imposed in accordance with subsection (2)(d) above shall be guilty of an offence and liable—

(a) on conviction on indictment, to imprisonment for a term not exceeding two years or to a fine or to both;

(b) on summary conviction, to imprisonment for a term not exceeding six months or to a fine not exceeding the statutory maximum or to both.

(6) A statement made by a person in compliance with a requirement imposed by virtue of this section may be used in evidence against him.

(7) In the application of subsection (1) above to Scotland, the reference to a justice of the peace includes a reference to a sheriff and for the reference to information on oath there shall be substituted a reference to evidence on oath; and in the application of that subsection to Northern Ireland for the reference to laying an information on oath there shall be substituted a reference to making a complaint on oath.

44. Obstruction of investigations

(1) A person who knows or suspects that an investigation is being or is likely to be carried out—

(a) under section 41 above; or

(b) into a suspected contravention of section 3 or 35 above,

shall be guilty of an offence if he falsifies, conceals, destroys or otherwise disposes of, or causes or permits the falsification, concealment, destruction or disposal of, documents which he knows or suspects are or would be relevant to such an investigation unless he proves that he had no intention of concealing facts disclosed by the documents from persons carrying out such an investigation.

(2) A person guilty of an offence under this section shall be liable—

(a) on conviction on indictment, to imprisonment for a term not exceeding two years or to a fine or to both;

(b) on summary conviction, to imprisonment for a term not exceeding six months or to a fine not exceeding the statutory maximum or to both.

Accounts and auditors

45. Audited accounts to be open to inspection

(1) An authorised institution shall at each of its offices in the United Kingdom at which it holds itself out as accepting deposits—

(a) keep a copy of its most recent audited accounts; and

(b) during normal business hours make that copy available for inspection by any person on request.

(2) An institution which fails to comply with paragraph (a) of subsection (1) above or with any request made in accordance with paragraph (b) of that subsection shall be guilty of an offence and liable on summary conviction to a fine not exceeding the fifth level on the standard scale.

(3) In the case of an institution incorporated in the United Kingdom the accounts referred to in subsection (1) above include the auditors' report on the accounts and, in the case of any other institution whose accounts are audited, the report of the auditors.

46. Notification in respect of auditors

(1) An authorised institution incorporated in the United Kingdom shall forthwith give written notice to the *Bank* **Authority** if the institution—

(a) proposes to give special notice to its shareholders of an ordinary resolution removing an auditor before the expiration of his term of office; or

(b) gives notice to its shareholders of an ordinary resolution replacing an auditor at the expiration of his term of office with a different auditor,

or if a person ceases to be an auditor of the institution otherwise than in consequence of such a resolution.

(2) An auditor of an authorised institution appointed under Chapter V of Part XI of the Companies Act 1985 shall forthwith give written notice to the *Bank* **Authority** if he—

(a)   resigns before the expiration of his term of office;

(b)   does not seek to be re-appointed. or

(c)   decides to include in his report on the institution's accounts any qualification as to a matter mentioned in section 235(2) or any statement pursuant to section 235(3) or section 237 of that Act.

(3)   The foregoing provisions of this section shall apply to a former authorised institution as they apply to an authorised institution.

(4)   In the application of subsection (2) above to Northern Ireland for the reference to Chapter V of Part XI and sections 235(2) and 235(3) and 237 of the Companies Act 1985 there shall be substituted references to Chapter V of Part XII and Articles 392, 243(2), 243(3) and 245 of the Companies (Northern Ireland) Order 1986.

(5)   An institution or auditor who fails to comply with this section shall be guilty of an offence and liable on summary conviction to a fine not exceeding the fifth level on the standard scale.

47.   Communication by auditor etc. with the Bank

(1)   No duty to which—

(a)   an auditor of an authorised institution; or

(b)   a person appointed to make a report under section 8(5) or 39(1)(b) above,

(c)   an auditor of a body with which an authorised institution which is a credit institution is closely linked by control who is also either—

(i)   an auditor of the institution; or

(ii)   a person appointed to make a report under section 8(5) or 39(1)(b) above in respect of the institution,

may be subject shall be regarded as contravened by reason of his communicating in good faith to the *Bank* **Authority**, whether or not in response to a request made by it, an information or opinion on a matter to which this section applies and which is relevant to any function of the *Bank* **Authority** under this Act.

(2)   In relation to an auditor of an authorised institution this section applies to any matter of which he becomes aware in his capacity as auditor and which relates to the business or affairs of the institution or any associated body.

(3)   In relation to a person appointed to make a report under section 8(5) or 39(1)(b) above this section applies to any matter of which he becomes aware in his capacity as the person making the report and which—

(a)   relates to the business of affairs of the institution in relation to which his report is made or any associated body of that institution; or

(b)   if by virtue of section 39(6) or (7) above the report relates to an associated body of an institution, to the business or affairs of that body.

(3A)   In relation to an auditor of a body with which an authorised institution which is a credit institution is closely linked by control, this section applies to any matter of which he becomes aware in his capacity as auditor of the body and which relates to the business or affairs of the institution.

(4)   In this section 'associated body', in relation to an institution, means any such body as is mentioned in section 39(6) or (7) above.

(5)   If it appears to the Treasury that any accountants or class of accountants who are persons to whom subsection (1) above applies are not subject to satisfactory rules made or guidance issued by a professional body specifying circumstances in which matters are to be communicated to the *Bank* **Authority** as mentioned in that subsection the Treasury may, after consultation with the *Bank* **Authority** and such bodies as appear to the Treasury to represent the interests of accountants and authorised institutions, make regulations applying to those accountants and specifying such circumstances; and it shall be the duty of an accountant to whom the regulations apply to communicate a matter to the *Bank* **Authority** in the circumstances specified by the regulations.

(6)   Regulations under this section may make different provision for different cases and no such regulations shall be made unless a draft of them has been laid before and approved by a resolution of each House of Parliament.

(7)   This section applies to the auditor of a former authorised institution as it applies to the auditor of an authorised institution.

Unauthorised acceptance of deposits

48.   Repayment of unauthorised deposits
(1)   If on the application of the *Bank* **Authority** it appears to the court that a person has accepted deposits in contravention of section 3 above the court may—
    (a)   order him and any other person who appears to the court to have been knowingly concerned in the contravention to repay the deposits forthwith or at such time as the court may direct; or
    (b)   except in Scotland, appoint a receiver to recover those deposits;
but in deciding whether and, if so, on what terms to make an order under this section the court shall have regard to the effect that repayment in accordance with the order would have on the solvency of the person concerned or otherwise on his ability to carry on his business in a manner satisfactory to his creditors.

(2)   The jurisdiction conferred by this section shall be exercisable by the High Court and the Court of Session.

49.   Profits from unauthorised deposits
(1)   If on the application of the *Bank* **Authority** the Court is satisfied that profits have accrued to a person as a result of deposits having been accepted in contravention of section 3 above the court may order him to pay into court or, except in Scotland, appoint a receiver to recover from him, such sum as appears to the court to be just having regard to the profits appearing to the court to have accrued to him.

(2)   In deciding whether, and if so, on what terms to make an order under this section the court shall have regard to the effect that payment in accordance with the order would have on the solvency of the person concerned or otherwise on his ability to carry on his business in a manner satisfactory to his creditors.

(3)   Any amount paid into court or recovered from a person in pursuance of an order under this section shall be paid out to such person or distributed among such persons as the court may direct, being a person or persons appearing to the court to

have made the deposits as a result of which the profits mentioned in subsection (1) above have accrued or such other person or persons as the court thinks just.

(4)   On an application under this section the court may require the person concerned to furnish it with such accounts or other information as it may require for determining whether any and if so, what profits have accrued to him as mentioned in subsection (1) above and for determining how any amounts are to be paid or distributed under subsection (3) above; and the court may require any such accounts or other information to be verified in such manner as it may direct.

(5)   The jurisdiction conferred by this section shall be exercisable by the High Court and the Court of Session.

PART II
THE DEPOSIT PROTECTION SCHEME

The Board and the Fund

50.   The Deposit Protection Board

(1)   The body corporate known as the Deposit Protection Board and the Fund known as the Deposit Protection Fund established by section 21 of the Banking Act 1979 shall continue to exist.

(2)   The Deposit Protection Board (in this Part of this Act referred to as 'the Board') shall—

(a)   hold, manage and apply the Fund in accordance with the provisions of this Part of this Act;

(b)   levy contributions for the Fund, in accordance with those provisions, from contributory institutions; and

(c)   have such other functions as are conferred on the Board by those provisions.

(3)   Schedule 4 to this Act shall have effect with respect to the Board.

51.   The Deposit Protection Fund

(1)   The Fund shall consist of—

(a)   any money which forms part of the Fund when this section comes into force;

(b)   initial, further and special contributions levied by the Board under this Part of this Act;

(c)   money borrowed by the Board under this Part of this Act; and

(d)   any other money required by any provision of this Part of this Act to be credited to the Fund or received by the Board and directed by it to be so credited.

(2)   The money constituting the Fund shall be placed by the Board in an account with the Bank.

(3)   As far as possible, the Bank shall invest money placed with it under subsection (2) above in Treasury bills; and any income from money so invested shall be credited to the Fund.

(3A)   In subsection (3) above, the reference to Treasury bills includes a reference to bills and other short-term instruments issued by the government of another EEA

State and appearing to the *Bank* **Authority** to correspond as nearly as may be to Treasury bills.

(4)   There shall be chargeable to the Fund—

(a)   repayments of special contributions under section 55(2) below;

(b)   payments under section 58 below;

(c)   money required for the repayment of, and the payment of interest on, money borrowed by the Board; and

(d)   the administrative and other necessary or incidental expenses incurred by the Board.

Contributions to the Fund

52.   Contributory institutions and general provisions as to contributions

(1)   All UK institutions and participating institutions shall be liable to contribute to the Fund and are in this Part of this Act referred to as contributory institutions.

(2)   Contributions to the Fund shall be levied on a contributory institution by the Board by the service on the institution a notice specifying the amount due, which shall be paid by the institution not later than twenty-one days after the date on which the notice is served.

(2A)   Where—

(a)   a notice under subsection (2) above is served on a contributory institution; and

(b)   the amount specified in the notice remains unpaid after the period of twenty-one days mentioned in that subsection,

the Board shall as soon as practicable give written notice of that fact to the *Bank* **Authority**.

(3)   Subject to section 56 below, on each occasion on which contributions are to be levied from contributory institutions (other than the occasion of the levy of an initial contribution from a particular institution under section 53 below)—

(a)   a contribution shall be levied from each of the contributory institutions; and

(b)   the amount of the contribution of each institution shall be ascertained by applying to the institution's deposit base the percentage determined by the Board for the purpose of the contribution levied on that occasion.

(4)   Subject to subsection (4B) and section 57 below, the deposit base of an institution in relation to any contribution is the amount which the Board determines as representing the average, over such period preceding the levying of the contribution as appears to the Board to be appropriate, of deposits in EEA currencies with the United Kingdom offices of that institution other than—

(a)   secured deposits;

(b)   deposits which are own funds within the meaning given by Article 2 of Directive 89/299/EEC;

(c)   deposits which fall within item 1 or 2 of Annex I to Directive 94/19/EC; and

(d)   deposits in respect of which the institution has in the United Kingdom issued a certificate of deposit in an EEA currency.

(4A)   In its application to UK institutions, subsection (4) above shall have effect as if the reference to United Kingdom office included a reference to offices in other EEA States.

(4B)   In the case of a participating EEA institution, the amount determined under subsection (4) above shall be reduced by the amount given by the formula—

$$PA \times \frac{HS}{UK}$$

where—

PA   = so much of the amount so determined as is attributable to deposits which are protected by the institution's home State scheme;

HS   = the level of protection (expressed in ecus) afforded by that scheme at the time when the determination is made, or the level of protection mentioned below, whichever is the less;

UK   = the level of protection (so expressed) afforded by this Part of this Act at that time.

(5)   In its application to this section, section 5(3) above shall have effect with the omission of paragraphs (b) and (c).

(6)   In this Part of this Act—

'the 1995 Regulations' means the Credit Institutions (Protection of Depositors) Regulations 1995;

'administrator', in relation to an institution, means an administrator of the institution under Part II of the Insolvency Act 1986 or Part III of the Insolvency (Northern Ireland) Order 1989;

'building society' means a building society incorporated (or deemed to be incorporated) under the Building Societies Act 1986;

'the deposit protection scheme' means the scheme for the protection of depositors continued in force by this Part of this Act;

'ecu' means—

(a)   the European currency unit as defined in Article 1 of Council Regulation No. 3320/94/EC; or

(b)   except in section 60(1) below, any other unit of account which is defined by reference to the European currency unit as so defined;

'EEA currency' means the currency of an EEA State or ecus;

'EEA State' means a State which is a Contracting Party to the Agreement on the European Economic Area signed at Oporto on 2 May 1992 as adjusted by the Protocol signed at Brussels on 17 March 1993;

'former authorised institution' does not include any institution which is a former UK institution or a former participating institution;

'former participating institution' means an institution which was formerly a participating institution and continues to have a liability in respect of any deposit for which it had a liability at a time when it was a participating institution, and 'former participating EEA institution' and 'former participating non-EEA institution' shall be construed accordingly;

'former UK institution' means an institution which was formerly a UK institution and continues to have a liability in respect of any deposit for which it had a liability at a time when it was a UK institution;

'home State Scheme' has the same meaning as in the 1995 Regulation;

'participating EEA institution' means a European authorised institution which, in accordance with Chapter I of Part II of the 1995 Regulations, is participating in the deposit protection scheme;

'participating institution' means a participating EEA institution or a participating non-EEA institution;

'participating non-EEA institution' means an authorised institution which is incorporated in or formed under the law of a country or territory outside the European Economic Area, not being one—

(a)   which has, in accordance with Chapter III of Part II of the 1995 Regulations, elected not to participate in the deposit protection scheme, and

(b)   whose election under that Chapter is still in force;

'UK institution' means an authorised institution which is incorporated in or formed under the law of any part of the United Kingdom.

(7)   In its application to this Part, section 5(3) above shall have effect as if—

(a)   the references in paragraph (a) to an authorised institution included references to a building society and to any credit institution which is incorporated in or formed under the law of a country or territory outside the United Kingdom; and

(b)   in Schedule 2 to this Act, paragraph 5 (building societies) were omitted.

53.   Initial contributions

(1)   Subject to subsection (4) below, where an institution becomes a contributory institution after the coming into force of this Part of this Act the Board shall levy from it, on or as soon as possible after the day on which it becomes a contributory institution, an initial contribution of an amount determined in accordance with subsection (2) or (3) below.

(2)   Where the institution concerned has a deposit base, then, subject to section 56(1) below, the amount of an initial contribution levied under this section shall be such percentage of the deposit base as the Board considers appropriate to put the institution on a basis of equality with the other contributory institutions, having regard to—

(a)   the initial contributions previously levied under this section or under section 24(1) of the Banking Act 1979; and

(b)   so far as they are attributable to an increase in the size of the Fund resulting from an order under subsection (2) of section 54 below or subsection (2) of section 25 of that Act, further contributions levied under either of those sections.

(2A)   In its application to participating EEA institutions, subsection (2) above shall have effect as if the reference to a basis of equality were a reference to a basis of parity.

(3)   Where the institution concerned has no deposit base the amount of an initial contribution levied under this section shall be the minimum amount for the time being provided for in section 56(1) below.

(4)   The Board may waive an initial contribution under this section if it appears to it that the institution concerned is to carry on substantially the same business as that previously carried on by one or more institutions which are or were contributory institutions.

54.   Further contributions

(1)   If at the end of any financial year of the Board the amount standing to the credit of the Fund is less than £3 million the Board may, with the approval of the Treasury, levy further contributions from contributory institutions so as to restore the amount standing to the credit of the Fund to a minimum of £5 million and a maximum of £6 million.

(2)   If at any time it appears to the Treasury to be desirable in the interests of depositors to increase the size of the Fund, the Treasury may, after consultation with the Board, by order amend subsection (1) above so as to substitute for the sums for the time being specified in that subsection such larger sums as may be specified in the order; but no such order shall be made unless a draft of it has been laid before and approved by a resolution of each House of Parliament.

(3)   An order under subsection (2) above may authorise the Board forthwith to levy further contributions from contributory institutions so as to raise the amount standing to the credit of the Fund to a figure between the new minimum and maximum amounts provided for by the order.

55.   Special contributions

(1)   If it appears to the Board that payments under section 58 below are likely to exhaust the Fund, the Board may, with the approval of the Treasury, levy special contributions from contributory institutions to meet the Fund's commitments under that section.

(2)   Where at the end of any financial year of the Board there is money in the Fund which represents special contributions and will not in the opinion of the Board be required for making payments under section 58 below in consequence of institutions having become insolvent or subject to administration orders before repayments are made under this subsection the Board—

(a)   shall repay to the institutions from which it was levied so much (if any) of that money as can be repaid without reducing the amount standing to the credit of the Fund below the maximum amount for the time being specified in subsection (1) of section 54 above; and

(b)   may repay to those institutions so much (if any) of that money as can be repaid without reducing the amount standing to the credit of the Fund below the minimum amount for the time being specified in that subsection.

(3)   Repayments to institutions under this section shall be made pro rata according to the amount of the special contribution made by each of them but the board may withhold the whole or part of any repayment due to an institution that has become

insolvent and, in the case of an institution that has ceased to be a contributory institution, may either withhold its repayment or make it to any other contributory institution which, in the opinion of the Board, is its successor.

56. Maximum and minimum contributions

(1)   The amount of the initial contribution levied from a contributory institution shall be no less than £10,000.

(2)   The amount of the initial contribution or any further contribution levied from a contributory institution shall not exceed £300,000.

(3)   No contributory institution shall be required to pay a further or special contribution if, or to the extent that, the amount of that contribution, together with previous initial, further and special contributions made by the institution, after allowing for any repayments made to it under section 55(2) above or section 63 below, amounts to more than 0.3 per cent of the institution's deposit base as ascertained for the purpose of the contribution in question.

(4)   Nothing in subsection (3) above—

(a)   shall entitle an institution to repayment of any contribution previously made; or

(b)   shall prevent the Board from proceeding to levy contributions from other contributory institutions in whose case the limit in that subsection has not been reached.

(5)   The Treasury may from time to time after consultation with the Board by order—

(a)   amend subsection (1) or (2) above so as to substitute for the sum for the time being specified in that subsection such other sum as may be specified in the order; or

(b)   amend subsection (3) above so as to substitute for the percentage for the time being specified in that subsection such other percentage as may be specified in the order.

(6)   No order shall be made under subsection (5) above unless a draft of it has been laid before and approved by a resolution of each House of Parliament.

57. Deposit base of transferee institutions

(1)   This section applies where the liabilities in respect of deposits of a person specified in Schedule 2 to this Act (an 'exempted person') are transferred to an institution which is not such a person (a 'transferee institution').

(2)   If the transferee institution becomes a contributory institution on the occasion of the transfer or immediately thereafter it shall be treated for the purposes of section 53 above as having such deposit base as it would have if—

(a)   deposits in EEA currencies with the United Kingdom offices of the exempted person at any time had at that time been deposits in EEA currencies with the United Kingdom offices of the transferee institution; and

(b)   certificates of deposit in EEA currencies issued by the exempted person had been issued by the transferee institution.

(3)   If the transferee institution is already a contributory institution at the time of the transfer, the Board shall levy from it, as soon as possible after the transfer, a

further initial contribution of an amount equal to the initial contribution which it would have been liable to make if—

(a)   it had become a contributory institution on the date of the transfer;

(b)   its deposit base were calculated by reference (and by reference opnly) to the deposits in EEA currencies with the United Kingdom offices of the exempted person, taking certificates of deposit in EEA currencies issued by the exempted person as having been issued by the transferee institution; and

(c)   the amount specified in section 56(2) above were reduced by the amount of any initial contribution which the transferee institution has already made.

(4)   Whether or not the transferee institution is already a contributory institution at the time of the transfer it shall be treated for the purposes of the levying from it of any further or special contribution as having such deposit base as it would have if the deposits in EEA currencies with its United Kingdom offices and the certificates of deposit in EEA currencies issued by it included respectively deposits in EEA currencies with the United Kingdom offices of the exempted person and certificates of deposit in EEA currencies issued by that person.

(4A)   In their application to UK institutions, subsections (2) to (4) above shall have effect as if references to United Kingdom offices included references to offices in other EEA States.

(5)   In its application to this section, section 5(3) above shall have effect with the omission of paragraphs (b) and (c).

Payments out of the Fund

58.   Compensation payments to depositors

(1)   Subject to the provisions of this section, if at any time an institution to which this subsection applies becomes insolvent, the Board—

(a)   shall as soon as practicable pay out of the Fund to depositors who have protected deposits with that institution which are due and payable amounts equal to nine-tenths of their protected deposits; and

(b)   shall in any event secure that, before the end of the relevant period, it is in a position to make those payments as soon as they fall to be made.

(2)   Subsection (1) above applies to an institution which—

(a)   is a UK institution or participating institution;

(b)   is a former UK institution or a former participating institution; or

(c)   is a former authorised institution (not being a recognised bank or licensed institution excluded by an order under section 23(2) of the Banking Act 1979);
and if at any time such an institution ceases to be insolvent, subsection (1) above shall cease to apply in relation to that institution.

(2A)   In subsection (1) above 'the relevant period' means—

(a)   the period of three months beginning with the time when the institution becomes insolvent; or

(b)   that period and such additional period or periods, being not more than three and of not more than three months each, as the *Bank* **Authority** may in exceptional circumstances allow.

(2B)   A person claiming to be entitled to a payment under subsection (1) above in respect of a protected deposit with a participating institution shall make his claim in such form, with such evidence proving it, and within such period, as the Board directs.

(2C)   The amount of any payment which falls to be made under subsection (1) above in respect of a protected deposit made with an office of a UK institution in another EEA State shall not exceed such amount as the Board may determine is or would be payable, in respect of an equivalent deposit made with an institution authorised in that State, under any corresponding scheme for the protection of depositors or investors which is in force in that State.

(2D)   Where, in the case of a participating EEA institution, the Board is satisfied that a depositor has received or is entitled to receive a payment in repect of his protected deposit under any home state scheme, the Board shall deduct an amount equal to that payment from the payment that would otherwise be made to the depositor under subsection (1) above.

(3)   Where, in the case of a UK institution or participating non-EEA institution, the Board is satisfied that a depositor has received or will receive a payment in respect of his protected deposit under any scheme for protecting depositors or investors which is comparable to that for which provision is made by this Part of this Act or under a guarantee given by a government or other authority the Board may–

(a)   deduct an amount equal to the whole or part of that payment from the payment that would otherwise be made to him under subsection (1) above; or

(b)   in pursuance of an agreement made by the Board with the authority responsible for the scheme or by which the guarantee was given, make in full the payment required by that subsection and recoup from that authority such contribution to it as may be specified in or determined under the agreement.

(4)   Where the Board makes such a deduction as is mentioned in paragraph (a) of subsection (3) above it may agree with the authority responsible for the scheme or by which the guarantee was given to reimburse that authority to the extent of the deduction or any lesser amount.

(5)   The Board may decline to make any payment under subsection (1) above to a person who, in the opinion of the Board, has any responsibility for, or may have profited directly or indirectly from, the circumstances giving rise to the institution's financial difficulties.

(6)   There shall be deducted from any payment to be made by the Board under subsection (1) above in respect of a deposit any payment already made in respect of that deposit by a liquidator or administrator of the institution; and in this subsection, in relation to an institution formed under the law of a country or territory outside the United Kingdom, the reference to a liquidator or administrator includes a reference to a person whose functions appear to the Board to correspond as nearly as may be to those of a liquidator or administrator.

(7)   The Treasury may, after consultation with the Board, by order amend subsection (1) above so as to substitute for the fraction for the time being specified in that subsection such other fraction as may be specified in the order; but no such

order shall be made unless a draft of it has been laid before and approved by a resolution of each House of Parliament.

(8) Notwithstanding that the Board may not yet have made or become liable to make a payment under subsection (1) above in relation to an institution falling within that subsection—

(a) the Board shall at all times be entitled to receive any notice or other document required to be sent to a creditor of the institution under Part II of the Insolvency Act 1986 or under Part III of the Insolvency (Northern Ireland) Order 1989, or required to be sent to a creditor of the institution whose debt has been proved; and

(b) a duly authorised representative of the Board shall be entitled—

(i) to attend any meeting of creditors of the institution and to make representations as to any matter for decision at that meeting;

(ii) to be a member of any committee established under section 26 or 301 of the Insolvency Act 1986;

(iii) to be a commissioner under section 30 of the Bankruptcy (Scotland) Act 1985; and

(iv) to be a member of a committee established for the purposes of Part IV or V of the Insolvency Act 1986 under section 101 of that Act or under section 141 or 142 of that Act;

(v) to be a member of any committee established under Article 38 or 274 of the Insolvency (Northern Ireland) Order 1989; and

(vi) to be a member of a committee established for the purposes of Part V or VI of the Insolvency (Northern Ireland) Order 1989 under Article 87 of that Order or under Article 120 of that Order.

(9) Where a representative of the Board exercises his right to be a member of such a committee as is mentioned in paragraph (b)(ii) or (iv) of subsection (8) above or to be a commissioner by virtue of paragraph (b)(iii) of that subsection he may not be removed except with the consent of the Board and his appointment under that subsection shall be disregarded for the purposes of any provision made by or under any enactment which specifies a minimum or maximum number of members of such a committee or commission.

(10) References in this section and sections 59 and 60 below to a former authorised institution include references to an institution which—

(a) was formerly a European authorised institution which accepted deposits in the United Kingdom; and

(b) continues to have a liability in respect of any deposit for which it had a liability when it was such an institution;

and references in section 60 below to ceasing to be an authorised institution include references to ceasing to be a European authorised institution which accepted deposits in the United Kingdom.

59. Meaning of insolvency etc.

(1) For the purposes of this Part of this Act, a UK institution or participating non-EEA institution becomes insolvent—

(a)   on the making by the *Bank* **Authority** of a determination that, for reasons which directly relate to the institution's financial circumstances, the institution—

  (i)   is unable to repay deposits which are due and payable; and

  (ii)   has no current prospect of being able to do so;

(b)   on the making by a court in any part of the United Kingdom, or in another EEA State, of a judicial ruling which—

  (i)   directly relates to the institution's financial circumstances; and

  (ii)   has the effect of suspending the ability of depositors to make claims against the institution; or

(c)   in the case of a participating non-EEA institution, on the making by a court in any country or territory outside the European Economic Area of a judicial ruling which appears to the Board to correspond as nearly as may be to such a judicial ruling as is mentioned in paragraph (b) above,

but only if deposits made with this institution have become due and payable and have not been repaid.

(2)   For those purposes, a participating EEA institution becomes insolvent—

(a)   on the making by the Supervisory authority in the institution's home State of a declaration that deposits held by the institution are no longer available; or

(b)   on the making by a court in any part of the United Kingdom, or in an EEA State other than the institution's home State, of a judicial ruling which—

  (i)   directly relates to the institution's financial circumstances; and

  (ii)   has the effect of suspending the ability of depositors to make claims against the institution,

but only if, in a case falling within paragraph (b) above, deposits made with the institution have become due and payable and have not been repaid.

(3)   For those purposes—

(a)   an institution which has become insolvent by virtue of such a determination or declaration as is mentioned in subsection (1)(a) or (2)(a) above ceases to be insolvent on any withdrawal of the determination or declaration; and

(b)   an institution which has become insolvent by virtue of such a judicial ruling as is mentioned in subsection (1)(b) or (c) or (2)(b) above ceases to be insolvent on any reversal of the ruling (whether on appeal or otherwise).

(4)   In relation to a UK institution or participating non-EEA institution, it shall be the duty of the *Bank* **Authority**—

(a)   to make such a determination as is mentioned in subsection (1)(a) above within 21 days of its being satisfied as there mentioned; and

(b)   to withdraw such a determination within 21 days of its ceasing to be so satisfied.

(5)   In this section—

(a)   any reference to a UK institution includes references to a former UK institution, and to a former authorised institution which is incorporated in or formed under the law of any part of the United Kingdom;

(b)   any reference to a participating EEA institution includes references to a former participating EEA institution, and to a former authorised institution which is incorporated in or formed under the law of an EEA State other than the United Kingdom; and

(c)   any reference to a participating non-EEA institution includes references to a former participating non-EEA institution, and to a former authorised institution which is incorporated in or formed under the law of a country or territory which is outside the European Economic Area.

60.   Protected deposits

(1)   Subject to the provisions of this section, in relation to an institution in respect of which a payment falls to be made under section 58(1) above, any reference in this Act to a depositor's protected deposit is a reference to the liability of the institution to him in respect of—

(a)   the principal amount of each deposit in an EEA currency which was made by him with a United Kingdom office of the institution before the time when the institution became insolvent and has become due and payable; and

(b)   accrued interest on any such deposit up to the time when it became due and payable,

but so that the total liability of the institution to him in respect of such deposits does not exceed £20,000, or the sterling equivalent of 22,222 ecus immediately before the time when the institution became insolvent, whichever is the greater.

(2)   In calculating a depositor's protected deposit for the purposes of subsection (1) above, the amount to be taken into account as regards any deposit made in another EEA currency shall be its sterling equivalent immediately before the time when the institution became insolvent, or the time when the deposit became due and payable, whichever is the later.

(2A)   In its application to UK institutions, subsection (1) above shall have effect as if any reference to United Kingdom offices included a reference to offices in other EEA States.

(3)   For the purposes of subsection (1) above no account shall be taken of any liability unless—

(a)   proof of the debt, or a claim for repayment of the deposit, which gives rise to the liability has been lodged with a liquidator or administrator of the institution; or

(b)   the depositor has provided the Board with all such written authorities, information and documents as, in the event of a liquidator or administrator being appointed, the Board will need for the purpose of lodging and pursuing, on the depositor's behalf, a proof of the debt, or a claim for the repayment of the deposit, which gives rise to the liability.

(4)   In subsection (3) above, in relation to an institution incorporated in or formed under the law of a country or territory outside the United Kingdom—

(a)   references to a liquidator or administrator include references to a person whose functions appear to the Board to correspond as nearly as may be to those of a liquidator or administrator; and

(b)   references to the lodging, or the lodging and pursuing, of a proof of the debt, or a claim for the repayment of the deposit, which gives rise to the liability include references to the doing of an act or acts which appear to the Board to correspond as nearly as may be to the lodging, or the lodging and pursuing, of such a proof or claim.

(5)   The Treasury may, after consultation with the Board, by order amend subsection (1) above so as to substitute for the sum for the time being specified in those subsections such larger sum as may be specified in the order; but no such order shall be made unless a draft of it has been laid before and approved by a resolution of each House of Parliament.

(6)   In determining the liability or total liability of an institution to a depositor for the purposes of subsection (1) above, no account shall be taken of any liability in respect of a deposit if—

(a)   it is a secured deposit; or

(b)   it is a deposit which is own funds within the meaning given by Article 2 of Directive 89/299/EEC; or

(c)   it is a deposit which the Board is satisfied was made in the course of a money-laundering transaction; or

(d)   it is a deposit by a person mentioned in item 1 or 2 of Annex I to Directive 94/19/EC which was made otherwise than as trustee for a person not so mentioned; or

(e)   the institution is a former UK institution or former authorised institution and the deposit was made after it ceased to be a UK institution or authorised institution unless, at the time the deposit was made, the depositor did not know, and could not reasonably be expected to have known, that it had ceased to be a UK institution or authorised institution; or

(f)   the institution is a former participating EEA institution and the deposit was made after it ceased to be a participating EEA institution; or

(g)   the institution is a former participating non-EEA institution and the deposit was made after it ceased to be a participating non-EEA institution unless the Board is satisfied—

(i)   that the depositor is entitled under the institution's home State scheme to a payment in respect of the deposit; and

(ii)   that he has not received, and has no prospect of receiving, the payment; and references in paragraph (e) above to an institution ceasing to be an authorised institution include references an institution ceasing to be a recognised bank or licensed institution under the Banking Act 1979.

(6A)   A transaction in connection with which an offence has been committed under—

(a)   any enactment specified in regulation 2(3) of the Money Laundering Regulations 1993; or

(b)   any enactment in force in another EEA State, or in a country or territory outside the European Economic Area, which has effect for the purpose of prohibiting money laundering within the meaning of Article 1 of Directive 91/308/EEC, is a money-laundering transaction for the purposes of subsection (6)(c) above at any time if, at that time, a person stands convicted of the offence or has been charged with the offence and has not been tried.

(7)   Unless the Board otherwise directs in any particular case, in determining the total liability of an institution to a depositor for the purposes of subsection (1) above there shall be deducted the amount of any liability of the depositor to the institution—

(a)   in respect of which a right of set off existed immediately before the institution became insolvent against any such deposit in an EEA currency as is referred to in subsection (1) above; or

(b)   in respect of which such right would then have existed if the deposit in question had been repayable on demand and the liability in question had fallen due.

(9)   For the purposes of this section and sections 61 and 62 below the definition of deposit in section 5 above—

(a)   shall be treated as including—

(i)   any sum that would otherwise be excluded by paragraph (a), (d) or (e) of subsection (3) of that section if the sum is paid as trustee for a person not falling within any of those paragraphs;

(ii)   any sum that would otherwise be excluded by paragraph (b) or (c) of that subsection;

(b)   subject to subsections (10) and (11) below, shall be treated as excluding any sum paid by a trustee for a person falling within paragraph (e) of subsection (3) of that section; and

(c)   shall be treated as including any sum the right to repayment of which is evidenced by a transferable certificate of deposit or other transferable instrument and which would be a deposit within the meaning of section 5 as extended by paragraph (a) and restricted by paragraph (b) above if it had been paid by the person who is entitled to it at the time when the institution in question becomes insolvent.

(10)   Where the trustee referred to in paragraph (b) of subsection (9) above is not a bare trustee and there are two or more beneficiaries that paragraph applies only if all the beneficiaries fall within section 5(3)(e) above.

(11)   Subsection (10) above does not extend to Scotland and, in Scotland, where there are two or more beneficiaries of a trust the trustee of which is referred to in paragraph (b) of subsection (9) above that paragraph applies only if all the beneficiaries fall within section 5(3)(e) above.

61.   Trustee deposits, joint deposits etc.

(1)   In the cases to which this section applies sections 58 and 60 above shall have effect with the following modifications.

(2)   Subject to the provisions of this section, where any persons are entitled to a deposit as trustees they shall be treated as a single and continuing body of persons distinct from the persons who may from time to time be the trustees, and if the same persons are entitled as trustees to different deposits under different trusts they shall be treated as a separate and distinct body with respect to each of those trusts.

(3)   Where a deposit is held for any person or for two or more persons jointly by a bare trustee, that person or, as the case may be, those persons jointly shall be treated as entitled to the deposit without the intervention of any trust.

(4)   Subsection (3) above does not extend to Scotland and, in Scotland, where a deposit is held by a person as nominee for another person or for two or more other persons jointly, that other person or, as the case may be, those other persons jointly shall be treated as entitled to the deposit.

(5)   A deposit to which two or more persons are entitled as members of a partnership (whether or not in equal shares) shall be treated as a single deposit.

(6)   Subject to subsection (5) above, where two or more persons are jointly entitled to a deposit and subsection (2) above does not apply each of them shall be treated as having a separate deposit of an amount produced by dividing the amount of the deposit to which they are jointly entitled by the number of persons who are so entitled.

(7)   Where a person is entitled (whether as trustee or otherwise) to a deposit made out of a clients' or other similar account containing money to which one or more other persons are entitled, that other person or, as the case may be, each of those other persons shall be treated (to the exclusion of the first-mentioned person) as entitled to such much of the deposit as corresponds to the proportion of the money in the account to which he is entitled.

(8)   Where an authorised institution is entitled as trustee to a sum which would be a deposit apart from section 5(3)(a) above and represents deposits made with the institution, each of the persons who made those deposits shall be treated as having made a deposit equal to so much of that sum as represents the deposit made by him.

(9)   The Board may decline to make any payment under section 58 above in respect of a deposit until the person claiming to be entitled to it informs the Board of the capacity in which he is entitled to the deposit and provides sufficient information to enable the Board to determine what payment (if any) should be made under that section and to whom.

(10)   In this section 'jointly entitled' means—

(a)   in England and Wales and in Northern Ireland, beneficially entitled as joint tenants, tenants in common or coparceners;

(b)   in Scotland, beneficially entitled as joint owners or owners in common.

(11)   In the application of this section in relation to deposits made with an office of a UK institution in another EEA State, references to persons entitled in any of the following capacities, namely—

(a)   as trustees;

(b)   as bare trustees;

(c)   as members of a partnership; or

(d)   as persons jointly entitled,

shall be construed as references to persons entitled under the law of that State in a capacity appearing to the Board to correspond as nearly as may be to that capacity.

62.   Liability of institution in respect of compensation payments

(1)   This section applies where—

(a)   an institution becomes insolvent; and

(b)   the Board has made, or is under a liability to make, a payment under section 58 above by virtue of the institution becoming insolvent;

and in the following provisions of this section a payment falling within paragraph (b) above, less any amount which the Board is entitled to recoup by virtue of any such agreement as is mentioned in subsection (3)(b) of that section, is referred to as 'a compensation payment' and the person to whom such a payment has been or is to be made is referred to as 'the depositor'.

(2) Where this section applies in respect of an institution that is being wound up—

(a) the institution shall become liable to the Board, as in respect of a contractual debt incurred immediately before the institution began to be wound up, for an amount equal to the compensation payment;

(b) the liability of the institution to the depositor in respect of any deposit or deposits of his ('the liability to the depositor') shall be reduced by an amount equal to the compensation payment made or to be made to him by the Board; and

(c) the duty of the liquidator of the insolvent institution to make payments to the Board on account of the liability referred to in paragraph (a) above ('the liability to the Board') and to the depositor on account of the liability to him (after taking account of paragraph (b) above) shall be varied in accordance with subsection (3) below.

(3) The variation referred to in subsection (2)(c) above is as follows—

(a) in the first instance the liquidator shall pay to the Board instead of to the depositor any amount which, apart from this section, would be payable on account of the liability to the depositor except insofar as that liability relates to any such deposit as is mentioned in section 60(6) above; and

(b) if at any time the total amount paid to the Board by virtue of paragraph (a) above and in respect of the liability to the Board equals the amount of the compensation payment made to the depositor, the liquidator shall thereafter pay to the depositor instead of to the Board any amount which, apart from this paragraph, would be payable to the Board in respect of the liability to the Board.

(4) Where this section applies in respect of an institution that is not being wound up—

(a) the institution shall, at the time when the compensation payment in respect of a deposit falls to be made by the Board, become liable to the Board for an amount equal to that payment; and

(b) the liability of the institution to the depositor in respect of that deposit shall be reduced by an amount equal to that payment.

(5) Where an institution is wound up after it becomes insolvent subsections (2) and (3) above shall not apply to any compensation payment to the extent to which the Board has received a payment in respect of it by virtue of subsection (4)(a) above.

(6) Where by virtue of section 61 above the compensation payment is or is to be made by the Board to a person other than the person to whom the institution is liable in respect of the deposit any reference in the foregoing provisions of this section to the liability to the depositor shall be construed as a reference to the liability of the institution to the person to whom that payment would fall to be made by the Board apart from that section.

(7) Where the Board makes a payment under section 58(4) above in respect of an amount deducted from a payment due to a depositor this section shall have effect as if the amount had been paid to the depositor.

(8)   Rules may be made—

(a)   for England and Wales, under sections 411 and 412 of the Insolvency Act 1986;

(b)   for Scotland—

(i)   under the said section 411; and

(ii)   in relation to an institution whose estate may be sequestrated under the Bankruptcy (Scotland) Act 1985, by the Secretary of State under the subsection; and

(c)   for Northern Ireland, under Article 359 of the Insolvency (Northern Ireland) Order 1989 and section 65 of the Judicature (Northern Ireland) Act 1978 or Part III of the Insolvency (Northern Ireland) Order 1989,

for the purpose of integrating the procedure provided for in this section into the general procedure on a winding-up, bankruptcy or sequestration or under Part II of the Insolvency Act 1986.

Repayments in respect of contributions

63.   Repayments in respect of contributions

(1)   Any money received by the board under section 62 above ('recovered money') shall not form part of the Fund but, for the remainder of the financial year of the Board in which it is received, shall be placed by the board in an account with the *Bank* **Authority** which shall as far as possible invest the money in Treasury bills; and any income arising from the money so invested during the remainder of the year shall be credited to the Fund.

(2)   The Board shall prepare a scheme for the making out of recovered money of repayments to institutions in respect of—

(a)   special contributions; and

(b)   so far as they are not attributable to an increase in the size of the Fund resulting from an order under subsection (2) of section 54 above, further contributions levied under that section,

which have been made in the financial year of the Board in which the money was received or in any previous such financial year.

(3)   A scheme under subsection (2) above—

(a)   shall provide for the making of repayments first in respect of special contributions and then, if those contributions can be repaid in full (taking into account any previous repayments under this section and under section 55(2) above) in respect of further contributions;

(b)   may make provision for repayments in respect of contributions made by an institution which has ceased to be a contributory institution to be made to a contributory institution which, in the opinion of the board, is its successor; and

(c)   subject to paragraph (b) above, may exclude from the scheme further contributions levied from institutions which have ceased to be contributory institutions.

(4)   Except where special or further contributions can be repaid in full, repayments to institutions under this section shall be made pro rata according to the amount of the special or further contribution made by each of them.

(5)   If at the end of a financial year of the board in which recovered money is received by it—

(a)   that money; and

(b)   the amount standing to the credit of the Fund, after any repayments made under section 55 above,

exceeds the maximum amount for the time being specified in section 54(1) above the Board shall as soon as practicable make out of the recovered money, up to an amount not greater than the excess, the repayments required by the scheme under subsection (2) above and may out of the recovered money make such further repayments required by the scheme as will not reduce the amounts mentioned in paragraphs (a) and (b) above below the minimum amount for the time being specified in section 54(1) above.

(6)   If in any financial year of the Board—

(a)   any of the recovered money is not applied in making payments in accordance with subsection (5) above; or

(b)   the payments made in accordance with that subsection are sufficient to provide for the repayment in full of all the contributions to which the scheme relates,

any balance of that money shall be credited to the Fund.

Supplementary provisions

64.   Borrowing powers

(1)   If in the course of operating the fund it appears to the Board desirable to do so, the Board may borrow up to a total outstanding at any time of £10 million or such larger sum as, after consultation with the Board, the Treasury may from time to time by order prescribe.

[£175 million is prescribed by the Deposit Protection Board (Increase of Borrowing Limit) Order 1991 (SI 1991/1684).]

(2)   An order under subsection (1) above shall be subject to annulment in pursuance of a resolution of either House of Parliament.

(3)   Any amount borrowed by virtue of this section shall be disregarded in ascertaining the amount standing to the credit of the Fund for the purposes of sections 54(1), 55(2) and 63(5) above.

65.   Power to obtain information

(1)   If required to do so by a request in writing made by the board, the *Bank* **Authority** may by notice in writing served on a contributory institution require the institution, within such time and at such place as may be specified in the notice, to provide the Board with such information and to produce to it such documents, or documents of such a description, as the Board may reasonably require for the purpose of determining the contributions of the institution under this Part of this Act.

(2)   Subsections (4), (5), (11) and (13) of section 39 above shall have effect in relation to any requirement imposed under subsection (1) above on a UK institution or participating non-EEA institution as they have effect in relation to a requirement imposed under this section.

(3)   The Board may by notice in writing served on an insolvent institution or, where a person has been appointed as liquidator or administrator of such an institution, on that person, require the institution or person, at such time or times and at such place as may be specified in the notice—

(a)   to provide the Board with such information; and

(b)   to produce to the Board such documents specified in the notice,

as the Board may reasonably require to enable it to carry out its functions under this Part of this Act.

(4)   Where, as a result of an institution being wound up, any documents have come into the possession of the Official Receiver or, in Northern Ireland, the Official Receiver for Northern Ireland, he shall permit any person duly authorised by the Board to inspect the documents for the purpose of establishing—

(a)   the identity of those of the institution's depositors to whom the Board are liable to make a payment under section 58 above; and

(b)   the amount of the protected deposit held by each of the depositors.

66.   Tax treatment of contributions and repayments

In computing for the purposes of the Tax Acts the profits or gains arising from the trade carried on by a contributory institution—

(a)   to the extent that it would not be deductible apart from this section, any sum expended by the institution in paying a contribution to the Fund may be deducted as an allowable expense;

(b)   any payment which is made to the institution by the Board under section 55(2) above or pursuant to a scheme under section 63(2) above shall be treated as a trading receipt.

PART III
BANKING NAMES AND DESCRIPTIONS

67.   Restriction on use of banking names

(1)   Subject to section 68 below, no person carrying on any business in the United Kingdom shall use any name which indicates or may reasonably be understood to indicate (whether in English or any other language) that he is a bank or banker or is carrying on a banking business unless he is an authorised institution to which this section applies.

(2)   This section applies to an authorised institution which—

(a)   is a company incorporated in the United Kingdom which has—

(i)   an issued share capital in respect of which the amount paid up is not less than £5 million (or an amount of equivalent value denominated wholly or partly otherwise than in sterling); or

(ii)   undistributable reserves falling within paragraph (a), (b) or (d) of section 264(3) of the Companies Act 1985 or Article 272(3)(a), (b) or (d) of the Companies (Northern Ireland) Order 1986 of not less than that sum (or such an equivalent amount); or

     (iii)   such undistributable reserves of an amount which together with the amount paid up in respect of its issued share capital equals not less than that sum (or such an equivalent amount); or

    (b)   is a partnership formed under the law of any part of the United Kingdom in respect of which one or more designated fixed capital accounts are maintained to which there has been credited not less than £5 million (or such an equivalent amount).

(3)   For the purposes of subsection (2)(a) above 'share capital' does not include share capital which under the terms on which it is issued is to be, or may at the option of the shareholder be, redeemed by the company.

(4)   For the purposes of subsection (2)(b) above 'designated fixed capital account', in relation to a partnership, means an account—

    (a)   which is prepared and designated as such under the terms of the partnership agreement;

    (b)   which shows capital contributed by the partners; and

    (c)   from which under the terms of that agreement an amount representing capital may only be withdrawn by a partner if—

     (i)   he ceases to be a partner and an equal amount is transferred to a designated fixed capital account by his former partners or any person replacing him as their partner; or

     (ii)   the partnership is otherwise dissolved or wound up.

(5)   An authorised institution to which subsection (2) above applies whose issued share capital, undistributable reserves or designated fixed capital account is denominated wholly or partly otherwise than in sterling shall not be regarded as ceasing to be such an institution by reason only of a fluctuation in the rate of exchange of sterling unless and until it has ceased to satisfy any of the conditions in that subsection for a continuous period of three months.

(6)   The Treasury may from time to time after consultation with the *Bank* **Authority** by order amend subsection (2)(a) and (b) above so as to substitute for the sum for the time being specified in that subsection such other sum as may be specified in the order; but an order under this subsection shall be subject to annulment in pursuance of a resolution of either House of Parliament.

68.   Exemption from s. 67

(1)   Section 67 above does not prohibit the use of a name by a relevant savings bank, a municipal bank or a school bank if the name contains an indication that the bank or body is a savings bank, municipal bank or, as the case may be, a school bank.

(2)   In subsection (1) above—

'relevant savings bank' means—

     (i)   the national Savings Bank; and

     (ii)   any penny savings bank;

'school bank' means a body of persons certified as a school bank by the National Savings Bank or an authorised institution.

(3)   Section 67 above does not prohibit the use by an authorised institution which is a company incorporated under the law of a country or territory outside the United

Kingdom or is formed under the law of a member State other than the United Kingdom of a name under which it carries on business in that country or territory or State (or an approximate translation in English of that name).

(4)   Section 67 above does not prohibit the use by—

(a)   an authorised institution which is a wholly-owned subsidiary of an authorised institution to which that section or subsection (3) above applies; or

(b)   a company which has a wholly-owned subsidiary which is an authorised institution to which that section or subsection applies,

of a name which includes the names of the authorised institution to which that section or subsection applies for the purpose of indicating the connection between the two companies.

(5)   Section 67 above does not prohibit the use by an overseas institution (within the meaning of Part IV of this Act) which has its principal place of business in a country or territory outside the United Kingdom and a representative office in the United Kingdom of the name under which it carries on business in that country or territory (or an approximate translation in English of that name) if—

(a)   the name is used in immediate conjunction with the description 'representative office'; and

(b)   where the name appears in writing, that description is at least as prominent as the name;

and in this subsection 'representative office' has the same meaning as in Part IV of this Act.

(6)   Section 67 above does not apply to—

(a)   the Bank;

(b)   the central bank of a member State other than the United Kingdom;

(c)   the European Investment Bank;

(d)   the International Bank for Reconstruction and Development;

(e)   the African Development Bank;

(f)   the Asian Development Bank;

(g)   the Caribbean Development Bank;

(h)   the Inter-American Development Bank.

(7)   The Treasury may, after consultation with the *Bank* **Authority**, by order provide—

(a)   that the prohibition in section 67 above shall not apply to any person or class of persons; or

(b)   that that prohibition shall apply to a person mentioned in any of paragraphs (c) to (h) of subsection (6) above or a person previously exempted from it by virtue of an order under paragraph (a) above.

(8)   An order under paragraph (a) of subsection (7) above shall be subject to annulment in pursuance of a resolution of either House of Parliament; and no order shall be made under paragraph (b) of that subsection unless a draft of it has been laid before and approved by a resolution of each House of Parliament.

(9)   Nothing in section 67 above shall prevent an institution which ceases to be an authorised institution to which that section or subsection (4) above applies or

ceases to be exempted from the prohibition in that section by virtue of subsection (1) above from continuing to use any name it was previously permitted to use by virtue of that provision during the period of six months beginning with the day when it ceases to be such an institution.

69. Restriction on use of banking descriptions

(1)   No person carrying on any business in the United Kingdom shall so describe himself or hold himself out as to indicate or reasonably be understood to indicate (whether in English or in any other language) that he is a bank or banker or is carrying on a banking business unless he is an authorised institution or is exempted from the requirements of this subsection under the following provisions of this section.

(2)   Subsection (1) above shall not be taken to authorise the use by an authorised institution to which the prohibition in section 67 above applies of any description of itself as a bank or banker or as carrying on a banking business which is in such immediate conjunction with the name of the institution that the description might reasonably be thought to be part of it.

(3)   Subsection (1) above does not prohibit the use by a building society authorised under the Building Societies Act 1986 of any description of itself as providing banking services unless the description is in such immediate conjunction with its name that it might reasonably be thought to be part of it.

(4)   Subsection (1) above does not prohibit a person from using the expression 'bank' or 'banker' (or a similar expression) where it is necessary for him to do so in order to be able to assert that he is complying with, or entitled to take advantage of, any enactment, any instrument made under an enactment, any international agreement, any rule of law or any commercial usage or practice which applies to a person by virtue of his being a bank or banker.

(5)   Subsection (1) above does not prohibit the use of a description by a relevant savings bank, a municipal bank or a school bank if the description is accompanied by a statement that the bank or body is a savings bank, a municipal bank or, as the case may be, a school bank; and for the purposes of this subsection 'relevant savings bank' and 'school bank' have the same meanings as in section 68 above.

(6)   Subsection (1) above does not apply to—
   (a)   the Bank;
   (b)   the central bank of a member State other than the United Kingdom;
   (c)   the European Investment Bank;
   (d)   the International Bank for Reconstruction and Development;
   (e)   the International Finance Corporation;
   (f)   the African Development Bank;
   (g)   the Asian Development Bank;
   (h)   the Caribbean Development Bank;
   (i)   the Inter-American Development Bank.

(7)   The Treasury may, after consultation with the *Bank* **Authority**, by order provide—
   (a)   that the prohibition in subsection (1) above shall not apply to any person or class of persons; or

(b)   that that prohibition shall apply to a person mentioned in any of paragraphs (c) to (i) of subsection (6) above or a person previously exempted from it by an order under paragraph (a) above.

(8)   An order under paragraph (a) of subsection (7) above shall be subject to annulment in pursuance of a resolution of either House of Parliament; and no order shall be made under paragraph (b) of that subsection unless a draft of it has been laid before and approved by a resolution of each House of Parliament.

70.   Power to object to institution's names

(1)   Where an institution applies for authorisation under this Act it shall give notice to the *Bank* **Authority** of any name it is using or proposes to use for the purposes of or in connection with any business carried on by it and the *Bank* **Authority** may give the institution notice in writing—

(a)   that it objects to the notified name; or

(b)   in the case of an institution which is or will be obliged to disclose any name in connection with any business carried on by it by virtue of section 4 of the Business Names Act 1985 or Article 6 of the Business Names (Northern Ireland) Order 1986, that it objects to that name.

(2)   Where an authorised institution proposes to change any name it uses for the purposes of or in connection with any business carried on by it or, in the case of such an institution as is mentioned in subsection (1)(b) above, any such name as is there mentioned, it shall give notice to the *Bank* **Authority** of the proposed name and the *Bank* **Authority** may within the period of two months beginning with the day on which it receives the notification give notice to the institution in writing that it objects to the proposed name.

(3)   The *Bank* **Authority** shall not give notice objecting to a name under subsection (1) or (2) above unless it considers that the name is misleading to the public or otherwise undesirable and, in the case of the use of a name by an authorised institution to which section 67 above applies—

(a)   the whole of the name shall be taken into account in considering whether it is misleading or undesirable; but

(b)   no objection may be made to so much of the name as it is entitled to use by virtue of that section.

(4)   Where as a result of a material change in circumstances since the time when notice was given to the *Bank* **Authority** under subsection (1) or (2) above or as a result of further information becoming available to the *Bank* **Authority** since that time, it appears to the *Bank* **Authority** that a name to which it might have objected under that subsection gives so misleading an indication of the nature of the institution's activities as to be likely to cause harm to the public, the *Bank* **Authority** may give notice in writing to the institution objecting to the name.

(5)   Any notice to be given by an institution under this section shall be given in such manner and form as the *Bank* **Authority** may specify and shall be accompanied by such information or documents as the *Bank* **Authority** may reasonably require.

71. Effect of notices under s. 70 and appeals

(1)   Where the *Bank* **Authority** has given notice to an authorised institution under section 70 above the institution shall not use the name to which the *Bank* **Authority** has objected for the purposes of or in connection with any business carried on in the United Kingdom after the objection has taken effect; and for the purposes of this subsection the disclosure of a name in connection with such a business by virtue of section 4 of the Business Names Act 1985 or Article 6 of the Business Names (Northern Ireland) Order 1986 shall be treated (if it would not otherwise be) as use for the purposes of that business.

(2)   For the purposes of this section an objection under section 70(1) or (2) above takes effect when the institution receives the notice of objection.

(3)   An institution to which a notice of objection is given under section 70(1) or (2) above may within the period of three weeks beginning with the day on which it receives the notice apply to the court to set aside the objection and on such an application the court may set it aside or confirm it (but without prejudice to its operation before that time).

(4)   For the purposes of this section on objection under section 70(4) above takes effect—

(a)   in a case where no application is made under subsection (5) below, at the expiry of the period of two months beginning with the day on which the institution receives the notice of objection or such longer period as the notice may specify; or

(b)   where an application is made under subsection (5) below and the court confirms the objection, after such period as the court may specify.

(5)   An institution to which a notice of objection is given under section 70(4) above may within the period of three weeks beginning with the day on which it receives the notice apply to the court to set aside the objection.

(6)   In this section 'the court' means the High Court, the Court of Session or the High Court in Northern Ireland according to whether—

(a)   if the institution concerned is a company registered in the United Kingdom, it is registered in England and Wales, Scotland or Northern Ireland; and

(b)   in the case of any other institution, its principal or prospective principal place of business in the United Kingdom is situated in England and Wales, Scotland or Northern Ireland.

72. Registration of substitute corporate name by oversea company

(1)   Where the *Bank* **Authority** gives notice under section 70 above objecting to the corporate name of a company incorporated outside the United Kingdom, subsection (4) of section 694 of the Companies Act 1985 or, in Northern Ireland, paragraph (4) of Article 644 of the Companies (Northern Ireland) Order 1986 shall apply, subject to subsection (2) below, as it applies where a notice is served on a company under subsection (1) or (2) of that section or, as the case may be, paragraph (1) or (2) of that Article.

(2)   No statement or further statement may be delivered under subsection (4) of section 694 or paragraph (4) of Article 644 by virtue of subsection (1) above unless

the *Bank* **Authority** has signified that it does not object to the name specified in the statement.

(3)　Section 70(2) above shall not apply to a proposed change of a name which has been registered under section 694(4) of the Companies Act 1985 or Article 644(4) of the Companies (Northern Ireland) Order 1986 by virtue of subsection (1) above.

73.　Offences under Part III

A person who contravenes any provision in this Part of this Act shall be guilty of an offence and liable on summary conviction to imprisonment for a term not exceeding six months or to a fine not exceeding the fifth level on the standard scale or to both and, where the contravention involves a public display or exhibition of any name or description, there shall be a fresh contravention on each day on which the person causes or permits the display or exhibition to continue.

PART IV
OVERSEAS INSTITUTIONS WITH REPRESENTATIVE OFFICES

74.　Meaning of 'overseas institution' and 'representative office'

(1)　In this Part of this Act 'overseas institution' means a person (other than an authorised institution or any person for the time being specified in Schedule 2 to this Act) who—

　　(a)　is a body corporate incorporated in a country or territory outside the United Kingdom or a partnership or other unincorporated association formed under the law of such a country or territory; or

　　(b)　has his principal place of business in such a country or territory,

being, in either case, a person who satisfies one of the conditions mentioned in subsection (2) below.

(2)　The condition referred to in subsection (1) above are—

　　(a)　that the person's principal place of business is outside the United Kingdom and the person is authorised by the relevant supervisory authority in a country or territory outside the United Kingdom;

　　(b)　that the person describes himself or holds himself out as being authorised by such an authority in a country or territory outside the United Kingdom;

　　(c)　that the person uses any name or in any other way so describes himself or holds himself out as to indicate or reasonably be understood to indicate (whether in English or any other language), that he is a bank or banker or is carrying on a banking business (whether in the United Kingdom or elsewhere).

(3)　In this Part of this Act 'representative office', in relation to any overseas institution, means premises from which the deposit-taking, lending or other financial or banking activities of the overseas institution are promoted or assisted in any way; and 'establishment', in relation to such an office, includes the making of any arrangements by virtue of which such activities are promoted or assisted from it.

75.　Notice of establishment of representative office

(1)　An overseas institution shall not establish a representative office in the United Kingdom unless it has given not less than two months' notice to the *Bank* **Authority** that it proposes to establish such an office and a notice under this subsection shall specify—

(a) any name the institution proposes to use in relation to activities conducted by it in the United Kingdom after the establishment of that office; and

(b) in the case of an institution which will be obliged to disclose any name in connection with those activities by virtue of section 4 of the Business Names Act 1985 or Article 6 of the Business Names (Northern Ireland) Order 1986, that name.

(2) Where an overseas institution has established a representative office in the United Kingdom before the date on which this Part of this Act comes into force and has not given notice of that fact to the *Bank* **Authority** under section 40 of the Banking Act 1979 it shall give notice in writing to the *Bank* **Authority** of the continued existenceof that office within the period of two months beginning with that date; and the obligation of an overseas institution to give notice under this subsection in respect of the establishment of an office established within the period of one month ending with that date shall supersede any obligation to give notice in respect of that matter under that section.

(3) A notice under this section shall be given in such manner and form as the *Bank* **Authority** may specify.

76. Power to object to names of overseas institutions

(1) An overseas institution which has established a representative office in the United Kingdom shall not change any name used by it in relation to activities conducted by it in the United Kingdom or, in the case of an institution which is obliged to disclose any name in connection with those activities as mentioned in section 75(1) above, that name unless it has given not less than two months' notice to the *Bank* **Authority** of the proposed name.

(2) Where notice of a name is given to the *Bank* **Authority** by an overseas institution under section 75(1) or subsection (1) above and it appears to the *Bank* **Authority** that the name is misleading to the public or otherwise undesirable it may, within the period of two months beginning with the day on which that notice was given, give notice in writing to the institution that it objects to that name.

(3) Where it appears to the *Bank* **Authority** that an overseas institution which has established a representative office in the United Kingdom before the date on which this Part of this Act comes into force is using a name in relation to activities conducted by it in the United Kingdom which is misleading to the public or otherwise undesirable, the *Bank* **Authority** may give notice in writing to the institution that it objects to the name—

(a) in a case where the *Bank* **Authority** was notified of the establishment of the representative office before that date, within the period of six months beginning with that date; and

(b) otherwise, within the period of six months beginning with the date on which the establishment of the representative office comes to the *Bank's* **Authority's** knowledge.

(4) Where, as a result of a material change in circumstances since the time when notice of a name was given to the *Bank* **Authority** under section 75(1) or subsection

(1) above or as a result of further information becoming available to the *Bank* **Authority** since that time, it appears to the *Bank* **Authority** that the name is so misleading as to be likely to cause harm to the public, the *Bank* **Authority** may give notice in writing to the overseas institution in question that it objects to the name.

77.   Effect of notices under s. 76 and appeals

(1)   Where the *Bank* **Authority** has given notice under section 76 above to an overseas institution the institution shall not use the name to which the *Bank* **Authority** has objected in relation to activities conducted by it in the United Kingdom after the objection has taken effect; and for the purposes of this subsection the disclosure of a name in connection with those activities as mentioned in section 75(1)(b) above shall be treated (if it would not otherwise be) as use of that name in relation to those activities.

(2)   For the purposes of this section an objection under section 76(2) above takes effect when the institution receives the notice of objection.

(3)   An institution to which a notice of objection is given under section 76(2) above may within the period of three weeks beginning with the day on which it receives the notice apply to the court to set aside the objection and on such an application the court may set it aside or confirm it (but without prejudice to its operation before that time).

(4)   For the purposes of this section an objection under section 76(3) or (4) above takes effect—

(a)   in a case where no application is made under subsection (5) below, at the expiry of the period of two months beginning with the day on which the institution receives the notice of objection or such longer period as the notice may specify; or

(b)   where an application is made under subsection (5) below and the court confirms the objection, after such period as the court may specify.

(5)   An institution to which a notice of objection is given under section 76(3) or (4) above may within the period of three weeks beginning with the day on which it receives the notice apply to the court to set aside the objection.

(6)   In this section 'the court' means the High Court, the Court of Session or the High Court in Northern Ireland according to whether the representative office of the institution in question is situated in England and Wales, Scotland or Northern Ireland.

78.   Registration of substitute corporate name by overseas institution

(1)   Where the *Bank* **Authority** gives notice under section 76 above objecting to the corporate name of an overseas institution, subsection (4) of section 694 of the Companies Act 1985, or, in Northern Ireland, paragraph (4) of Article 644 of the Companies (Northern Ireland) Order 1986 shall apply, subject to subsection (2) below, as it applies where a notice is served on a company under subsection (1) or (2) of that section or, as the case may be, paragraph (1) or (2) of that Article.

(2)   No statement or further statement may be delivered under subsection (4) of section 694 or paragraph (4) of Article 644 by virtue of subsection (1) above unless the *Bank* **Authority** has signified that it does not object to the name specified in the statement.

(3)   Section 76(1) above shall not apply to a change of a name which has been registered under section 694(4) of the Companies Act 1985 or Article 644(4) of the Companies (Northern Ireland) Order 1986 by virtue of subsection (1) above.

79.   Duty to provide information and documents

(1)   The *Bank* **Authority** may by notice in writing require any overseas institution which has established a representative office in the United Kingdom or has given notice to the *Bank* **Authority** under section 75(1) above of its intention to establish such an office to provide the Bank with such information or documents as the *Bank* **Authority** may reasonably require.

(2)   Without prejudice to the generality of subsection (1) above, the *Bank* **Authority** may by notice in writing require such an overseas institution to deliver to the *Bank* **Authority**—

(a)   in the case of an overseas institution which is a company incorporated in the United Kingdom, copies of the documents which the company is required to send to the registrar of companies under section 10 of the Companies Act 1985 or Article 21 of the Companies (Northern Ireland) Order 1986;

(aa)   in the case of an overseas institution to which section 690A of that Act applies, copies of the documents which it is required to deliver for registration in accordance with paragraph 1(1) or (2) of Schedule 2A of that Act;

(b)   in the case of an overseas institution to which section 691(1) of that Act or Article 641(1) of that Order applies, copies of the document which it is required to deliver for registration in accordance with that section or Article;

(c)   in the case of any other overseas institution (other than an individual), information corresponding to that which would be contained in the documents which it would be required to deliver as mentioned in paragraph (b) above if it were a company to which section 691(1) applied;

(d)   in the case of an overseas institution which is authorised to take deposits or conduct banking business in a country or territory outside the United Kingdom by the relevant supervisory authority in that country or territory, a certified copy of any certificate from that authority conferring such authorisation on it.

(3)   An overseas institution to which a notice is given under subsection (1) or (2) above shall comply with the notice—

(a)   in the case of an institution which has established a representative office in the United Kingdom, before the end of such period as is specified in the notice; and

(b)   in the case of an institution which has given notice under section 75(1) above of its intention to establish such an office, before it establishes the office.

(4)   If at any time an overseas institution which has been required to deliver information or documents to the *Bank* **Authority** under subsection (2) above is required to deliver any document or give notice to the registrar of companies under section 18 or 288(2) of the said Act of 1985 or Article 29 or 296(2) of the said Order of 1986, it shall no later than the time by which it must have complied with that requirement deliver a copy of that document or give notice to the *Bank* **Authority**.

(5)   If at any time an overseas institution is required to furnish any document or give notice to the registrar of companies under section 692, 695A(3) or 696 of, or paragraph 7 or 8 of Schedule 21A to the said Act of 1985 or Article 642 or 646 of the said Order of 1986 (or would be so required if it were a company to which that section, paragraph or Article applied), it shall no later than the time by which it must have complied with that requirement deliver a copy of that document to the *Bank* **Authority**.

(6)   If at any time a certificate of authorisation of which a copy was required to be delivered to the *Bank* **Authority** under subsection (2)(d) above is amended or the authorisation is withdrawn, the overseas institution shall no later than one month after the amendment or withdrawal deliver a copy of the amended certificate or, as the case may be, a notice stating that the authorisation has been withdrawn to the *Bank* **Authority**.

(7)   The Treasury may after consultation with the *Bank* **Authority** by order provide that sections 39 and 40 above shall apply in relation to overseas institutions as they apply in relation to authorised institutions; but no order shall be made under this section unless a draft of it has been laid before and approved by a resolution of each House of Parliament.

80.   Regulations imposing requirements on overseas-based banks

(1)   The Treasury may, after consultation with the *Bank* **Authority**, by regulations impose on overseas institutions which have established or propose to establish representative offices in the United Kingdom such requirements as the Treasury consider appropriate in connection with those offices and the activities conducted from them.

(2)   Regulations under this section may in particular require the establishment or continued existence of a representative office to be authorised by the *Bank* **Authority** and such regulations may make provision for—

(a)   the granting and revocation of such authorisations;

(b)   the imposition of conditions in connection with the grant or retention of such authorisations; and

(c)   appeals against the refusal or withdrawal of such authorisations or the imposition of such conditions.

(3)   No regulations shall be made under this section unless a draft of the regulations has been laid before and approved by a resolution of each House of Parliament.

81.   Offences under Part IV

A person who contravenes any provision in this Part of this Act or any requirement imposed under it shall be guilty of an offence and liable on summary conviction to imprisonment for a term not exceeding six months or to a fine not exceeding the fifth level on the standard scale or to both and, where the contravention involves a public display or exhibition of any name or description, there shall be a fresh contravention on each day on which the person causes or permits the display or exhibition to continue.

PART V
RESTRICTION ON DISCLOSURE OF INFORMATION

82. Restricted information

(1)   Except as provided by the subsequent provisions of this Part of this Act—

(a)   no person who under or for the purposes of this Act receives information relating to the business or other affairs of any person; and

(b)   no person who obtains any such information directly or indirectly from a person who has received it as aforesaid, shall disclose the information without the consent of the person to whom it relates and (if different) the person from whom it was received as aforesaid.

(2)   This section does not apply to information which at the time of the disclosure is or has already been made available to the public from other sources or to information in the form of a summary or collection of information so framed as not to enable information relating to any particular person to be ascertained from it.

(3)   Any person who discloses information in contravention of this section shall be guilty of an offence and liable—

(a)   on conviction on indictment, to imprisonment for a term not exceeding two years or to a fine or to both;

(b)   on summary conviction, to imprisonment for a term not exceeding three months or to a fine not exceeding the statutory maximum or to both.

83. Disclosure for facilitating discharge of functions by the Bank

(1)   Section 82 above does not preclude the disclosure of information in any case in which disclosure is for the purpose of enabling or assisting the *Bank* **Authority** to discharge—

(a)   its functions under this Act;

(aa)   **its functions in its capacity as a designated agency within the meaning of the Financial Services Act 1986; or**

(b)   *its functions as a monetary authority;*

(c)   its functions as a supervisory of money market *and gilt market* institutions. *or*

(d)   *its functions as a supervisor of systems for the transfer of funds between credit institutions and their customers.*

(2)   Without prejudice to the generality of subsection (1) above, that section does not preclude the disclosure of information by the *Bank* **Authority** to the auditor of an authorised institution or former authorised institution if it appears to the *Bank* **Authority** that disclosing the information would enable or assist the *Bank* **Authority** to discharge the functions mentioned in that subsection or would otherwise be in the interests of depositors.

(3)   If, in order to enable or assist the *Bank* **Authority** properly to discharge any of its functions under this Act, the *Bank* **Authority** considers it necessary to seek advice from any qualified person on any matter of law, accountancy, valuation or other matter requiring the exercise of professional skill, section 82 above does not preclude the disclosure by the *Bank* **Authority** to that person of such information as

appears to the *Bank* **Authority** to be necessary to ensure that he is properly informed with respect to the matters on which his advice is sought.

84. Disclosure for facilitating discharge of functions by other supervisory authorities

(1)   Section 82 above does not preclude the disclosure by the *Bank* **Authority** of information to any person specified in the first column of the following Table if the *Bank* **Authority** considers that the disclosure would enable or assist that person to discharge the functions specified in relation to him in the second column of that Table.

TABLE

Person	*Functions*
1 The Secretary of State.	Functions under the Insurance Companies Act 1982, Part XIV of the Companies Act 1985, Part XIII of the Insolvency Act 1986, the Financial Services Act 1986 or Part II, III or VII of the Companies Act 1989.
2 The Secretary of State	Functions under the Insurance Companies Act 1982, under the Financial Services Act 1986 or under Part III or VII of the Companies Act
3 An inspector appointed under Part XIV of the Companies Act 1985 or section 94 or 177 of the Financial Services Act 1986.	Functions under that Part or that section.
4 A person authorised to exercise powers under section 43A or 44 of the Insurance Companies Act 1982, section 447 of the Companies Act 1985, section 106 of the Financial Services Act 1986 or section 84 of the Companies Act 1989.	Functions under that section.
4A The Bank of England	**Functions in its capacity as a monetary authority or supervisor of systems for the transfer of funds between credit institutions and their customers.**
5 The Chief Registrar of friendly societies and the Assistant Registrar of Friendly Societies for Scotland.	Functions under the enactments relating to friendly societies.
5A The Friendly Societies Commission.	Functions under the enactments relating to friendly societies or under the Financial Services Act 1986.
6 The Industrial Assurance Commissioner and the Industrial Assurance Commissioner for Northern Ireland.	Functions under the enactments relating to industrial assurance.

7	The Building Societies Commission.	Functions under the Building Societies Act 1986 and protecting the interests of the shareholders and depositors of building societies.
8	The Director General of Fair Trading.	Functions under the Consumer Credit Act 1974.
9	A designated agency (within the meaning of the Financial Services Act 1986).	Functions under the Financial Services Act 1986 or Part VII of the Companies Act 1989.
10	A transferee body or the competent authority (within the meaning of the Financial Services Act 1986).	Functions under the Financial Services Act 1986.
11	A recognised self-regulating organisation, recognised professional body, recognised investment exchange or recognised self-regulating organisation for friendly societies (within the meaning of the Financial Services Act 1986).	Functions in its capacity as an organisation, body or exchange recognised under the Financial Services Act 1986.
11A	A recognised clearing house (within the meaning of the Financial Services Act 1986).	Functions in its capacity as a clearing house under the Financial Services Act 1986 so far as they are exercisable in relation to defaults or potential defaults by market participants.
11B	A person approved under the Uncertificated Securities Regulations 1995 as an operator of a relevant system (within the meaning of those Regulations).	Functions as a person so approved so far as they are exercisable in relation to defaults or potential defaults by market participants.
11C	A recognised supervisory body (within the meaning of Part II of the Companies Act 1989).	Functions in its capacity as such a body under that Part or functions in relation to disciplinary proceedings against auditors.
12	A recognised professional body (within the meaning of section 391 of the Insolvency Act 1986).	Functions in its capacity as such a body under the Insolvency Act 1986 or functions in relation to disciplinary proceedings against insolvency practitioners (within the meaning of that Act).
13	The Department of Economic Development in Northern Ireland.	Functions under Part XV of the Companies (Northern Ireland) Order 1986 or Part XII of the

Insolvency (Northern Ireland)
Order 1989 or Part III of the
Companies (Northern Ireland)
Order 1990 or Part II or V of the
Companies (No. 2) (Northern
Ireland) Order 1990.

14	An inspector appointed under Part XV of the Companies (Northern Ireland) Order 1986.	Functions under that Part.
15	A person authorised to exercise powers under Article 440 of the Companies (Northern Ireland) Order 1986.	Functions under that Article.
16	The Official Receiver or, in Northern Ireland, the Official Receiver for Northern Ireland.	Investigating the cause of the failure of an authorised institution or former authorised institution in respect of which a winding-up order or bankruptcy order has been made.
17	The Panel on Take-overs and Mergers.	All its functions.
18	A person included in the list maintained by the *Bank* **Authority** for the purposes of section 171 of the Companies Act 1989.	Functions under settlement arrangements to which regulations under that section relate.
19	A recognised professional body (within the meaning of Article 350 of the Insolvency (Northern Ireland) Order 1989).	Functions in its capacity as such a body under the Insolvency (Northern Ireland) Order 1989 or functions in relation to disciplinary proceedings against insolvency practitioners (within the meaning of that Order).
20	A recognised supervisory body (within the meaning of Part III of the Companies (Northern Ireland) Order 1990).	Functions in its capacity as such a body under that Part, or functions in relation to disciplinary proceedings against auditors.

(2)   The Treasury may after consultation with the *Bank* **Authority** by order amend the Table in subsection (1) above by—

(a)   adding any person exercising regulatory functions and specifying functions in relation to that person;

(b)   removing any person for the time being specified in the Table; or

(c)   altering the functions for the time being specified in the Table in relation to any person;

and the Treasury may also after consultation with the *Bank* **Authority** by order restrict the circumstances in which, or impose conditions subject to which, disclosure is permitted in the case of any person for the time being specified in the Table.

(3)   An order under subsection (2) above shall be subject to annulment in pursuance of a resolution of either House of Parliament.

(4)   Section 82 above does not preclude the disclosure by any person specified in the first column of the Table in subsection (1) above of information obtained by him by virtue of that subsection if he makes the disclosure with the consent of the *Bank* **Authority** and for the purpose of enabling or assisting him to discharge any functions specified in relation to him in the second column of that Table; and before deciding whether to give its consent to such a disclosure by any person the *Bank* **Authority** shall take account of such representations made by him as to the desirability of or the necessity for the disclosure.

(5)   Section 82 above does not preclude the disclosure by the *Bank* **Authority** of information to the Treasury if disclosure appears to the *Bank* **Authority** to be—

   (a)   desirable or expedient in the interests of depositors; or

   (b)   in the public interest,

and (in either case) in accordance with article 12(7) of the First Council Directive.

(5A)   Section 82 above does not preclude the disclosure by the *Bank* **Authority** of information to the Secretary of State for purposes other than those specified in relation to him in subsection (1) above if the disclosure is made with the consent of the Treasury and—

   (a)   the information relates to an authorised institution or former authorised institution and does not enable the financial affairs of any other identifiable person to be ascertained and disclosure appears to the *Bank* **Authority** to be necessary in the interests of depositors or in the public interest; or

   (b)   in any case, disclosure appears to the *Bank* **Authority** to be necessary in the interests of depositors;

and (in either case) disclosure appears to the *Bank* **Authority** to be in accordance with article 12(7) of the First Council Directive.

(6)   Section 82 above does not preclude the disclosure of information for the purpose of enabling or assisting an authority in a country or territory outside the United Kingdom to exercise—

   (a)   functions corresponding to those of—

      (i)   the *Bank* **Authority** under this Act or the Banking Coordination (Second Council Directive) Regulations 1992;

      (ii)   the Secretary of State or the Treasury under the Insurance Companies Act 1982, Part XIII of the Insolvency Act 1986 or the Financial Services Act 1986; or

      (iii)   the competent authority under Part IV of the Financial Services Act 1986;

   (b)   functions in connection with rules of law corresponding to any of the provisions of Part V of the Criminal Justice Act 1993 (insider dealing) or Part VII of the Finncial Services Act 1986;

   (c)   supervisory functions in respect of bodies carrying on business corresponding to that of building societies.

(d)   in the case of a supervisory authority in another EEA State, its functions as a supervisor of systems for the transfer of funds between credit institutions and their customers.

(7)   Subsection (6) above does not apply in relation to disclosures to an authority which is not a supervisory authority in another member State unless the *Bank* **Authority** is satisfied that the authority is subject to restrictions on further disclosures at least equivalent to those imposed by this Part of this Act.

(8)   Information which is disclosed to a person in pursuance of subsection (1), (4) or (6) above shall not be used otherwise than for the purpose mentioned in that subsection.

(9)   Any person who uses information in contravention of subsection (8) above shall be liable on summary conviction to imprisonment for a term not exceeding three months or to a fine not exceeding the fifth level on the standard scale or to both.

(10)   Subject to subsection (11) below, any reference in this section to enabling or assisting any person to discharge or exercise any functions is a reference to enabling or assisting that person to discharge or exercise those functions in relation to—

(a)   a financial market; or

(b)   persons carrying on the business of banking or insurance, Consumer Credit Act businesses or the business of providing other financial services;
and in this subsection 'Consumer Credit Act business' has the same meaning as in the Banking Coordination (Second Council Directive) Regulations 1992.

(11)   Subsection (10) above shall not apply in relation to references to enabling or assisting the discharge or exercise of the following functions, namely—

(a)   functions of the Secretary of State under Part XIV of the Companies Act 1985, Part XIII of the Insolvency Act 1986 or Part II of the Companies Act 1989 or, so far as relating to the breach of any law relating to companies, under section 83 of the Companies Act 1989;

(b)   functions of an inspector under Part XIV of the Companies Act 1985 or, so far as relating to offences involving securities of a company, under section 177 of the Financial Services Act 1986;

(c)   functions of a person authorised to exercise powers under section 84 of the Companies Act 1989, so far as relating to the breach of any law relating to companies;

(d)   functions of a recognised clearing house (within the meaning of the Financial Services Act 1986);

(e)   functions of a person approved under the Uncertificated Securities Regulations 1995 as an operator of a relevant system (within the meaning of those Regulations);

(f)   functions of a recognised supervisory body (within the meaning of Part II of the Companies Act 1989);

(g)   functions of a recognised professional body (within the meaning of section 391 of the Insolvency Act 1986);

(h)   functions of the Department of Economic Development in Northern Ireland under Part XV of the Companies (Northern Ireland) Order 1986, Part XII of the Insolvency (Northern Ireland) Order 1989 or Part III of the Companies (Northern Ireland) Order 1990;

(i)   functions of an inspector under Part XV of the Companies (Northern Ireland) Order 1986;

(j)   functions of a recognised professional body (within the meaning of Article 350 of the Insolvency (Northern Ireland) Order 1989);

(k)   functions of a recognised supervisory body (within the meaning of Part III of the Companies (Northern Ireland) Order 1990);

(l)   functions of a supervisory authority in another EEA State in its capacity as a supervisor of systems for the transfer of funds between credit institutions and their customers.

(12)   In this section 'another EEA State' means a State other than the United Kingdom which is a contracting party to the agreement on the European Economic Area signed at Oporto on 2 May 1992 as adjusted by the Protocol signed at Brussels on 17 March 1993.

85.   Other permitted disclosures

(1)   Section 82 above does not preclude the disclosure of information—

(a)   for the purpose of enabling or assisting the Board of Banking Supervision or the Deposit Protection Board or any other person to discharge its or his functions under this Act;

(b)   for the purpose of enabling or assisting a person to do anything which he is required to do in pursuance of a requirement imposed under section 39(1)(b) above;

(c)   with a view to the institution of, or otherwise for the purposes of, any criminal proceedings, whether under this Act or otherwise;

(d)   in connection with any other proceedings arising out of this Act;

(e)   with a view to the institution of, or otherwise for the purposes of, proceedings under section 7 or 8 of the Company Directors Disqualification Act 1986 or Article 10 or 11 of the Companies (Northern Ireland) Order 1989 in respect of a director or former director of an authorised institution or former authorised institution;

(f)   in connection with any proceedings in respect of an authorised institution or former authorised institution under the Bankruptcy (Scotland) Act 1985 or Parts I to VII or IX to XI of the Insolvency Act 1986 or Parts II to VII or IX and X of the Insolvency (Northern Ireland) Order 1989 which the *Bank* **Authority** has instituted or in which it has a right to be heard;

(g)   in pursuance of a Community obligation.

(1A)   The disclosures permitted by subsection (1)(f) above do not include the disclosure of information relating to a person who (not being a director, controller or manager of the institution) is or has been, to the knowledge of the person making the disclosure, involved in an attempt to secure the survival of the institution as a going concern.

(2)   Section 82 above does not preclude the disclosure by the *Bank* **Authority** to the Director of Public Prosecutions, the Director of Public Prosecutions for Northern

Ireland, the Lord Advocate, a procurator fiscal or a constable of information obtained by virtue of section 41, 42 or 43 above or of information in the possession of the *Bank* **Authority** as to any suspected contravention in relation to which the powers conferred by those sections are exercisable.

(3)   Section 82 above does not preclude the disclosure of information by the Deposit Protection Board to any person or body responsible for a scheme for protecting depositors or investors (whether in the United Kingdom or elsewhere) similar to that for which provision is made by Part II of this Act if it appears to the Board that disclosing the information would enable or assist the recipient of the information or the Board to discharge his or its functions.

86.   Information supplied to Bank by relevant overseas authority etc.

(1)   Section 82 above applies also to information which—

(a)   has been supplied to the *Bank* **Authority** for the purposes of any relevant functions by the relevant supervisory authority in a country or territory outside the United Kingdom; or

(b)   has been obtained for those purposes by the *Bank* **Authority**, or by a person acting on its behalf, in another member State.

(2)   Subject to subsections (3) and (4) below, information supplied or obtained as mentioned in subsection (1)(a) or (b) above shall not be disclosed except as provided by section 82 above or—

(a)   for the purpose of enabling or assisting the *Bank* **Authority** to discharge any relevant function **or any functions in its capacity as a designated agency within the meaning of the Financial Services Act 1986**; or

(b)   with a view to the institution of, or otherwise for the purposes of, criminal proceedings, whether under this Act or otherwise.

(3)   Information supplied to the Bank for the purposes of any relevant functions by the relevant supervisory authority in another member State may be disclosed—

(a)   to a relevant recipient, if the authority consents to its disclosure and the case is one in which information to which section 82 above applies could be so disclosed by virtue of section 84(1) or (2) above; or

(b)   to the Treasury or the Secretary of State, if the authority consents to its disclosure and the case is one in which information to which section 82 above applies could be so disclosed by virtue of section 84(5) or (5A) above.

(4)   Information obtained as mentioned in subsection (1)(b) above may be disclosed—

(a)   to a relevant recipient, if the relevant supervisory authority in the member State concerned consents to its disclosure and the case is one in which information to which section 82 above applies could be so disclosed by virtue of section 84(1) or (2) above; or

(b)   to the Treasury or the Secretary of State, if that authority consents to its disclosure and the case is one in which information to which section 82 above applies could be so disclosed by virtue of section 84(5) or (5A) above.

(4A)   Before the *Bank* **Authority** discloses information to any person under subsection (3) above, it shall notify the relevant supervisory authority which supplied the information of the name and responsibilities of that person.

(5)   In this section—

'relevant functions', in relation to the Bank, means its functions under this Act, its functions as a monetary authority and its functions as a supervisor of money market and gilt market institutions;

'relevant functions', in relation to the authority, means its functions under this Act and its functions as a supervisor of money market institutions;

'relevant recipient' means a person specified in any of entries 1 to 8, 13 to 15 and 17 in the Table in section 84(1) above.

87.   Disclosure of information obtained under other Acts

(1)   After section 174(3) or the Consumer Credit Act 1974 there shall be inserted—

'(3A)   Subsections (1) and (2) do not apply to any disclosure of information by the Director to the Bank of England for the purpose of enabling or assisting the Bank or discharge its functions under the Banking Act 1987 or the Director to discharge his functions under this Act.'

[The Consumer Credit Act 1974, s. 174(3A), is amended by the Banking Act 1998, s. 23(1) and sch. 5, para. 60.]

(2)   Information disclosed to the *Bank* **Authority** under subsection (1) of section 449 of the Companies Act 1985 for the purpose of enabling or assisting it to discharge its functions under this Act or in its capacity as a competent authority under *subsection (3)* **subsection (3)(ha)** of that section may be disclosed—

(a)   with the consent of the Secretary of State, in any case in which information to which section 82 applies could be disclosed by virtue of section 84(1) or (2) above; and

(b)   in any case in which information to which section 82 above applies could be disclosed by virtue of any of the other provisions of this part of this Act.

(3)   Information disclosed in the *Bank* **Authority** under paragraph (1) of Article 442 of the Companies (Northern Ireland) Order 1986 for the purpose of enabling or assisting it to discharge its functions under this Act or in its capacity as a competent authority under paragraph (3) of that Article may be disclosed—

(a)   with the consent of the Department of Economic Development in Northern Ireland, in any case in which information to which section 82 above applies could be disclosed by virtue of section 84(1) or (2) above; and

(b)   in any case in which information to which section 82 above applies could be disclosed by virtue of any of the other provisions of this Part of this Act.

(3A)   Information disclosed by the Building Societies Commission to the *Bank* **Authority** for the purpose of enabling or assisting it to discharge any relevant functions may be disclosed—

(a)   to a relevant recipient, if the Commission consents to its disclosure and the case is one in which information to which section 82 above applies could be so disclosed by virtue of section 84(1) or (2) above; or

(b)   to the Treasury or the Secretary of State, if the Commission consents to its disclosure and the case is one in which information to which section 82 above applies could be so disclosed by virtue of section 84(5)(a) or (5A) above;
and in this subsection 'relevant functions' has the same meaning as in section 86 above and 'relevant recipient' means a person specified in any of entries 1 to 8, 13 to 15 and 17 in the Table in section 84(1) above.

(4)   Any information which has been lawfully disclosed to the *Bank* **Authority** may be disclosed by it to the Board of Banking Supervision so far as necessary for enabling or assisting the Board to discharge its functions under this Act.

[PARALLEL VERSION OF PART V

When the Bank of England Act 1998 is brought into force (1 June 1998) ss. 86 and 87(2), (3) and (3A) of the Banking Act 1987 will have effect both in the form set out above and in the form set out below, and, in their application in the form set out below, those provisions will have effect as if the rest of part V were worded as set out below. This parallel version of part V is set out as amended by the Bank of England Act 1998, s. 36(2) and (3) and sch. 5, paras 57 and 59.]

PART V
RESTRICTION ON DISCLOSURE OF INFORMATION

82.   Restricted information
   (1)   Except as provided by the subsequent provisions of this Part of this Act—
   (a)   no person who under or for the purposes of this Act receives information relating to the business or other affairs of any person; and
   (b)   no person who obtains any such information directly or indirectly from a person who has received it as aforesaid,
shall disclose the information without the consent of the person to whom it relates and (if different) the person from whom it was received as aforesaid.
   (2)   This section does not apply to information which at the time of the disclosure is or has already been made available to the public from other sources or to information in the form of a summary or collection of information so framed as not to enable information relating to any particular person to be ascertained from it.
   (3)   Any person who discloses information in contravention of this section shall be guilty of an offence and liable—
   (a)   on conviction on indictment, to imprisonment for a term not exceeding two years or to a fine or to both;
   (b)   on summary conviction, to imprisonment for a term not exceeding three months or to a fine not exceeding the statutory maximum or to both.

83.   Disclosure for facilitating discharge of functions by the Bank
   (1)   Section 82 above does not preclude the disclosure of information in any case in which disclosure is for the purpose of enabling or assisting the Bank to discharge—

(a)   its functions under this Act;

(b)   its functions as a monetary authority;

(c)   its functions as a supervisor of money market and gilt market institutions; or

(d)   its functions as a supervisor of systems for the transfer of funds between credit institutions and their customers.

(2)   Without prejudice to the generality of subsection (1) above, that section does not preclude the disclosure of information by the Bank to the auditor of an authorised institution or former authorised institution if it appears to the Bank that disclosing the information would enable or assist the Bank to discharge the functions mentioned in that subsection or would otherwise be in the interests of depositors.

(3)   If, in order to enable or assist the Bank properly to discharge any of its functions under this Act, the Bank considers it necessary to seek advice from any qualified person on any matter of law, accountancy, valuation or other matter requiring the exercise of professional skill, section 82 above does not preclude the disclosure by the Bank to that person of such information as appears to the Bank to be necessary to ensure that he is properly informed with respect to the matters on which his advice is sought.

84.   Disclosure for facilitating discharge of functions by other supervisory authorities

(1)   section 82 above does not preclude the disclosure by the Bank of information to any person specified in the first column of the following Table if the Bank considers that the disclosure would enable or assist that person to discharge the functions specified in relation to him in the second column of that Table.

TABLE

Person	Functions
1 The Secretary of State.	Functions under the Insurance Companies Act 1982, Part XIV of the Companies Act 1985, Part XIII of the Insolvency Act 1986, the Financial Services Act 1986 or Part II, III or VII of the Companies Act 1989.
1A The Authority.	Functions under the Financial Services Act 1986 (other than as a designated agency within the meaning of that Act), the Banking Act 1987 or section 171 of the Companies Act 1989.
2 The Secretary of State	Functions under the Insurance Companies Act 1982, under the Financial Services Act 1986 or under Part III or VII of the Companies Act 1989
3 An inspector appointed under Part XIV of the Companies Act 1985 or section 94 or 177 of the Financial Services Act 1986.	Functions under that Part or that section.
4 A person authorised to exercise powers under section 43A or 44 of the Insurance Companies Act 1982, section 447 of the Companies Act 1985, section 106 of the Financial Services Act 1986 or section 84 of the Companies Act 1989.	Functions under that section.
5 The Chief Registrar of friendly societies and the Assistant Registrar of Friendly Societies for Scotland.	Functions under the enactments relating to friendly societies.
5A The Friendly Societies Commission.	Functions under the enactments relating to friendly societies or under the Financial Services Act 1986.
6 The Industrial Assurance Commissioner and the Industrial Assurance Commissioner for Northern Ireland.	Functions under the enactments relating to industrial assurance.

7	The Building Societies Commission.	Functions under the Building Societies Act 1986 and protecting the interests of the shareholders and depositors of building societies.
8	The Director General of Fair Trading.	Functions under the consumer Credit Act 1974.
9	A designated agency (within the meaning of the Financial Services Act 1986).	Functions under the Financial Services Act 1986 or Part VII of the Companies Act 1989.
10	A transferee body or the competent authority (within the meaning of the Financial Services Act 1986).	Functions under the Financial Services Act 1986.
11	A recognised self-regulating organisation, recognised professional body, recognised investment exchange or recognised self-regulating organisation for friendly societies (within the meaning of the Financial Services Act 1986).	Functions in its capacity as an organisation, body or exchange recognised under the Financial Services Act 1986.
11A	A recognised clearing house (within the meaning of the Financial Services Act 1986).	Functions in its capacity as a clearing house under the Financial Services Act 1986 so far as they are exercisable in relation to defaults or potential defaults by market participants.
11B	A person approved under the Uncertificated Securities Regulations 1995 as an operator of a relevant system (within the meaning of those Regulations).	Functions as a person so approved so far as they are exercisable in relation to defaults or potential defaults by market participants.
11C	A recognised supervisory body (within the meaning of Part II of the Companies Act 1989).	Functions in its capacity as such a body under that Part or functions in relation to disciplinary proceedings against auditors.
12	A recognised professional body (within the meaning of section 391 of the Insolvency Act 1986).	Functions in its capacity as such a body under the Insolvency Act 1986 or functions in relation to disciplinary proceedings against insolvency practitioners (within the meaning of that Act).

13	The Department of Economic Development in Northern Ireland.	Functions under Part XV of the Companies (Northern Ireland) Order 1986 or Part XII of the Insolvency (Northern Ireland) Order 1989 or Part III of the Companies (Northern Ireland) Order 1990 or Part II or V of the Companies (No. 2) (Northern Ireland) Order 1990.
14	An inspector appointed under Part XV of the Companies (Northern Ireland) Order 1986.	Functions under that Part.
15	A person authorised to exercise powers under Article 440 of the Companies (Northern Ireland) Order 1986.	Functions under that Article.
16	The Official Receiver or, in Northern Ireland, the Official Receiver for Northern Ireland.	Investigating the cause of the failure of an authorised institution or former authorised institution in respect of which a winding-up order or bankruptcy order has been made.
17	The Panel on Take-overs and Mergers.	All its functions.
18	A person included in the list maintained by the Bank for the purposes of section 171 of the Companies Act Act 1989.	Functions under settlement arrangements to which regulations under that section relate.

[By mistake the Bank of England Act 1998 does not change 'Bank' to 'Authority' in item 18 in this parallel version, because paras 57(2) and 59(4) of sch. 5 to the 1998 Act provide that sch. 5, para. 54(4), which makes that change in the main version, is not to apply to the parallel version.]

19	A recognised professional body (within the meaning of Article 350 of the Insolvency (Northern Ireland) Order 1989).	Functions in its capacity as such a body under the Insolvency (Northern Ireland) Order 1989 or functions in relation to disciplinary proceedings against insolvency practitioners (within the meaning of that Order).
20	A recognised supervisory body (within the meaning of Part III of the Companies (Northern Ireland) Order 1990).	Functions in its capacity as such a body under that Part, or functions in relation to disciplinary proceedings against auditors.

(2)   The Treasury may after consultation with the Bank by order amend the Table in subsection (1) above by—

(a)   adding any person exercising regulatory functions and specifying functions in relation to that person;

(b)   removing any person for the time being specified in the Table; or

(c)   altering the functions for the time being specified in the Table in relation to any person;

and the Treasury may also after consultation with the Bank by order restrict the circumstances in which, or impose conditions subject to which, disclosure is permitted in the case of any person for the time being specified in the Table.

(3)   An order under subsection (2) above shall be subject to annulment in pursuance of a resolution of either House of Parliament.

(4)   Section 82 above does not preclude the disclosure by any person specified in the first column of the Table in subsection (1) above of information obtained by him by virtue of that subsection if he makes the disclosure with the consent of the Bank and for the purpose of enabling or assisting him to discharge any functions specified in relation to him in the second column of that Table; and before deciding whether to give its consent to such a disclosure by any person the Bank shall take account of such representations made by him as to the desirability of or the necessity for the disclosure.

[The first version of s. 84(5) printed below applies for the purposes of s. 86 as printed below. The second version of s. 84(5) printed below applies for the purposes of s. 87(2), (3) and (3A) as printed below.]

(5)   Section 82 above does not preclude the disclosure by the Bank of information to the Treasury if disclosure appears to the Bank to be in the public interest and in accordance with article 12(7) of the First Council Directive.

(5)   Section 82 above does not preclude the disclosure by the Bank of information to the Treasury if disclosure appears to the Bank to be—

(a)   desirable or expedient in the interests of depositors; or

(b)   in the public interest,

and (in either case) in accordance with article 12(7) of the First Council Directive.

(5A)   Section 82 above does not preclude the disclosure by the Bank of information to the Secretary of State for purposes other than those specified in relation to him in subsection (1) above if—

(a)   the disclosure is made with the consent of the Treasury,

(b)   the information relates to an authorised institution or former authorised institution and does not enable the financial affairs of any other identifiable person to be ascertained, and

(c)   disclosure appears to the Bank to be—

(i)   in the pubic interest, and

(ii)   in accordance with article 12(7) of the First Council Directive.

(6)   Section 82 above does not preclude the disclosure of information for the purpose of enabling or assisting an authority in a country or territory outside the United Kingdom to exercise—

(a)   functions corresponding to those of—

(i)   the Bank under this Act or the Banking Coordination (Second Council Directive) Regulations 1992;

(ii)   the Secretary of State or the Treasury under the Insurance Companies Act 1982, Part XIII of the Insolvency Act 1986 or the Financial Services Act 1986; or

(iii)   the competent authority under Part IV of the Financial Services Act 1986;

(b)   functions in connection with rules of law corresponding to any of the provisions of Part V of the Criminal Justice Act 1993 (insider dealing) or Part VII of the Financial Services Act 1986;

(c)   supervisory functions in respect of bodies carrying on business corresponding to that of building societies.

(d)   in the case of a supervisory authority in another EEA State, its functions as a supervisor of systems for the transfer of funds between credit institutions and their customers.

(7)   Subsection (6) above does not apply in relation to disclosures to an authority which is not a supervisory authority in another member State unless the Bank is satisfied that the authority is subject to restrictions on further disclosures at least equivalent to those imposed by this Part of this Act.

(8)   Information which is disclosed to a person in pursuance of subsection (1), (4) or (6) above shall not be used otherwise than for the purpose mentioned in that subsection.

(9)   Any person who uses information in contravention of subsection (8) above shall be liable on summary conviction to imprisonment for a term not exceeding three months or to a fine not exceeding the fifth level on the standard scale or to both.

(10)   Subject to subsection (11) below, any reference in this section to enabling or assisting any person to discharge or exercise any functions is a reference to enabling or assisting that person to discharge or exercise those functions in relation to—

(a)   a financial market; or

(b)   persons carrying on the business of banking or insurance, Consumer Credit Act businesses or the business of providing other financial services;
and in this subsection 'Consumer Credit Act business' has the same meaning as in the Banking Coordination (Second Council Directive) Regulations 1992.

(11)   Subsection (10) above shall not apply in relation to references to enabling or assisting the discharge or exercise of the following functions, namely—

(a)   functions of the Secretary of State under Part XIV of the Companies Act 1985, Part XIII of the Insolvency Act 1986 or Part II of the Companies Act 1989 or, so far as relating to the breach of any law relating to companies, under section 83 of the Companies Act 1989;

(b)   functions of an inspector under Part XIV of the Companies Act 1985 or, so far as relating to offences involving securities of a company, under section 177 of the Financial Services Act 1986;

(c)   functions of a person authorised to exercise powers under section 84 of the Companies Act 1989, so far as relating to the breach of any law relating to companies;

(d)   functions of a recognised clearing house (within the meaning of the Financial Services Act 1986);

(e)   functions of a person approved under the Uncertificated Securities Regulations 1995 as an operator of a relevant system (within the meaning of those Regulations);

(f)   functions of a recognised supervisory body (within the meaning of Part II of the Companies Act 1989);

(g)   functions of a recognised professional body (within the meaning of section 391 of the Insolvency Act 1986);

(h)   functions of the Department of Economic Development in Northern Ireland under Part XV of the Companies (Northern Ireland) Order 1986, Part XII of the Insolvency (Northern Ireland) Order 1989 or Part III of the Companies (Northern Ireland) Order 1990;

(i)   functions of an inspector under Part XV of the Companies (Northern Ireland) Order 1986;

(j)   functions of a recognised professional body (within the meaning of Article 350 of the Insolvency (Northern Ireland) Order 1989);

(k)   functions of a recognised supervisory body (within the meaning of Part III of the Companies (Northern Ireland) Order 1990);

(l)   functions of a supervisory authority in another EEA State in its capacity as a supervisor of systems for the transfer of funds between credit institutions and their customers.

(12)   In this section 'another EEA State' means a State other than the United Kingdom which is a contracting party to the agreement on the European Economic Area signed at Oporto on 2 May 1992 as adjusted by the Protocol signed at Brussels on 17 March 1993.

85.   Other permitted disclosures

(1)   Section 82 above does not preclude the disclosure of information—

(a)   for the purpose of enabling or assisting the Board of Banking Supervision or the Deposit Protection Board or any other person to discharge its or his functions under this Act;

(b)   for the purpose of enabling or assisting a person to do anything which he is required to do in pursuance of a requirement imposed under section 39(1)(b) above;

(c)   with a view to the institution of, or otherwise for the purposes of, any criminal proceedings, whether under this Act or otherwise;

(d)   in connection with any other proceedings arising out of this Act;

(e)   with a view to the institution of, or otherwise for the purposes of, proceedings under section 7 or 8 of the Company Directors Disqualification Act 1986 or Article 10 or 11 of the Companies (Northern Ireland) Order 1989 in respect of a director or former director of an authorised institution or former authorised institution;

(f)   in connection with any proceedings in respect of an authorised institution or former authorised institution under the Bankruptcy (Scotland) Act 1985 or Parts I to VII or IX to XI of the Insolvency Act 1986 or Parts II to VII or IX and X of the Insolvency (Northern Ireland) Order 1989 which the Bank has instituted or in which it has a right to be heard;

(g)   in pursuance of a Community obligation.

(1A)   The disclosures permitted by subsection (1)(f) above do not include the disclosure of information relating to a person who (not being a director, controller or manager of the institution) is or has been, to the knowledge of the person making the disclosure, involved in an attempt to secure the survival of the institution as a going concern.

(2)   Section 82 above does not preclude the disclosure by the Bank to the Director of Public Prosecutions, the Director of Public Prosecutions for Northern Ireland, the Lord Advocate, a procurator fiscal or a constable of information obtained by virtue of section 41, 42 or 43 above or of information in the possession of the Bank as to any suspected contravention in relation to which the powers conferred by those sections are exercisable.

(3)   Section 82 above does not preclude the disclosure of information by the Deposit Protection Board to any person or body responsible for a scheme for protecting depositors or investors (whether in the United Kingdom or elsewhere) similar to that for which provision is made by Part II of this Act if it appears to the Board that disclosing the information would enable or assist the recipient of the information or the Board to discharge his or its functions.

86.   Information supplied to Bank by relevant overseas authority etc.

(1)   Section 82 above applies also to information which—

(a)   has been supplied to the Bank for the purposes of any relevant functions by the relevant supervisory authority in a country or territory outside the United Kingdom; or

(b)   has been obtained for those purposes by the Bank, or by a person acting on its behalf, in another member State.

(2)   Subject to subsections (3) and (4) below, information supplied or obtained as mentioned in subsection (1)(a) or (b) above shall not be disclosed except as provided by section 82 above or—

(a)   for the purpose of enabling or assisting the Bank to discharge any relevant functions; or

(b)   with a view to the institution of, or otherwise for the purposes of, criminal proceedings, whether under this Act or otherwise.

(3)   Information supplied to the Bank for the purposes of any relevant functions by the relevant supervisory authority in another member State may be disclosed—

(a)   to a relevant recipient, if the authority consents to its disclosure and the case is one in which information to which section 82 above applies could be so disclosed by virtue of section 84(1) or (2) above; or

(b)   to the Treasury or the Secretary of State, if the authority consents to its disclosure and the case is one in which information to which section 82 above applies could be so disclosed by virtue of section 84(5) or (5A) above.

(4)   Information obtained as mentioned in subsection (1)(b) above may be disclosed—

(a)   to a relevant recipient, if the relevant supervisory authority in the member State concerned consents to its disclosure and the case is one in which information to which section 82 above applies could be so disclosed by virtue of section 84(1) or (2) above; or

(b)   to the Treasury or the Secretary of State, if that authority consents to its disclosure and the case is one in which information to which section 82 above applies could be so disclosed by virtue of section 84(5) or (5A) above.

(4A)   Before the Bank discloses information to any person under subsection (3) above, it shall notify the relevant supervisory authority which supplied the information of the name and responsibilities of that person.

(5)   In this section—

'relevant functions', in relation to the Bank, means its functions as a monetary authority and its functions as a supervisor of systems for the transfer of funds between credit institutions and their customers;

'relevant recipient' means a person specified in any of entries 1 to 9, 13 to 15 and 17 in the Table in section 84(1) above.

87.   Disclosure of information obtained under other Acts

(2)   Information disclosed to the Bank under subsection (1) of section 449 of the Companies Act 1985 in its capacity as a competent authority under subsection (3) of that section may be disclosed—

(a)   with the consent of the Secretary of State, in any case in which information to which section 82 applies could be disclosed by virtue of section 84(1) or (2) above; and

(b)   in any case in which information to which section 82 above applies could be disclosed by virtue of any of the other provisions of this part of this Act.

(3)   Information disclosed in the Bank under paragraph (1) of Article 442 of the Companies (Northern Ireland) Order 1986 in its capacity as a competent authority under paragraph (3) of that Article may be disclosed—

(a)   with the consent of the Department of Economic Development in Northern Ireland, in any case in which information to which section 82 above applies could be disclosed by virtue of section 84(1) or (2) above; and

(b)   in any case in which information to which section 82 above applies could be disclosed by virtue of any of the other provisions of this Part of this Act.

(3A)   Information disclosed by the Building Societies Commission to the Bank for the purpose of enabling or assisting it to discharge any relevant functions may be disclosed—

(a)   to a relevant recipient, if the Commission consents to its disclosure and the case is one in which information to which section 82 above applies could be so disclosed by virtue of section 84(1) or (2) above; or

(b)   to the Treasury or the Secretary of Sate, if the Commission consents to its disclosure and the case is one in which information to which section 82 above applies could be so disclosed by virtue of section 84(5A) above;

and in this subsection 'relevant functions' in relation to the Bank, means its functions as a monetary authority and its functions as a supervisor of systems for the transfer of funds between credit institutions and their customers; and 'relevant recipient' means a person specified in any of entries 1 to 9, 13 to 15 and 17 in the Table in section 84(1) above.

PART VI
MISCELLANEOUS AND SUPPLEMENTARY

88.   Exclusion of authorised institution's agreements from Consumer Credit Act 1974

(1)   The Consumer Credit Act 1974 shall be amended as follows.

(2)   In section 16(1) (consumer credit agreements with certain bodies exempt from regulation) after paragraph (g) there shall be inserted ', or

(h)   an authorised institution or wholly-owned subsidiary (within the meaning of the Companies Act 1985) or such an institution.'.

(3)   In section 16(3) (Secretary of State's duty to consult before making orders) after paragraph (e) there shall be inserted 'or

(f)   under subsection (1)(h) without consulting the Treasury and the Bank of England.'.

(4)   In section 189(1) (definitions) after the definition of 'association' there shall be inserted—

'authorised institution' means an institution authorised under the Banking Act 1987;'.

89.   Electronic transfer of funds

After section 187(3) of the Consumer Credit Act 1974 (arrangements to be disregarded in determining whether a consumer credit agreement is to be treated as entered into in accordance with prior or in contemplation of future arrangements between creditor and supplier) there shall be inserted—

'(3A)   Arrangements shall also be disregarded for the purposes of subsection (1) and (2) if they are arrangements for the electronic transfer of funds from a current account at a bank within the meaning of the Bankers' Books Evidence Act 1879.'

90.   Disclosure of transactions by authorised institutions with chief executives and managers

(1)   For section 233(3) of the Companies Act 1985 there shall be substituted—

'(3)   Subsections (1) and (2) do not apply in relation to any transaction, arrangement or agreement made by an authorised institution for any officer of the institution or for any officer of its holding company unless the officer is a chief executive or manager within the meaning of the Banking Act 1987; and references to officer in Part II of Schedule 6 shall be construed accordingly.'

(2)   For Article 241(3) of the Companies (Northern Ireland) Order 1986 there shall be substituted—

'(3)   Paragraphs (1) and (2) do not apply in relation to any transaction, arrangement or agreement made by an authorised institution for any officer of the institution or for any officer of its holding company unless that officer is a chief executive or manager within the meaning of the Banking Act 1987; and references to officers in Part II of Schedule 6 shall be construed accordingly.'

[Section 90(1) would be repealed if the relevant provision of the Companies Act 1989, s. 212 and sch. 24, were brought into force. The repeal should have been brought into force by the Companies Act 1989 (Commencement No. 4 and Transitional and Saving Provisions) Order 1990 (SI 1990/355), but has been overlooked.]

91.   Powers for securing reciprocal facilities for banking and other financial business

For the avoidance of doubt it is hereby declared that a notice under section 183 of the Financial Services Act 1986 (disqualification or restriction of persons connected with overseas countries which do not afford reciprocal facilities for financial business) may be served on any person connected with the country in question who is carrying on or appears to the Secretary of State or the Treasury to intend to carry on in, or in relation to, the United Kingdom business of any of the descriptions specified in subsection (1) of that section whether or not it is of the same description as that affected by the less favourable terms which are the occasion for the service of the notice.

92.   Winding up on petition from the Bank

(1)   On a petition presented by the *Bank* **Authority** by virtue of this section the court having jurisdiction under the Insolvency Act 1986 may wind up an authorised institution or former authorised institution if—

(a)   the institution is unable to pay its debts within the meaning of section 123 or, as the case may be, section 221 of that Act; or

(b)   the court is of the opinion that it is just and equitable that the institution should be wound up;

and for the purposes of such a petition an institution which defaults in an obligation to pay any sum due and payable in respect of a deposit shall be deemed to be unable to pay its debts as mentioned in paragraph (a) above.

(2)   Where a petition is presented under subsection (1) above for the winding up of a partnership on the ground mentioned in paragraph (b) of that subsection or, in

Scotland, on the ground mentioned in paragraph (a) or (b) of that subsection, the court shall have jurisdiction and the Insolvency Act 1986 shall have effect as if the partnership were an unregistered company within the meaning of section 220 of that Act.

(3) On a petition presented by the *Bank* **Authority** by virtue of this section the High Court in Northern Ireland may wind up an authorised institution if—

(a) the institution is unable to pay its debts within the meaning of Article 103 or, as the case may be, Article 185 of the Insolvency (Northern Ireland) Order 1989; or

(b) the court is of the opinion that it is just and equitble that the institution should be wound up;

and for the purposes of such a petition an institution which defaults in an obligation to pay any sum due and payable in respect of a deposit shall be deemed to be unable to pay its debts as mentioned in paragraph (a) above.

(4) Where a petition is presented under subsection (3) above for the winding up of a partnership on the ground mentioned in paragraph (b) of that subsection, the court shall have jurisdiction and the said Order of 1989 shall have effect as if the partnership were an unregistered company within the meaning of Article 184 of that Order.

(5) For the purposes of this section the definition of deposit in section 5 above shall be treated as including any sum that would otherwise be excluded by subsection (3)(a), (b) or (c) of that section.

(6) This section applies to a company or partnership which has contravened section 3 above as it applies to an authorised institution.

93. Injunctions

(1) If on the application of the *Bank* **Authority**, the Director of Public Prosecutions, the Lord Advocate or the Director of Public Prosecutions for Northern Ireland the court is satisfied—

(a) that there is a reasonable likelihood that a person will contravene section 3, 18, 35, 67, 69, 71 or 77 above, a direction under section 19 above or regulations under section 32, 24 or 80 above; or

(b) that any person has been guilty of any such contravention and that there is a reasonable likelihood that the contravention will continue or be repeated,

the court may grant an injunction restraining, or in Scotland an interdict prohibiting, the contravention.

(2) If on the application of the *Bank* **Authority**, the Director of Public Prosecutions, the Lord Advocate or the Director of Public Prosecutions for Northern Ireland it appears to the court that a person may have been guilty of such a contravention as is mentioned in subsection (1) above the court may grant an injunction restraining, or in Scotland an interdict prohibiting, him from disposing of or otherwise dealing with any of his assets while the suspected contravention is investigated.

(3) The jurisdiction conferred by this section shall be exercisable by the High Court and the Court of Session.

94.   False and misleading information

(1)   Any person who knowingly or recklessly provides the *Bank* **Authority** or any other person with information which is false or misleading in a material particular shall be guilty of an offence if the information is provided—

(a)   in purported compliance with a requirement imposed by or under this Act; or

(b)   otherwise than as mentioned in paragraph (a) above but in circumstances in which the person providing the information intends, or could reasonably be expected to know, that the information would be used by the *Bank* **Authority** for the purpose of exercising its functions under this Act.

(2)   Any person who knowingly or recklessly provides the *Bank* **Authority** or any other person with information which is false or misleading in a material particular shall be guilty of an offence if the information is provided in connection with an application for authorisation under this Act.

(3)   An authorised institution or former authorised institution shall be guilty of an offence if it fails to provide the *Bank* **Authority** with any information in its possession knowing or having reasonable cause to believe—

(a)   that the information is relevant to the exercise by the *Bank* **Authority** of its functions under this Act in relation to the institution; and

(b)   that the withholding of the information is likely to result in the *Bank* **Authority** being misled as to any matter which is relevant to and of material significance for the exercise of those functions in relation to the institution.

(4)   Any person who knowingly or recklessly provides any person appointed under section 41 above with information which is false or misleading in a material particular shall be guilty of an offence.

(5)   Any person guilty of an offence under this section shall be liable—

(a)   on conviction on indictment, to imprisonment for a term not exceeding two years or to a fine or to both;

(b)   on summary conviction, to imprisonment for a term not exceeding six months or to a fine not exceeding the statutory maximum or to both.

95.   Restriction of Rehabilitation of Offenders Act 1974

(1)   The Rehabilitation of Offenders Act 1974 shall have effect subject to the provisions of this section in cases where the spent conviction is for—

(a)   an offence involving fraud or other dishonesty; or

(b)   an offence under legislation (whether or not of the United Kingdom) relating to companies (including insider dealing), building societies, industrial and provident societies, credit unions, friendly societies, insurance, banking or other financial services, insolvency, consumer credit or consumer protection.

(2)   Nothing in section 4(1) (restriction on evidence as to spent convictions in proceedings) shall prevent the determination in any proceeding arising out of any such decision of the *Bank* **Authority** as is mentioned in section 27(1) or (3) above (including proceedings on appeal to any court) of any issue, or prevent the admission or requirement in any such proceedings of any evidence, relating to a person's

previous convictions for any such offence as is mentioned in subsection (1) above or the circumstances ancillary thereto.

(3) A conviction for such an offence as is mentioned in subsection (1) above shall not be regarded as spent for the purposes of section 4(2) (questions relating to an individual's previous convictions) if—

(a) the question is put by or on behalf of the *Bank* **Authority** and the individual is a person who is or is seeking to become a director, controller or manager of an authorised institution, a former authorised institution or an institution which has made an application for authorisation which has not been disposed of; or

(b) the question is put by or on behalf of any such institution and the individual is or is seeking to become a director, controller or manager of that institution, and the person questioned is informed that by virtue of this section convictions for any such offence are to be disclosed.

(4) Section 4(3)(b) (spent conviction not to be ground for excluding person from office, occupation etc.) shall not—

(a) prevent the *Bank* **Authority** from refusing to grant or revoking an authorisation on the ground that an individual is not a fit and proper person to be a director, controller or manager of the institution in question or from imposing a restriction or giving a direction requiring the removal of an individual as director, controller or manager of an institution; or

(b) prevent an authorised institution, a former authorised institution or an institution which has made an application for authorisation which has not yet been disposed of from dismissing or excluding an individual from being a director, controller or manager of the institution, by reason, or partly by reason, of a spent conviction of that individual for such an offence as is mentioned in subsection (1) above or any circumstances ancillary to such a conviction or of a failure (whether or not by that individual) to disclose such a conviction or any such circumstances.

(5) For the purposes of subsections (3) and (4) above an application by an institution is not disposed of until the decision of the *Bank* **Authority** on the application is communicated to the institution.

(6) This section shall apply to Northern Ireland with the substitution for the references to the said Act of 1974 and section 4(1), (2) and (3)(b) of that Act of references to the Rehabilitation of Offenders (Northern Ireland) Order 1978 and Article 5(1), (2) and (3)(b) of that Order.

[Section 95 will be repealed when the relevant provision of the Police Act 1997, s. 134(2) and sch. 10, is brought into force.]

96. Offences

(1) Where an offence under this Act committed by a body corporate is proved to have been committed with the consent or connivance of, or to be attributable to any neglect on the part of any director, manager, secretary or other similar officer of the body corporate, or any person who was purporting to act in any such capacity, he, as

well as the body corporate, shall be guilty of that offence and be liable to be proceeded against and punished accordingly.

(2)   Where the affairs of a body corporate are managed by its members, subsection (1) above shall apply in relation to the acts and defaults of a member in connection with his functions of management as if he were a director of the body corporate.

(3)   In the case of a person who by virtue of subsection (1) or (2) above or section 98(6) or (7) below is guilty of an offence under section 12(6) or 19(6) above the penalty that can be imposed on conviction on indictment shall be imprisonment for a term not exceeding two years or a fine or both.

(4)   In any proceedings for an offence under this Act it shall be a defence for the person charged to prove that he took all reasonable precautions and exercised all due diligence to avoid the commission of such an offence by himself or any person under his control.

(5)   No proceedings for an offence under this Act shall be instituted—

(a)   in England and Wales, except by or with the consent of the Director of Public Prosecutions or the *Bank* **Authority**; or

(b)   in Northern Ireland, except by or with the consent of the Director of Public Prosecutions for Northern Ireland or the *Bank* **Authority**.

(6)   In relation to proceedings against a building society incorporated (or deemed to be incorporated) under the Building Societies Act 1986 subsection (5) above shall have effect with the substitution for references to the *Bank* **Authority** of references to the Building Societies Commission.

(7)   In relation to proceedings against a friendly society within the meaning of section 7(1)(a) of the Friendly Societies Act 1974 the reference in paragraph (a) of subsection (5) above to the *Bank* **Authority** shall include a reference to the Chief Registrar of friendly societies.

97.   Summary proceedings

(1)   Summary proceedings for any offence under this Act may, without prejudice to any jurisdiction exercisable apart from this subsection, be taken against an institution, including an unincorporated institution, at any place at which it has a place of business, and against an individual at any place at which he is for the time being.

(2)   Notwithstanding anything in section 127(1) of the Magistrates' Courts Act 1980, any information relating to an offence under this Act which is triable by a magistrates' court in England and Wales may be so tried if it is laid at any time within three years after the commission of the offence and within six months after the relevant date.

(3)   Notwithstanding anything in section 136 of the Criminal Procedure (Scotland) Act 1995, summary proceedings for such an offence may be commenced in Scotland at any time within three years after the commission of the offence and within six months after the relevant date; and subsection (3) of that section shall apply for the purposes of this subsection as it applies for the purposes of that section.

(4)   Notwithstanding anything in Article 19(1) of the Magistrates' Courts (Northern Ireland) Order 1981, a complaint relating to such an offence which is

triable by a court of summary jurisdiction in Northern Ireland may be so tried if it is made at any time within three years after the commission of the offence and within six months after the relevant date.

(5)   In this section—

'the relevant date' means the date on which evidence sufficient in the opinion of the prosecuting authority to justify proceedings comes to its knowledge; and

'the prosecuting authority' means the authority by or with whose consent the proceedings are instituted in accordance with section 96 above or, in Scotland, the Lord Advocate.

(6)   For the purposes of subsection (5) above, a certificate of any prosecuting authority as to the date on which such evidence as is there mentioned came to its knowledge shall be conclusive evidence of that fact.

98.   Offences committed by unincorporated associations

(1)   Proceedings for an offence alleged to have been committed under this Act by an unincorporated association shall be brought in the name of that association (and not in that of any of its members) and, for the purposes of any such proceedings, any rules of court relating to the service of documents shall have effect as if the association were a corporation.

(2)   A fine imposed on an unincorporated association on its conviction of an offence under this Act shall be paid out of the funds of the association.

(3)   Section 33 of the Criminal Justice Act 1925 and Schedule 3 to the Magistrates' Courts Act 1980 (procedure on charge of offence against a corporation) shall have effect in a case in which an unincorporated association is charged in England or Wales with an offence under this Act in like manner as they have effect in the case of a corporation so charged.

(4)   In relation to any proceedings on indictment in Scotland for an offence alleged to have been committed under this Act by an unincorporated association, section 70 of the Criminal Procedure (Scotland) Act 1995 (proceedings on indictment against bodies corporate) shall have effect as if the association were a body corporate.

(5)   Section 18 of the Criminal Justice Act (Northern Ireland) 1945 and Schedule 4 to the Magistrates' Courts (Northern Ireland) Order 1981 (procedure on charge of offence against a corporation) shall have effect in a case in which an unincorporated association is charged in Northern Ireland with an offence under this Act in like manner as they have effect in the case of a corporation so charged.

(6)   Where a partnership is guilty of an offence under this Act, every partner, other than a partner who is proved to have been ignorant of, or to have attempted to prevent the commission of the offence, shall also be guilty of that offence and be liable to be proceeded against and punished accordingly.

(7)   Where any other unincorporated association is guilty of an offence under this Act, every officer of the association who is bound to fulfil any duty whereof the offence is a breach, or if there is no such officer then every member of the committee or other similar governing body, other than a member who is proved to have been ignorant of, or to have attempted to prevent the commission of

the offence, shall also be guilty of that offence and be liable to be proceeded against and punished accordingly.

99. Service of notices on the Bank

(1)   No notice required by this Act to be given to or served on the *Bank* **Authority** shall be regarded as given or served until it is received.

(2)   Subject to subsection (1) above, any such notice may be given or served by telex or other similar means which produce a document containing the text of the communication.

100. Service of other notices

(1)   This section has effect in relation to any notice, direction or other document required or authorised by or under this Act to be given to or served on any person other than the *Bank* **Authority**.

(2)   Any such document may be given to or served on the person in question—

(a)   by delivering it to him; or

(b)   by leaving it at his proper address; or

(c)   by sending it by post to him at that address; or

(d)   by sending it to him at that address by telex or other similar means which produce a document containing the text of the communication.

(3)   Any such document may—

(a)   in the case of a body corporate, by given to or served on the secretary or clerk of that body; and

(b)   in the case of any other description of institution, be given to or served on a controller of the institution.

(4)   For the purposes of this section and section 7 of the Interpretation Act 1978 (service of documents by post) in its application to this section, the proper address of any person to or on whom a document is to be given or served shall be his last known address, except that—

(a)   in the case of a body corporate or its secretary or clerk, it shall be the address of the registered or principal office of that body in the United Kingdom; and

(b)   in the case of any other description of institution or a person having control or management of its business, it shall be that of the principal office of the institution in the United Kingdom.

(5)   If the person to or on whom any document mentioned in subsection (1) above is to be given or served has notified the *Bank* **Authority** of an address within the United Kingdom, other than his proper address within the meaning of subsection (4) above, as the one at which he or someone on his behalf will accept documents of the same description as that document, that address shall also be treated for the purposes of this section and section 7 of the Interpretation Act 1978 as his proper address.

101. Evidence

(1)   In any proceedings, a certificate purporting to be signed on behalf of the *Bank* **Authority** and certifying—

(a)   that a particular person is or is not an authorised institution or was or was not such an institution at a particular time;

(b) the date on which a particular institution became or ceased to be authorised;

(c) whether or not a particular institution's authorisation is or was restricted;

(d) the date on which a restricted authorisation expires; or

(e) the date on which a particular institution became or ceased to be a recognised bank or licensed institution under the Banking Act 1979,

shall be admissible in evidence and, in Scotland, shall be sufficient evidence of the facts stated in the certificate.

(2) A certificate purporting to be signed as mentioned in subsection (1) above shall be deemed to have been duly signed unless the contrary is shown.

102. Orders and regulations

Any power of the Treasury to make orders or regulations under this Act shall be exercisable by statutory instrument.

103. Municipal banks

(1) References in this Act to a municipal bank are to a company within the meaning of the Companies Act 1985 which—

(a) carries on a deposit-taking business,

(b) is connected with a local authority as mentioned in subsection (2) below, and

(c) has its deposits guaranteed by that local authority in accordance with subsection (5) below.

(2) The connection referred to in paragraph (b) of subsection (1) above between a company and a local authority is that—

(a) the company's articles of association provide that the shares in the company are to be held only by members of the local authority; and

(b) substantially all the funds lent by the company are lent to the local authority.

(3) Where on 9 November 1978 a company or its predecesor—

(a) was carrying on a deposit-taking business, and

(b) was connected with a local authority as mentioned in subsection (2) above, that local authority or its successor may for the purposes of this Act resolve to guarantee deposits with the company.

(4) A resolution passed by a local authority under subsection (3) above may not be rescinded.

(5) Where a local authority has passed a resolution under subsection (3) above or under section 48(3) of the Banking Act 1979, that local authority and any local authority which is its successor shall be liable, if the company concerned defaults in payment, to make a good to a depositor the principal and interest owing in respect of any deposit with the company, whether made before or after the passing of the resolution.

(6) For the purposes of this section—

(a) one company is the predecessor of another if that other succeeds to its obligations in respect of its deposit-taking business; and

(b)   one local authority is the successor of another if, as a result of, or in connection with, an order under Part IV of the Local Government Act 1972, Part II of the Local Government Act 1992 or Part II of the Local Government and Rating Act 1997 or under Part II of the Local Government (Scotland) Act 1973 (change of local government area), it becomes connected as mentioned in subsection (2) above with a company formerly so connected with that other local authority.

104.   Scottish 1819 savings banks

(1)   This section applies to any saving bank established before 28 July 1863 under an Act passed in the 59th year of King George III entitled an Act for the Protection of Banks for Savings in Scotland.

(2)   For the purposes of Part II of this Act a savings bank to which this section applies becomes insolvent on the making of a winding-up order against it under Part V of the Insolvency Act 1986 or on the making of an award of sequestration on the estate of the bank.

(3)   A savings bank to which this section applies shall be regarded as a relevant savings bank for the purposes of sections 68 and 69 above.

105.   Meaning of 'director', 'controller', 'manager', and 'associate'

(1)   In the provisions of this Act other than section 96 'director', 'controller', 'manager' and 'associate' shall be construed in accordance with the provisions of this section.

(2)   'Director', in relation to an institution, includes—

(a)   any person who occupies the position of a director, by whatever name called; and

(b)   in the case of an institution established in a country or territory outside the United Kingdom, any person, including a member of a managing board, who occupies a position appearing to the *Bank* **Authority** to be analogous to that of a director of a company registered under the Companies Act 1985;

and in the case of a partnership 'director', where it is used in subsections (6) and (7) below, includes a partner.

(3)   'Controller', in relation to an institution, means—

(a)   a managing director of the institution or of another institution of which it is a subsidiary or, in the case of an institution which is a partnership, a partner;

(b)   a chief executive of the institution or of another institution of which it is a subsidiary;

(c)   a person who satisfies the requirements of this paragraph;

(d)   a person in accordance with whose directions or instructions the directors of the institution or of another institution of which it is a subsidiary or persons who are controllers of the institution by virtue of paragraph (c) above (or any of them) are accustomed to act; and

(e)   a person who is, or would be if he were an undertaking, a parent undertaking of the institution.

(3A)   A person satisfies the requirements of subsection (3)(c) above in relation to an institution if, either alone or with any associate or associates—

(a) he holds 10 per cent or more of the shares in the institution or another institution of which it is a subsidiary undertaking;

(b) he is entitled to exercise, or control the exercise of, 10 per cent or more of the voting power at any general meeting of the institution or another institution of which it is such an undertaking; or

(c) he is able to exercise a significant influence over the management of the institution or another institution of which it is such an undertaking by virtue of—

(i) a holding of shares in; or

(ii) an entitlement to exercise, or control the exercise of, the voting power at any general meeting of,

the institution or, as the case may be, the other institution concerned;

and in this subsection 'share' has the same meaning as in Part VII of the Companies Act 1985 or Part VIII of the Companies (Northern Ireland) Order 1986.

(4) A person who is a controller of an institution by virtue of subsection (3)(c) above is in this Act referred to as a 'shareholder controller' of the institution; and in this Act—

(a) a 'minority shareholder controller' means a shareholder controller not falling within paragraph (a) or (b) of subsection (3A) above;

(b) a '10 per cent shareholder controller' means a shareholder controller in whose case the percentage referred to in the relevant paragraph is 10 or more but less than 20;

(c) a '20 per cent shareholder controller' means a shareholder controller in whose case that percentage is 20 or more but less than 33;

(d) a '33 per cent shareholder controller' means a shareholder controller in whose case that percentage is 33 or more but less than 50;

(e) a '50 per cent shareholder controller' means a shareholder controller in whose case that percentage is 50 or more;

(f) a 'majority shareholder controller' means a shareholder controller in whose case that percentage is 50 or more but less than 75; and

(g) a 'principal shareholder controller' means a shareholder in whose case that percentage is 75 or more;

and in this subsection 'the relevant paragraph', in relation to a shareholder controller, means whichever one of paragraphs (a) and (b) of subsection (3A) above gives the greater percentge in his case.

(5) A person who is a controller of an institution by virtue of subsection (3)(d) above is in this Act referred to as 'an indirect controller' of the institution.

(5A) A person who is a controller of an institution by virtue of subsection (3)(e) above is in this Act referred to as a 'parent controller' of the institution.

(6) 'Manager', in relation to an institution, means a person (other than a chief executive) who, under the immediate authority of a director or chief executive of the institution—

(a) exercises managerial functions; or

(b) is responsible for maintaining accounts or other records of the institution.

(7) In this section 'chief executive', in relation to an institution, means a person who, either alone or jointly with one or more other persons, is responsible under the

immediate authority of the directors for the conduct of the business of the institution.

(8)   Without prejudice to subsection (7) above, in relation to an institution whose principal place of busines is in a country or territory outside the United Kingdom, 'chief executive' also includes a person who, either alone or jointly with one or more other persons, is responsible for the conduct of its business in the United Kingdom.

(9)   In this Act 'associate', in relation to a person entitled to exercise or control the exercise of voting power in relation to, or holding shares in, an undertaking, means—

(a)   the wife or husband or son or daughter of that person;

(b)   the trustees of any settlement under which that person has a life interest in possession or, in Scotland, a life interest;

(c)   any company of which that person is a director;

(d)   any person who is an employee or partner of that person;

(e)   if that person is a company—

    (i)   any director of that company;

    (ii)   any subsdidiary undertaking of that company; and

    (iii)   any director or employee of any such subsidiary undertaking; and

(f)   if that person has with any other person an agreement or arrangement with respect to the acquisition, holding or disposal of shares or other interests in that undertaking or body corporate or under which they undertake to act together in exercising their voting power in relation to it, that other person.

(10)   For the purposes of subsection (9) above—

'son' includes stepson and 'daughter' includes stepdaughter;

'settlement' includes any disposition or arrangement under which property is held in trust.

105A.   Meaning of 'related company'

(1)   In this Act a 'related company', in relation to an institution or the parent undertaking of an institution, means a body corporate (other than a subsidiary undertaking) in which the institution or parent undertaking holds a qualifying capital interest.

(2)   A qualifying capital interest means an interest in relevant shares of the body corporate which the institution or parent undertaking holds on a long-term basis for the purpose of securing a contribution to its own activities by the exercise of control or influence arising from that interest.

(3)   Relevant shares means shares comprised in the equity share capital of the body corporate of a class carrying rights to vote in all circumstances at general meetings of the body.

(4)   A holding of 20 per cent or more of the nominal value of the relevant shares of a body corporate shall be presumed to be a qualifying capital interest unless the contrary is shown.

(5)   In this paragraph 'equity share capital' has the same meaning as in the Companies Act 1985 and the Companies (Northern Ireland) Order 1986.

106. Interpretation

(1) In this Act—

'associate' has the meaning given in section 105(9) above;

'authorisation' means authorisation granted by the *Bank* **Authority** under this Act and 'authorised' shall be construed accordingly;

'the Authority' means the Financial Services Authority;

'the Bank' means the Bank of England;

'bare trustee', in relation to a deposit, means a person holding the deposit on trust for another person who has the exclusive right to direct how it shall be dealt with subject only to satisfying any outstanding charge, lien or other right of the trustee to resort to it for the payment of duty, taxes, costs or other outgoings;

'controller' has the meaning given in section 105(3) above;

'director' has the meaning given in section 105(2) above;

'debenture' has the same meaning as in the Companies Act 1985;

'deposit' and 'deposit-taking business' have the meaning given in sections 5 and 6 above but subject to any order under section 7 above;

'documents' includes information recorded in any form and, in relation to information recorded otherwise than in legible form, references to its production include references to producing a copy of the information in legible form;

'former authorised institution' means an institution which was formerly an authorised institution or a recognised bank or licensed institution under the Banking Act 1979 and continues to have a liability in respect of any deposit for which it had a liability at a time when it was an authorised institution, recognised bank or licensed institution;

'group', in relation to a body corporate, means that body corporate, any other body corporate which is its holding company or subsidiary and any other body corporate which is a subsidiary of that holding company;

'indirect controller' has the meaning given in section 105(5) above;

'institution', except in the expression 'overseas institution' means—

(a) a body corporate wherever incorporated;

(b) a partnership formed under the law of any part of the United Kingdom;

(c) a partnership or other unincorporated association of two or more persons formed under the law of a member State other than the United Kingdom; or

(d) a savings bank to which section 104 above applies;

'liquidator', in relation to a partnership having its principal place of business in Scotland, includes a trustee appointed on the sequestrated estate of the partnership under the Bankruptcy (Scotland) Act 1985;

'local authority' means—

(a) in England and Wales, a local authority within the meaning of the Local Government Act 1972, the Common Council of the City of London or the Council of the Isles of Scilly;

(b) in Scotland, a local authority within the meaning of the Local Government (Scotland) Act 1973; and

(c) in Northern Ireland, a district council within the meaning of the Local Government Act (Northern Ireland) 1972;

'manager' has the meaning given in section 105(6) above;

'municipal bank' has the meaning given in section 103 above;

'parent controller' has the meaning given in section 105(5A) above;

'penny savings bank' has the same meaning as in the National Savings Bank Act 1971;

'related company' has the meaning given by section 105A above;

'relevant supervisory authority'—

(a) in relation to another member State, has the meaning given in regulation 2 of the Banking Coordination (Second Council Directive) Regulations 1992;

(b) in relation to any other country or territory outside the United Kingdom, means the authority discharging in that country or territory functions corresponding to those of the *Bank* **Authority** under this Act;

'shareholder controller', 'minority shareholder controller', '10 per cent shareholder controller', '20 per cent shareholder controller', '33 per cent shareholder controller', '50 per cent shareholder controller', 'majority shareholder controller' and 'principal shareholder controller' have the meanings given in section 105(4) above.

(2)   Section 736 of the Companies Act 1985 (meaning of subsidiary and holding company) shall apply for the purposes of this Act.

(2A)   In this Act the following expressions, namely—

another member State;

connected UK authority;

credit institution;

European authorised institution;

the First Council Directive;

home State;

listed activity;

parent undertaking;

recognised self-regulating organisation;

relevant supervisory authority;

the Second Council Directive;

subsidiary undertaking;

supervisory authority;

undertaking,

have the same meanings as in the Banking Coordination (Second Council Directive) Regulations 1992.

(2B)   Any reference in this Act to the First Council Directive or the Second Council Directive is a reference to that Directive as amended by the Prudential

Supervision Directive (within the meaning of the Financial Institutions (Prudential Supervision) Regulations 1996).

(2C) Any reference in this Act—

(a) to an undertaking being closely linked with any person, or being closely linked with any person by control; or

(b) to an undertaking's close links with any person,

shall be construed in accordance with regulation 2 of those Regulations.

(3) Any reference in this Act to any provision of Northern Ireland legislation within the meaning of section 24 of the Interpretation Act 1978 includes a reference to any subsequent provision of that legislation which, with or without modification, re-enacts the provision referred to in this Act.

107. Transitional provisions

Schedule 5 to this Act shall have effect with respect to the transitional matters there mentioned.

108. Minor and consequential amendments, repeals and revocations

(1) The enactments mentioned in Schedule 6 to this Act, shall have effect with the amendments there specified, being minor amendments and amendments consequential on the provisions of this Act, but subject to any savings there mentioned.

(2) The enactments mentioned in Part I of Schedule 7 to this Act and the instruments mentioned in Part II of that Schedule are hereby repealed or revoked to the extent specified in the third column of those Parts.

109. Northern Ireland

(1) This Act extends to Northern Ireland.

(2) Subject to any Order made after the passing of this Act by virtue of subsection (1)(a) of section 3 of the Northern Ireland Constitution Act 1973, the regulation of banking shall not be a transferred matter for the purposes of that Act but shall for the purposes of subsection (2) of that section be treated as specified in Schedule 3 to that Act.

110. Short title and commencement

(1) This Act may be cited as the Banking Act 1987.

(2) Section 91 above shall come into force on the passing of this Act and the other provisions of this Act shall come into force on such day as the Treasury may by order appoint; and different days may be appointed for different provisions or different purposes.

[All provisions of the Act have been brought into force by the Banking Act (Commencement No. 1) Order 1987 (SI 1987/1189), the Banking Act (Commencement No. 2) Order 1987 (SI 1987/1664), the Banking Act (Commencement No. 3) Order 1988 (SI 1988/502), the Banking Act (Commencement No. 4) Order 1988 (SI 1988/644).]

SCHEDULES

Section 2   SCHEDULE 1
THE BOARD OF BANKING SUPERVISION

Terms of office

1.—(1)   The independent members of the Board shall hold office for five years
except that some of those first appointed may be appointed to hold office for shorter
and different periods so as to secure that all the members do not retire simultaneously.

(2)   An independent member may resign his office by written notice to the *Bank*
Authority and the Chancellor of the Exchequer.

(3)   A person shall vacate his office as an independent member if he takes up a
post with executive responsibility in the *Bank* **Authority**.

(4)   Subject to sub-paragraph (3) above, a person who has ceased to be an
independent member of the Board shall be eligible for re-appointment.

Removal from office

2.   An independent member may be removed by the *Bank* **Authority** with the
consent of the Chancellor of the Exchequer if it is satisfied—

(a)   that he has been absent from meetings of the Board for more than three
months without the permission of the Board;

(b)   that he has become bankrupt, that his estate has been sequestrated or that
he has made an arrangement with or granted a trust deed for his creditors;

(c)   that he is incapacitated by physical or mental illness; or

(d)   that he is otherwise unable or unfit to discharge his functions as a member
of the Board.

Increase in number of members

3.—(1)   The Treasury may, after consultation with the *Bank* **Authority**, by order
increase or, subject to section 2(2) of this Act, reduce the number of ex officio or
independent members of the Board, provided always that there shall be a majority of
independent members on the Board.

(2)   Any order under this paragraph shall be subject to annulment in pursuance
of a resolution of either House of Parliament.

Proceedings

4.—(1)   The quorum for a meeting of the Board shall be one ex officio member
and three independent members.

(2)   Subject to sub-paragraph (1) above, the Board shall determine its own
procedure.

Facilities, remuneration and allowances

5.   The *Bank* **Authority** shall make such provision as it thinks necessary for
providing the Board with facilities for the exercise of its functions and for providing

remuneration, allowances or other benefits for or in respect of the independent members.

Section 4(1)   SCHEDULE 2
                              EXEMPTED PERSONS

1.   The central bank of a member State other than the United Kingdom.

2.   The National Savings Bank.

3.   A penny savings bank.

4.   A municipal bank.

5.   A building society incorporated (or deemed to be incorporated) under the Building Societies Act 1986.

6.—(1)   A friendly society within the meaning of section 7(1)(a) of the Friendly Societies Act 1974.

(2)   This paragraph applies only to the acceptance of deposits in the course of carrying out transactions permitted by the rules of the society.

7.   A society registered under either of the Acts mentioned in paragraph 6 above other than such a society as is there mentioned.

8.—(1)   Any institution which is for the time being authorised under section 3 or 4 of the Insurance Companies Act 1982 to carry on insurance business of a class specified in Schedule 1 or 2 to that Act.

(2)   This paragraph applies only to the acceptance of deposits in the course of carrying on the authorised insurance business.

9.   A loan society whose rules are certified, deposited and enrolled in accordance with the Loan Societies Act 1840.

10.   A credit union within the meaning of the Credit Unions Act 1979 or the Credit Unions (Northern Ireland) Order 1985.

11.   A body of persons certified as a school bank by the National Savings Bank or an authorised institution.

12.   A local authority.

13.   Any other body which by virtue of any enactment has power to issue a precept to a local authority in England or Wales or a requisition to a local authority in Scotland.

15.   The European Atomic Energy Community.

16.   The European Coal and Steel Community.

17.   The European Economic Community.

18.   The European Investment Bank.

19.   The International Bank for Reconstruction and Development.

20.   The International Finance Corporation.

21.   The International Monetary Fund.

22.   The African Development Bank.

23.   The Asian Development Bank.

24.   The Caribbean Development Bank.

25.   The Inter-American Development Bank.

26.   The European Bank for Reconstruction and Development.

27.   The Council of Europe Resettlement Fund.

Sections 9, 11, 13(4),   SCHEDULE 3
16(1) and 22   MINIMUM CRITERIA FOR AUTHORISATION

Directors etc. to be fit and proper persons

1.—(1)   Every person who is, or is to be, a director, controller or manager of the institution is a fit and proper person to hold the particular position which he holds or is to hold.

(2)   In determining whether a person is a fit and proper person to hold any particular position, regard shall be had to his probity, to his competence and soundness of judgment for fulfilling the responsibilities of that position, to the diligence with which he is fulfilling or likely to fulfil those responsibilities and to whether the interests of depositors or potential depositors of the institution are, or are likely to be, in any way threatened by his holding that position.

(3)   Without prejudice to the generality of the foregoing provisions, regard may be had to the previous conduct and activities in business or financial matters of the person in question and, in particular, to any evidence that he has—

(a)   committed an offence involving fraud or other dishonesty or violence;

(b)   contravened any provision made by or under any enactment appearing to the *Bank* **Authority** to be designed for protecting members of the public against financial loss due to dishonesty, incompetence or malpractice by persons concerned in the provision of banking, insurance, investment or other financial services or the management of companies or against financial loss due to the conduct of discharged or undischarged bankrupts;

(c)   engaged in any business practices appearing to the *Bank* **Authority** to be deceitful or oppressive or otherwise improper (whether unlawful or not) or which otherwise reflect discredit on his method of conducting business;

(d)   engaged in or been associated with any other business practices or otherwise conducted himself in such a way as to cast doubt on his competence and soundness of judgement.

Business to be directed by at least two individuals

2.   At least two individuals effectively direct the business of the institution.

Composition of board of directors

3.   In the case of an institution incorporated in the United Kingdom the directors include such number (if any) of directors without executive responsibility for the management of its business as the *Bank* **Authority** considers appropriate having regard to the circumstances of the institution and the nature and scale of its operations.

Business to be conducted in prudent manner

4.—(1)   The institution conducts, or, in the case of an institution which is not yet carrying on a deposit-taking business, will conduct its business in a prudent manner.

(2)   An institution shall not be regarded as conducting its business in a prudent manner unless it maintains or, as the case may be, will maintain own funds which,

together with other financial resources available to the institution of such nature and amount as are considered appropriate by the *Bank* **Authority**, are—

(a) of an amount which is commensurate with the nature and scale of the institution's operations; and

(b) of an amount and nature sufficient to safeguard the interests of its depositors and potential depositors, having regard to the particular factors mentioned in sub-paragraph (3) below and any other factors appearing to the *Bank* **Authority** to be relevant.

(3) The particular factors referred to above are—

(a) the nature and scale of the institution's operations; and

(b) the risks inherent in those operations and in the operations of any other undertaking in the same group so far as capable of affecting the institution.

(3A) An institution shall not be regarded as conducting its business in a prudent manner unless it maintains or, as the case may be, will maintain own funds which amount to not less than ecu 5 million (or an amount of equal value denominated wholly or partly in another unit of account).

(4) An institution shall not be regarded as conducting its business in a prudent manner unless it maintains or, as the case may be, will maintain adequate liquidity, having regard to the relationship between its liquid assets and its actual and contingent liabilities, to the times at which those liabilities will or may fall due and its assets mature, to the factors mentioned in sub-paragraph (3) above and to any other factors appearing to the *Bank* **Authority** to be relevant.

(5) For the purposes of sub-paragraph (4) above the *Bank* **Authority** may, to such extent as it thinks appropriate, take into account as liquid assets, assets of the institution and facilities available to it which are capable of providing liquidity within a reasonable period.

(6) An institution shall not be regarded as conducting its business in a prudent manner unless it makes or, as the case may be, will make adequate provision for depreciation or diminution in the value of its assets (including provision for bad or doubtful debts), for liabilities which will or may fall to be discharged by it and for losses which it will or may incur.

(7) An institution shall not be regarded as conducting its business in a prudent manner unless it maintains or, as the case may be, will maintain adequate accounting and other records of its business and adequate systems of control of its business and records.

(8) Those records and systems shall not be regarded as adequate unless they are such as to enable the business of the institution to be prudently managed and the institution to comply with the duties imposed on it by or under this Act and in determining whether those systems are adequate the *Bank* **Authority** shall have regard to the functions and responsibilities in respect of them of any such directors of the institution as are mentioned in paragraph 3 above.

(9) Sub-paragraph (2) to (7) above are without prejudice to the generality of sub-paragraph (1) above.

(10) In this paragraph 'ecu' and 'own funds' have the same meaning as in the Banking Coordination (Second Council Directive) Regulations 1992.

Integrity and skill

5.   The business of the institution is or in the case of an institution which is not yet carrying on a deposit-taking business, will be carried on with integrity and the professional skills appropriate to the nature and scale of its activities.

Minimum net assets

6.—(1)   The institution will at the time when authorisation is granted to it have initial capital amounting to not less than ecu 5 million (or an amount of equal value denominated wholly or partly in another unit of account).

(2) . In this paragraph 'ecu' and 'initial capital' have the same meanings as in the Banking Coordination (Second Council Directive) Regulations 1992.

Section 50   SCHEDULE 4
                    THE DEPOSIT PROTECTION BOARD

Constitution

1.—(1)   The Board shall consist of three ex offiio members, namely—

(*a*)   *the Governor of the Bank for the time being, who shall be the chairman of the Board;*

(*b*)   *the Deputy Governor of the Bank for the time being; and*

(*c*)   *the Chief Cashier of the Bank for the time being;*

(a)   the Chairman of the Authority, who shall chair the Board;

(b)   the holder of such other office within the Authority as the Chairman of the Authority may designate for the purposes of this provision; and

(c)   the Deputy Governor of the Bank of England responsible for financial stability;

and such ordinary members as shall from time to time be appointed under sub-paragraph (2) below.

(*2*)   *The Governor of the Bank shall appoint as ordinary members of the Board—*

(*a*)   *three persons who are directors, controllers or managers of contributory institutions; and*

(*b*)   *persons who are officers or employees of the Bank.*

(2)   The Chairman of the Authority shall appoint as ordinary members of the Board—

(a)   three persons who are directors, controllers or managers of contributory institutions; and

(b)   persons who are officers or employees of the Authority.

(*3*)   *Each ex officio member of the Board may appoint an alternate member, being an officer or employee of the Bank, to perform his duties as a member in his absence.*

(3)   An ex officio member of the Board may appoint an alternate member to perform his duties as a member in his absence as follows—

(a)   the Chairman of the Authority or the holder of a designated office within the Authority may appoint an officer or employee of the Authority, and

(b)   the Deputy Governor of the Bank of England may appoint an officer or employee of the Bank.

(4)   Each ordinary member of the Board may appoint an appropriately qualified person as an alternate member to perform his duties as a member in his absence; and for this purpose a person is appropriately qualified for appointment as an alternate—

(a)   by a member appointed under paragraph (a) of sub-paragraph (2) above, if he is a director, controller or manager of a contributory institution; and

(b)   by a member appointed under paragraph (b) of that sub-paragraph, if he is either an officer or an employee of the *Bank* **Authority**.

(5)   Ordinary and alternate members of the Board shall hold and vacate office in accordance with the terms of their appointment.

Expenses

2.   The Board may pay to its members such allowances in respect of expenses as the Board may determine.

Proceedings

3.—(1)   The Board shall determine its own procedure, including the quorum necessary for its meetings.

(2)   The validity of any proceedings of the Board shall not be affected by any vacancy among the ex officio members of the Board or by any defect in the appointment of any ordinary or alternate member.

4.—(1)   The fixing of the common seal of the Board shall be authenticated by the signature of the chairman of the Board or some other person authorised by the Board to act for that purpose.

(2)   A document purporting to be duly executed under the seal of the Board shall be received in evidence and deemed to be so executed unless the contrary is proved.

Accounts, audit and annual report

5.—(1)   The Board may determine its own financial year.

(2)   It shall be the duty of the Board—

(a)   to keep proper accounts and proper records in relation to the accounts; and

(b)   to prepare in respect of each of its financial years a statement of accounts showing the state of affairs and income and expenditure of the Board.

(3)   A statement of accounts prepared in accordance with sub-paragraph (2)(b) above shall be audited by auditors appointed by the board and the auditors shall report to the Board stating whether in their opinion the provisions of sub-paragraph (2) above have been complied with.

(4)   A person shall not be appointed as auditor by the Board under sub-paragraph (3) above unless he is eligible for appointment as a company auditor under section 25 of the Companies Act 1989.

(5)   It shall be the duty of the Board, as soon as practicable after the end of each of its financial year, to prepare a report on the performance of its functions during that year.

(6) It shall be the duty of the Board to publish, in such manner as it thinks appropriate, every statement of account prepared in accordance with sub-paragraph (2)(b) above and every report prepared in accordance with sub-paragraph (5) above.

Section 107   SCHEDULE 5
                          TRANSITIONAL PROVISIONS

First report by Bank of England

1. If this Act comes into force in the course of a financial year of the Bank of England its first report under section 1 of this Act shall include a report on its activities during that year under the Banking Act 1979 (in this Schedule referred to as 'the former Act').

Existing recognised banks and licensed institutions

2.—(1) Any institution (within the meaning of this Act) which at the coming into force of section 3 of this Act or by virtue of paragraph 4 or 5 below is—

(a)   a recognised bank; or

(b)   a licensed institution,

under the former Act shall be deemed to have been granted an authorisation under this Act.

(2) In relation to any such institution the reference in paragraph (a) of section 11(2) of this Act to the day on which it was authorised shall be construed as a reference to the day on which it was recognised or licensed under the former Act; and in relation to an institution recognised under the former Act by virtue of Part II of Schedule 3 to that Act that paragraph shall have effect with the omission of the words 'in the United Kingdom'.

(3) In relation to any such institution the reference in section 70(4) of this Act to the time when notice was given to the Bank under subsection (1) shall be construed as a reference to the day on which it first applied for recognition or a licence under the former Act.

Conditional licences

3.—(1) Any conditional licence in force under the former Act when section 3 of this Act comes into force or granted by virtue of paragraph 4 or 5 below shall be treated as an authorisation granted under this Act subject to restrictions (as to duration and conditions) corresponding to those applying to the conditional licence; but no institution shall be guilty of an offence under section 12 of this Act by reason only of a contravention of or failure to comply with a condition which is treated as a restriction of such an authorisation except so far as the condition is attributable to a variation under this Act.

(2) In relation to an application for authorisation made by an institution holding a conditional licence which by virtue of this paragraph is treated as a restricted authorisation, paragraph 6(1) of Schedule 3 to this Act shall have effect with the substitution for the reference to £1 million of a reference to £250,000.

Applications subject to appeal

4.—(1)   Where an application for recognition or a licence under the former Act has been refused by the Bank and at the coming into force of section 3 of this Act—

(a)   an appeal is pending against that refusal; or

(b)   the time for appealing against that refusal has not expired,

the repeal of the former Act shall not preclude the determination, or the bringing and determination, of the appeal and the grant or refusal of recognition or a licence as a result of that determination.

(2)   Sub-paragraph (1) above does not apply to an appeal by a licensed institution against a refusal to grant it recognition.

Revocation

5.—(1)   Where the Bank has given an institution a notice under section 7(3) or (4) of the former Act and the proceedings pursuant to that notice under the provisions of Schedule 4 to that Act have not been concluded at the coming into force of section 3 of this Act the repeal of that Act shall not affect the operation of those provisions in relation to that notice.

(2)   Paragraph 2 above does not apply to an institution which is a recognised bank or licensed institution at the coming into force of section 3 of this Act if its recognition or licence is subsequently revoked by virtue of this paragraph.

Directions

6.—(1)   The repeal of the former Act shall not affect the continued operation of any direction under section 8 of that Act which has been confirmed in accordance with section 9 before the repeal and any such direction may be varied or revoked as if given under section 19 of this Act.

(2)   A direction may be given under section 19 of this Act to an institution which was a recognised bank or licensed institution under the former Act if—

(a)   its recognition or licence under that Act was revoked or surrendered; or

(b)   a disqualification notice has been served on it under section 183 of the Financial Services Act 1986;

but subsection (5) of section 19 shall apply to it as it applies to an authorised institution, taking references to the time when it was authorised as references to the time when it was recognised or licensed under the former Act.

Information and investigations

7.—(1)   The repeal of the former Act shall not affect the operation of any requirement imposed under section 16 of that Act before the repeal or any powers exercisable under that section in relation to any such requirement.

(2)   The repeal of the former Act shall not affect the operation of section 17 of that Act in any case in which a person or persons to carry out an investigation under that section have been appointed before the repeal.

(3) Sections 42, 43 and 44 of this Act shall have effect in relation to a contravention of section 1 or 39 of the former Act as they have effect in relation to a contravention of section 3 or 35 of this Act.

Members of Deposit Protection Board

8. Any person who is an ordinary member or alternate member of the Deposit Protection Board at the coming into force of Part II of this Act shall be treated as having been appointed under Schedule 4 to this Act.

Initial contributions by excluded institutions

9.—(1) On or as soon as possible after the coming into force of Part II of this Act the Deposit Protection Board shall levy an initial contribution from each authorised institution which by virtue of an order under section 23(2) of the former Act did not have such a contribution levied from it under section 24 of that Act.

(2) The amount of the initial contribution to be levied from an institution under this paragraph shall be the amount of the initial contribution that would have been levied from it under that section if it had not been exempted from levy by virtue of the order.

Maximum contributions

10. For the purposes of section 56(3) of this Act there shall be taken into account any contribution or repayment made under any provision of the former Act which corresponds to any provision of this Act.

Insolvencies before commencement of Part II

11. This Act does not affect the operation of sections 28 to 31 of the former Act in relation to any insolvency occurring before the coming into force of Part II of this Act; but section 63 of this Act shall apply (instead of section 32 of that Act) to any money received by the Board under section 31.

Borrowing

12. Any sum borrowed by virtue of section 26(3) of the said Act of 1979 shall, so far as outstanding at the coming into force of Part II of this Act, be treated as having been borrowed under section 64 of this Act.

Use of banking names

13.—(1) Subject to sub-paragraph (2) below, section 67 of this Act does not prohibit the use by an institution which is incorporated in or is a partnership formed under the law of any part of the United Kingdom and is deemed to be an authorised institution by virtue of paragraph 2 above of a name which was its registered business or compay name immediately before the coming into force of Part III of this Act or of section 36 of the former Act.

(2) Sub-paragraph (1) above shall cease to apply—

(a)   in the case of an incorporated institution, if the total value in sterling of its issued share capital and undistributable reserves falls below their total value at the coming into force of Part III of this Act; or

(b)   in the case of a partnership in respect of which one or more designated fixed capital accounts are maintained, if the total value in sterling of those accounts falls below their value at that time.

(3)   Section 67 of this Act does not prohibit the use by—

(a)   an authorised institution which is a wholly-owned subsidiary of an institution to which sub-paragraph (1) above applies; or

(b)   a company which has a wholly-owned subsidiary which is an institution to which that sub-paragraph applies,

or a name which includes the name of the institution to which the sub-paragraph applies for the purpose of indicating the connection between the two companies.

(4)   In sub-paragraph (2) above 'share capital' and 'designated fixed capital account' have the same meaning as in subsection (2) of section 67 of this Act and 'undistributable reserves' means such reserves as mentioned in paragraph (a)(ii) of that subsection.

Restriction on disclosure of information

14.   In section 82(1) of this Act the reference to information received under or for the purposes of this Act includes a reference to information received under or for the purposes of the former Act.

[Schedules 6 (minor and consequential amendments) and 7 (repeals and revocations) are omitted.]

Sources of amendments incorporated in the text printed here

S. 1: Bank of England Act 1998, sch. 5, para. 2. **S. 2:** Bank of England Act 1998, s. 28(1) and (2). **S. 3:** Bank of England Act 1998, sch. 5, para. 3. **S. 4:** Bank of England Act 1998, sch. 5, para. 3. **S. 5:** SI 1995/1442, reg. 45. **S. 7:** Bank of England Act 1998, sch. 5, para. 4. **S. 8:** SI 1992/3218, reg. 25; Bank of England Act 1998, sch. 5, para. 4. **S. 9:** SI 1992/3218, reg. 26; SI 1996/1669, reg. 3(1); Bank of England Act 1998, sch. 5, para. 4. **S. 10:** SI 1989/2405, sch. 9, para. 49; SI 1992/3218, reg. 32(2)(a); Bank of England Act 1998, sch. 5, para. 4. **S. 11:** SI 1989/2405 (NI 19), sch. 9, para. 49; SI 1992/3218, reg. 28; SI 1996/1669, reg. 3(2); Bank of England Act 1998, sch. 5, para. 5. **S. 12:** Bank of England Act 1998, sch. 5, para. 6. **S. 12A:** SI 1992/3218, reg. 29; Bank of England Act 1998, sch. 5, para. 7. **S. 13:** SI 1992/3218, reg. 30(1); Bank of England Act 1998, sch. 5, para. 7. **S. 14:** Bank of England Act 1998, sch. 5, para. 7. **S. 15:** SI 1992/3218, reg. 30(2); Bank of England Act 1998, sch. 5, para. 7. **S. 16:** Bank of England Act 1998, sch. 5, para. 7. **S. 17:** Bank of England Act 1998, sch. 5, para. 7. **S. 19:** Bank of England Act 1998, sch. 5, para. 8. **S. 20:** Bank of England Act 1998, sch. 5, para. 9. **S. 21:** SI 1992/3218, reg. 31(1) (this amendment does not apply to institutions which are not credit institutions incorporated in or formed under the law of a part of the United Kingdom:

SI 1992/3218, reg. 46(a)); Bank of England Act 1998, sch. 5, para. 9. **S. 22:** SI 1992/3218, reg. 31(2); Bank of England Act 1998, sch. 5, para. 9. **S. 23:** SI 1992/3218, reg. 32(2)(b); Bank of England Act 1998, sch. 5, para. 9. **S. 24:** Bank of England Act 1998, sch. 5, para. 9. **S. 25:** Bank of England Act 1998, sch. 5, para. 9. **S. 26:** Bank of England Act 1998, sch. 5, para. 9. **S. 26A:** SI 1992/3218, reg. 32(1); Bank of England Act 1998, sch. 5, para. 9. **S. 27:** SI 1992/3218, reg. 32(2)(c); Bank of England Act 1998, sch. 5, para. 9. **S. 28:** Courts and Legal Services Act 1990, sch. 10, para. 69; Judicial Pensions and Retirement Act 1993, sch. 6, para. 65. **S. 29:** Bank of England Act 1998, sch. 5, para. 10. **S. 30:** Tribunals and Inquiries Act 1992, sch. 4; Bank of England Act 1998, sch. 5, para. 11. **S. 31:** Bank of England Act 1998, sch. 5, para. 11. **S. 32:** Bank of England Act 1998, sch. 5, para. 11. **S. 33:** Bank of England Act 1998, sch. 5, para. 11. **S. 34:** Bank of England Act 1998, sch. 5, para. 11. **S. 36:** Bank of England Act 1998, sch. 5, para. 11. **S. 36A:** SI 1992/3218, reg. 35; Bank of England Act 1998, sch. 5, para. 11.. **S. 37:** SI 1992/3218, reg. 34 (this amendment does not apply to institutions which are not credit institutions incorporated in or formed under the law of a part of the United Kingdom: SI 1992/3218, reg. 46(a)); Bank of England Act 1998, sch. 5, para. 11. **S. 37A:** SI 1992/3218, reg. 35; Bank of England Act 1998, sch. 5, para. 11. **S. 38:** Bank of England Act 1998, sch. 5, para. 11. **S. 39:** SI 1992/3218, reg. 36 (this amendment does not apply to institutions which are not credit institutions incorporated in or formed under the law of a part of the United Kingdom: SI 1992/3218, reg. 46(a)); Bank of England Act 1998, s. 27 and sch. 5, para. 11. **S. 40:** Bank of England Act 1998, sch. 5, para. 11. **S. 41:** SI 1992/3218, reg. 37 (this amendment does not apply to institutions which are not credit institutions incorporated in or formed under the law of a part of the United Kingdom: SI 1992/3218, reg. 46(a)); Bank of England Act 1998, sch. 5, para. 11. **S. 42:** Bank of England Act 1998, sch. 5, para. 11. **S. 43:** Bank of England Act 1998, sch. 5, para. 12. **S. 46:** Companies Act 1989, s. 119(3) and sch. 10, para. 37; SI 1990/593 (NI 5), sch. 10, para. 29; SI 1990/1504 (NI 10), art. 54(3); Bank of England Act 1998, sch. 5, para. 13. **S. 47:** SI 1996/1669, reg. 4; Bank of England Act 1998, sch. 5, para. 13. **S. 48:** Bank of England Act 1998, sch. 5, para. 13. **S. 49:** Bank of England Act 1998, sch. 5, para. 13. **S. 50:** SI 1995/1442, reg. 25. **S. 51:** SI 1995/1442, reg. 26. **S. 52:** SI 1995/1442, reg. 27; Bank of England Act 1998, sch. 5, para. 14. **S. 53:** SI 1995/1442, reg. 28. **S. 57:** SI 1995/1442, reg. 29. **S. 58:** SI 1989/2405 (NI 19), sch. 9, para. 50(b); SI 1995/1442, reg. 30; Bank of England Act 1998, sch. 5, para. 14. **S. 59:** SI 1995/1442, reg. 31; Bank of England Act 1998, sch. 5, para. 14. **S. 60:** SI 1995/1442, reg. 32. **S. 61:** SI 1995/1442, reg. 33. **S. 62:** SI 1989/2405 (NI 19), sch. 9, para. 52; SI 1995/1442, reg. 34. **S. 65:** SI 1995/1442, reg. 35; Bank of England Act 1998, sch. 5, para. 14. **S. 67:** Bank of England Act 1998, sch. 5, para. 14. **S. 68:** Bank of England Act 1998, sch. 5, para. 14. **S. 69:** Bank of England Act 1998, sch. 5, para. 14. **S. 70:** Bank of England Act 1998, sch. 5, para. 15. **S. 71:** Bank of England Act 1998, sch. 5, para. 15. **S. 72:** Bank of England Act 1998, sch. 5, para. 15. **S. 75:** Bank of England Act 1998, sch. 5, para. 15. **S. 76:** Bank of England Act 1998, sch. 5, para. 16. **S. 77:** Bank of England Act 1998, sch. 5, para. 17. **S. 78:** Bank of England Act 1998, sch. 5, para. 17. **S. 79:** SI 1992/3179, sch. 3, para. 10; Bank of England Act 1998, sch. 5, para. 17. **S. 80:** Bank of England Act 1998, sch. 5, para. 17. **S. 83:** SI 1992/3218, reg. 38; SI 1996/1669, reg. 5(1); (until the Banking Act 1998, s. 36(4), is brought into force the amendments made by SI 1992/3218 and SI 1996/1669 do not apply to information relating to the business or other affairs of institutions which are authorised institutions, but not credit institutions: SI 1992/3218, reg. 46(b); SI 1996/1669, reg. 5(6)); Bank of England Act 1998, sch. 5, para. 53, and sch. 9, part I. **S. 84:** SI 1987/1292; Companies Act 1989, ss. 81, 171(7) and s. 212 and sch. 24; SI 1989/2405 (NI 19), sch. 9, para. 54; SI 1990/1504 (NI 10), art. 25; Friendly Societies Act 1992, s. 120, sch. 21, para. 9 and sch. 22, part I; SI 1992/1315, art. 10(1) and sch. 4, para. 11; SI 1992/3218, reg. 39; Criminal Justice Act 1993, sch. 5, para. 13, and sch. 6, part I; SI 1994/3132, reg. 11; SI 1996/1669, reg. 5(2), (3) and (4) and sch. 5, para. 1; (until the Banking Act 1998, s. 36(4), is brought into force the amendments made by SI 1992/3218, reg. 39(2) to (4), and SI 1996/1669 do not apply to information relating to the business or other affairs of institutions which are authorised institutions, but not credit institutions: SI 1992/3218, reg. 46(b); SI 1996/1669, reg. 5(6)); SI 1997/2781, art. 8(1) and sch., para. 113; Bank of England Act 1998, sch. 5, para. 54; amendment made by SI 1993/491 revoked by SI 1993/836. **S. 85:** SI 1989/2404, sch. 4, para. 5; SI 1989/2405, sch. 9, para. 55; SI 1992/3218, reg. 40 (until the Banking Act 1998, s. 36(4), is brought into force the amendments made by SI 1992/3218 do not apply to information relating to the business or other affairs of institutions which are authorised institutions, but not credit institutions: SI 1992/3218, reg. 46(b)); Bank of England Act 1998, sch. 5, para. 55. **S. 86:** SI 1992/3218, reg. 41; SI 1996/1669, reg. 5(5); (until the Banking Act 1998, s. 36(4), is brought into force the amendments made by SI 1992/3218 and SI 1996/1669 do not apply to information relating to the business or other affairs of institutions which are authorised institutions, but not credit institutions: SI 1992/3218, reg. 46(b); SI 1996/1669, reg. 5(6)); Bank of England Act 1998, s. 36(1) and sch. 5, para. 56. **S. 87:** SI 1989/2404 (NI 18), sch. 4, para. 13; SI 1992/3218, reg. 42 (until the Banking Act 1998, s. 36(4), is brought into force the amendment made by SI 1992/3218 does not apply to information relating to the business or other affairs of institutions which are authorised institutions, but not credit institutions: SI 1992/3218, reg. 46(b)); Bank of England Act 1998, sch. 5, para. 58. **S. 92:** SI 1989/2405 (NI 19), sch. 9, para. 56; Bank of England Act 1998, sch. 5, para. 18. **S. 93:** Bank of England Act 1998, sch. 5, para. 18. **S. 94:** Bank of England Act 1998, sch. 5, para. 18. **S. 95:** Bank of England Act 1998, sch. 5, para. 18. **S. 96:** Friendly Societies Act 1992, s. 120(2) and sch. 22, part I; Bank of England Act 1998, sch. 5, para. 18. **S. 97:** Criminal Procedure (Consequential Provisions) (Scotland) Act 1995, s. 5 and sch. 4, para. 67. **S. 98:** Criminal Procedure (Consequential Provisions) (Scotland) Act 1995, s. 5 and sch. 4, para. 67. **S. 99:** Bank of England Act 1998, sch. 5, para. 18. **S. 100:** Bank of England Act 1998, sch. 5, para. 18. **S. 101:** Bank of England Act 1998, sch. 5, para. 18. **S. 103:** Local Government Act 1992, sch. 3, para. 22; Local Government and Rating Act 1997, s. 33(1) and sch. 3, para. 21 (this amendment does not extend to Northern Ireland). **S. 105:** SI 1992/3218, reg. 43 (this

Appendix 3
Bank of England Act 1946

Apart from headings, *words in italics* will be repealed and **words in bold** will be inserted when the relevant provisions of the Bank of England Act 1998 are brought into force (1 June 1998).

9 & 10 GEO 6 CHAPTER 27

An Act to bring the capital stock of the Bank of England into public ownership and bring the Bank under public control, to make provision with respect to the relations between the Treasury, the Bank of England and other banks and for purposes connected with the matters aforesaid. [14 February 1946]

Be it enacted by the King's most Excellent Majesty, by and with the advice and consent of the Lords Spiritual and Temporal, and Commons, in this present Parliament assembled, and by the authority of the same, as follows:—

1. Transfer of Bank stock to Treasury

(1) On the appointed day—

(a) the whole of the existing capital stock of the Bank (hereinafter referred to as 'Bank stock') shall, by virtue of this section, be transferred, free of all trusts, liabilities and incumbrances, to such person as the Treasury may by order nominate, to be held by that person on behalf of the Treasury;

(b) the Treasury shall issue, to the person who immediately before the appointed day is registered in the books of the Bank as the holder of any Bank stock, the equivalent amount of stock created by the Treasury for the purpose (hereinafter referred to as the 'Government stock').

(2) The Government stock shall bear interest at the rate of three per cent, per annum; and the equivalent amount of Government stock shall, in relation to any person, be taken to be such that the sum payable annually by way of interest thereon is equal to the average annual gross dividend declared during the period of twenty years immediately preceding the thirty-first day of March, nineteen hundred and forty-five, upon the amount of Bank stock of which that person was the registered holder immediately before the appointed day.

(3)   The Government stock may be redeemed at par by the Treasury on or at any time after the fifth day of April, nineteen hundred and sixty-six, after giving not less than three months' notice in the London Gazette of their intention to do so.

(4)   After the appointed day, no dividends on Bank stock shall be declared but in lieu of any such dividends the Bank shall pay to the Treasury, on every fifth day of April and of October, *the sum of eight hundred and seventy-three thousand, one hundred and eighty pounds, or such less or greater sum as may from time to time be agreed upon between the Treasury and the Bank* **a sum equal to 25 per cent of the Bank's net profits for its previous financial year, or such other sum as the Treasury and the Bank may agree**.

(5)   The incidental and supplemental provisions set out in the First Schedule to this Act shall have effect with respect to the Government stock and to the sums payable to the Treasury under the last foregoing subsection.

(6)   **In subsection (4) of this section, the reference to the Bank's net profits for its previous financial year is to the profits shown in the audited accounts for that year less the amount of the tax charge so shown.**

2.   *Court of directors of the Bank*

(1)   On the appointed day, all persons who are, immediately before that day, holding office as Governor, Deputy Governor or director of the Bank shall vacate their office, and on and after that day there shall be a Governor, a Deputy Governor and sixteen directors of the Bank, who shall be the court of directors.

(2)   The Governor, Deputy Governor and other members of the court of directors shall be appointed by His Majesty.

(3)   The provisions of the Second Schedule to this Act shall have effect as respects the tenure of office, qualifications and employment of members of the court of directors and meetings of the court.

3.   Consequential provisions as to constitution and powers of the Bank

(1)   So much of any enactment as limits the duration of the Bank as a body corporate shall cease to have effect.

(2)   As from the appointed day every member of the court of directors of the Bank shall be a member of the said body corporate, notwithstanding that he holds no Bank stock, and accordingly the members of the said body shall be the members for the time being of that court together with the person who for the time being holds the Bank stock on behalf of the Treasury.

(3)   As from the appointed day His Majesty may revoke all or any of the provisions of the charters of the Bank except in so far as they incorporate the Bank, and thereafter, subject to the provisions of this Act **and the Bank of England Act 1998**, the Bank shall be constituted and regulated in accordance with so much of the said charters as remains unrevoked and such other charters as may from time to time be granted by His Majesty and accepted on behalf of the Bank by the court of directors.

4. Treasury directions to the Bank and relations of the Bank with other banks

(1) The Treasury may from time to time give such directions to the Bank as, after consultation with the Governor of the Bank, they think necessary in the public interest, **except in relation to monetary policy.**

(2) Subject to any such directions, the affairs of the Bank shall be managed by the court of directors in accordance with such provisions (if any) in that behalf as may be contained in any charter of the Bank for the time being in force and any byelaws made thereunder.

(3) The Bank, if they think it necessary in the public interest, may request information from and make recommendations to bankers, and may, if so authorised by the Treasury, issue directions to any banker for the purpose of securing that effect is given to any such request or recommendation:

Provided that:

(a) no such request or recommendations shall be made with respect to the affairs of any particular customer of a banker; and

(b) before authorising the issue of any such directions the Treasury shall give the banker concerned, or such person as appears to them to represent him, an opportunity of making representations with respect thereto.

(6) In this section the expression 'banker' means any such person carrying on a banking undertaking as may be declared by order of the Treasury to be a banker for the purposes of this section.

(7) Any order under the last foregoing subsection may be varied or revoked by a subsequent order.

5. Interpretation

For the purpose of this Act—

(a) the expression 'the Bank' means the Bank of England;

(b) the appointed day shall be such day as the Treasury may by order appoint. [The appointed day is 1 March 1946, by the Bank of England (Appointed Day) Order 1946 (SR & O 1946/237).]

6. Short title

This Act may be cited as the Bank of England Act, 1946.

SCHEDULES

Section 1   FIRST SCHEDULE

INCIDENTAL AND SUPPLEMENTAL PROVISIONS AS TO THE GOVERNMENT STOCK AND SUMS PAYABLE BY THE BANK TO THE TREASURY

1. The principal of and interest on the Government stock, and any expenses incurred in connection with the issue or redemption thereof, shall be charged on and issued out of the Consolidated Fund of the United Kingdom (hereafter in this Schedule referred to as 'the Consolidated Fund').

3.   The interest on the Government stock shall be payable on the fifth day of April and the fifth day of October in each year.

4.   A full half year's interest on the Government stock shall be payable on whichever of the dates mentioned in the last foregoing paragraph occurs first after the appointed day, and shall be deemed to have accrued from day to day during the six months preceding that date.

6.   Section forty-seven of the Finance Act, 1942 (which empowers the Treasury to make regulations as respects the transfer and registration of stock and registered bonds of the descriptions specified in Part I of the Eleventh Schedule to that Act), and any regulations made thereunder which are in force immediately before the appointed day, shall have effect as if the Government stock were included among the stocks to which the said regulations apply.

7.   Where immediately before the appointed day any dead person is registered in the books of the Bank as the holder or one of the joint holders of any Bank stock, any · Government stock purporting to be issued to him, or to him and the other joint holders, shall be deemed to be duly issued to his personal representatives, or to the joint holders, as the case may be; and, in the case of administrators, as well as in the case of executors, this paragraph shall have effect notwithstanding that there is no grant of representation to them until after the appointed day.

8.   The Government stock issued in substitution for any Bank stock shall be held in the same rights and on the same trusts and subject to the same powers, privileges, provisions, charges, restraints and liabilities as those in, on or subject to which the Bank stock was held immediately before the appointed day, and so as to give effect to and not revoke any deed, will, order, mandate, notice or other instrument or testamentary or other disposition disposing of or affecting the Bank stock, and every such instrument or disposition shall take effect with reference to the whole or a proportionate part, as the case may be, of the substituted Government stock.

9.   Trustees, executors and all other holders in any representative or fiduciary capacity of any Bank stock may hold, dispose of or otherwise deal with the Government stock issued in substitution therefor in all respects as they might have held, disposed of or otherwise dealt with the Bank stock.

10.   Paragraphs 3 and 5 of the Second Schedule to the National Loans Act 1939 (which applies certain enactments to securities issued under that Act), shall have effect as if references to securities issued under that Act included references to the Government stock.

[Paragraph 10 is repealed by the Statute Law (Repeals) Act 1993, s. 1(1) and sch. 1, part IX, group 1, but, so far as relating to stock registered in the National Savings Stock Register, this repeal will not have effect until the coming into force of the first regulations made by virtue of the National Debt Act 1972, s. 3(1)(bb) (Statute Law (Repeals) Act 1993, s. 4(2)).]

11.   The Government stock shall be subject to the provisions of the National Debt Act 1870, so far as is consistent with the tenor of this Act.

11A.—(1)   If, when a payment falls to be made under section 1(4) of this Act, the Bank's accounts for the previous financial year have not been audited, the

payment shall be made on the basis of the Bank's estimate of the relevant amounts.

(2)   If an amount estimated under sub-paragraph (1) of this paragraph differs from the amount shown in the audited accounts, an appropriate adjustment shall be made to the next payment under section 1(4) of this Act to be made after the difference becomes apparent.

13.   The sums paid by the Bank to the Treasury in lieu of dividends on Bank stock shall be paid into the Exchequer.

14.   In charging the profits and gains of the Bank for the purposes of income tax for any year of assessment, the sums paid by the Bank as aforesaid in that year shall be allowed as a deduction.

14.   Any sum paid by the Bank to the Treasury in lieu of dividends shall be allowed as a deduction in assessing the Bank to corporation tax for the accounting period by reference to which the payment is calculated.

Section 2   *SECOND SCHEDULE*
SUPPLEMENTAL PROVISIONS AS TO COURT OF DIRECTORS

1.   The term of office of the Governor and of the Deputy Governor shall be five years.

2.   The term of office of the directors shall be four years, and four of them shall retire each year on the anniversary of the appointed day:

Provided that, of the directors appointed to take office on the appointed day, four shall be appointed to hold office until the first anniversary of that day and shall then retire, four shall be appointed to hold office until the second anniversary of that day and shall then retire, and four shall be appointed to hold office until the third anniversary of that day and shall then retire.

3.   A person who has held the office of Governor, Deputy Governor or director shall be eligible for re-appointment to that office or for appointment to any other of those offices.

4.   A person shall be disqualified for holding the office of Governor, Deputy Governor or director if—

(a)   he is a Minister of the Crown, or a person serving in a Government Department in employment in respect of which remuneration is payable out of moneys provided by Parliament; or

(b)   he is an alien within the meaning of the British Nationality and Status of Aliens Acts 1914 to 1943; or

(c)   he is subject to any disqualification which may be imposed by the charter of the Bank;

and a person shall vacate any such office if he becomes subject to any such disqualification.

5.   Where the office of a director is vacated under the foregoing paragraph, or by death or resignation, a person appointed to fill the vacancy shall hold office until the time when the person in whose place he was appointed would regularly have retired, and shall then retire.

6. *Not more than four of the directors may be employed to give their exclusive services to the Bank.*

7. *The following provisions shall have effect as respects any meeting of the court of directors held on or after the appointed day but before a charter making provision for the matters dealt with by this paragraph has been granted and accepted under this Act:*

    (a)   the meeting may be called by the Governor or Deputy Governor in such manner as he may determine;

    (b)   a quorum shall consist of not less than eight directors together with the Governor or Deputy Governor;

    (c)   when a quorum is present the court may act notwithstanding that a vacancy exists among the members of the court.

Sources of amendments incorporated in the text printed here

S. 1: Bank of England Act 1998, s. 8(1) and (2). **S. 2:** Bank of England Act 1998, s. 43 and sch. 9, part I. **S. 3(3):** Bank of England Act 1998, s. 9(3). **S. 3(4):** repealed by the Statute Law Revision Act 1950, s. 1(1) and sch. 1. **S. 4(1):** Bank of England Act 1998, s. 10. **S. 4(2):** Bank of England Act 1998, s. 43 and sch. 9, part I. **S. 4(4) and (5):** repealed by the Official Secrets Act 1989, s. 16(4) and sch. 2. **S. 4(8):** repealed by the Statute Law Revision Act 1950, s. 1(1) and sch. 1. **S. 5:** Statute Law (Repeals) Act 1976, s. 1 and sch. 1, part XI. **Sch. 1, para. 1:** Statute Law Revision Act 1963, s. 1 and sch. **Sch. 1, para. 2:** repealed by the National Loans Act 1968, s. 24(2) and sch. 6. **Sch. 1, para. 5:** repealed by the Finance Act 1954, s. 35(9) and sch. 6. **Sch. 1, para. 10:** Income Tax Act 1952, s. 527(1) and sch. 25, part I. **Sch. 1, para. 11A:** Bank of England Act 1998, s. 8(3). **Sch. 1, para. 12:** repealed by the National Loans Act 1968, s. 24(2) and sch. 6. **Sch. 1, para. 13:** National Loans Act 1968, s. 24(2) and sch. 6. **Sch. 1, para. 14:** Bank of England Act 1998, s. 8(4). **Sch. 2:** House of Commons Disqualification Act 1957, s. 14 and sch. 4; Bank of England Act 1998, s. 43 and sch. 9, part I. **Sch. 3:** repealed by the Statute Law Revision Act 1950, s. 1(1) and sch. 1.

[Here the Names of the said several subscribers are repeated]
and all and every other Person and Persons, Natives and Foreigners, Bodies Politick
or Corporate, who, over and above the Persons before especially named, have at any
Time or Times before the making of these Presents, subscribed and contributed any
Sum or Sums of Money towards the said Sum of Twelve Hundred Thousand Pounds
so subscribed, pursuant to the said Act, and our said Commission, and have paid the
fourth Part thereof upon their said Subscriptions, and who are now living or existent,
and have not assigned their Interest in the said Subscriptions; and all and every the
Heirs and Successors of any of the said original Subscribers, who are now dead, and
have not in their Life-times assigned their Interests in the said Subscriptions, and the
Heirs and Successors of such of the said Assignees who are now dead, and did not in
their Life-times assign or depart with their interest in the said Stock and annual Fond,
and all and every Person and Persons, Natives or Foreigners, Bodies Politick and
Corporate, who, either as original Subscribers of the said Sum of Twelve Hundred
Thousand Pounds so subscribed and not having parted with their Interests in their
Subscriptions, or as Heirs, Successors, or Assignees, or by any other lawful Title
derived, or to be derived from, by, or under the said original Subscribers of the said
Sum of Twelve Hundred Thousand Pounds so subscribed, or any of them now have,
or at any Time or Times hereafter shall have, or be entitled to any Part, Share, or
Interest of or in the Principal or Capital Stock of the said Corporation, or the said
yearly Fond of One Hundred Thousand Pounds, granted by the said Act of
Parliament, or any Part thereof, so long as they respectively shall have any such Part,
Share, or Interest therein, shall be, and be called one Body Politick and Corporate, of
themselves, in Deed and in Name, by the Name of *The Governor and Company of
the Bank of England*; and them by that Name, one Body Politick and Corporate, in
Deed and in Name, We do, for Us, our Heirs, and Successors, make, create, erect,
establish, and confirm for ever, by these Presents, and by the same Name, they and
their Successors shall have perpetual Succession, and shall and may have and use a
Common Seal, for the Use, Business, or Affairs of the said Body Politick and
Corporate, and their Successors, with Power to break, alter, and to make anew their
Seal from Time to Time, at their Pleasure, and as they shall see Cause. And by the
same Name, they and their Successors in all Times coming, shall be able and capable
in Law, to have, take, purchase, receive, hold, keep, possess, enjoy, and retain to them
and their Successors, any Manors, Messuages, Lands, Rents, Tenements, Liberties,
Privileges, Franchises, Hereditaments, and Possessions whatsoever, and of what
Kind, Nature, or Quality soever; and moreover, to purchase and acquire all Goods
and Chattels whatsoever, wherein they are not restrained by the said Act, and also to
sell, grant, demise, alien, and dispose of the same Manors, Messuages, Lands, Rents,
Tenements, Privileges, Franchises, Hereditaments, Possessions, Goods and Chattels,
or any of them. And by the same Name they and their successors shall and may sue
and implead, and be sued and impleaded, answer and defend, and be answered and
defended in Courts of Record, or any other Place whatsoever, and before whatsoever
Judges, Justices, Officers and Ministers of Us, our Heirs and Successors; and in all
and singular Pleas, Actions, Suits, Causes and Demands whatsoever, of what Kind,

Nature, or Sort soever, and in as large, ample and beneficial Manner and Form as any other Body Politick and Corporate, or any other the Liege People of *England*, or other our Dominions, being Persons able and capable in law, may or can have, take, purchase, receive, hold, keep, possess, enjoy, sell, grant, demise, alien, dispose, sue, implead, defend, or answer, or be sued, impleaded, defended, or answered in any manner of wise,
...

And we do hereby for Us, our Heirs and Successors, declare, limit, direct and appoint, that the aforesaid Sum of Twelve Hundred Thousand Pounds so subscribed as aforesaid, shall be, and be called, accepted, esteemed, reputed and taken, *The Common Capital and Principal Stock of the Corporation hereby constituted.*
...

In *Witness* whereof, we have caused these our Letters to be made Patents, *Witness* our selves at *Westminster*, the seven and twentieth day of *July*, in the sixth Year of our Reign.

By *Writ of Privy Seal*,

Pigott.

Intrat. int. Record. Domini Regis Willielmi Tertii, infra Recept. Scaccarii ss. remanen, in Officio Clerici Thesaurarii al. Clerici Pellium decimo die Junii, 1695. Annoq; Regni dicti Domini Regis septimo.[1]

---

[1] 'Entered among the Records of the Lord King William III, within the Receipt of the Exchequer; to wit, remaining in the Office of the Clerk of the Treasurer, otherwise the Clerk of the Pells, 10 June 1695. And in the seventh year of the reign of the said Lord King.' The pells were the Exchequer's parchment accounting records and the Clerk of the Pells was in charge of them.

THE CHARTER OF THE CORPORATION
OF THE
GOVERNOR AND COMPANY
OF THE
BANK OF ENGLAND

[1 March 1946]

GEORGE THE SIXTH, by the Grace of God, of Great Britain, Ireland and the British Dominions beyond the Seas King, Defender of the Faith, Emperor of India:

To all to whom these Presents shall come, Greeting!

WHEREAS by a Charter granted by Their Majesties King William and Queen Mary by Letters Patent under the Great Seal in pursuance of the Bank of England Act 1694 and dated the twenty-seventh day of July in the sixth year of their reign the Governor and Company of the Bank of England (hereinafter called 'the Bank of England') were duly incorporated with perpetual succession and a common seal and such rights, powers and privileges as are therein described:

AND WHEREAS by a Supplemental Charter granted by Her Majesty Queen Victoria by Letters Patent under the Great Seal in pursuance of the Bank Act 1892 and dated the nineteenth day of August in the sixtieth year of Her reign the internal affairs of the Bank of England were further regulated:

AND WHEREAS the Bank of England Act 1946 by section one enacted that on a day to be appointed (hereinafter called 'the appointed day') the whole of the existing capital stock of the Bank of England should be transferred to such person as the Treasury might by order nominate: and by section two enacted that on and after the appointed day there should be a Governor a Deputy Governor and sixteen Directors of the Bank of England who should be the Court of Directors and should be appointed by Us Our Heirs and Successors and that the provisions of the Second Schedule to that Act should have effect as respects the tenure of office qualifications and employment of members of the Court of Directors: and by section three enacted that as from the appointed day the members of the said body corporate should be the members for the time being of the Court of Directors together with the person who for the time being should hold the capital stock of the Bank of England on behalf of the Treasury and by section five enacted that the appointed day should be such day as the Treasury might by order appoint:

AND WHEREAS the Bank of England Act 1946 by section three further enacted that as from the appointed day all or any of the provisions of the Charters of the Bank of England might be revoked except in so far as they incorporate the Bank of England and that thereafter, subject to the provisions of that Act, the Bank of England should be constituted and regulated in accordance with so much of the said Charters as remained unrevoked and such other Charters as might from time to time be granted by Us Our Heirs and Successors and accepted on behalf of the Bank of England by the Court of Directors:

AND WHEREAS by the Bank of England (Appointed Day) Order 1946 the Treasury have appointed the first day of March nineteen hundred and forty-six as the appointed day for the purposes of the Bank of England Act 1946:

AND WHEREAS it is Our pleasure in pursuance of section three of the Bank of England Act 1946 to revoke the existing Charters of the Bank of England except in so far as they incorporate the Bank of England, constitute its capital stock, authorise it to have a common seal, to hold land and other property as therein mentioned and to sue and be sued and in place thereof to grant such new Charter as is herein set forth:

NOW THEREFORE know ye that We, taking the premises into Our consideration and of Our especial grace, certain knowledge, and mere motion do, in pursuance of the Bank of England Act 1946 and of all other powers enabling Us in that behalf, by these Presents for Us Our Heirs and Successors give, grant, ordain and declare as follows, that is to say:

1. Revocation of Charters in part

As from the appointed day the Charter of the Bank of England dated the 27th day of July 1694 (except in so far as it incorporates the Bank of England, constitutes its capital stock and authorises it to have a common seal, to hold land and other property as therein mentioned and to sue and be sued) and the Supplemental Charter of the Bank of England dated the 19th day of August 1896 shall be and the same are hereby revoked.

2. Stock to vest in nominee of Treasury

If at any time the Treasury direct that the capital stock of the Bank of England or any part thereof shall be transferred from the person nominated by them under section one of the Bank of England Act 1946 to any other person nominated by them the said stock or such part thereof shall without any instrument of transfer vest in the person so nominated by them to be held by him on behalf of the Treasury accordingly.

3. Powers of the Court of Directors

The Court of Directors may and shall choose and appoint and remove officers servants and agents and determine their remuneration and conditions of service and generally in all matters do whatsoever they may judge necessary for the well ordering and managing of the Bank of England and the affairs thereof.

4. Power to make By-Laws

The By-Laws of the Bank of England heretofore made under the said Charter and Supplemental Charter ceasing to have effect as from the appointed day, the Court of Directors shall have power hereunder to make such By-Laws as appear to them to be required for the good order and management of the Bank of England and from time to time to repeal alter or supplement any By-Laws so made: provided always that the said By-Laws and any repeal alteration or supplement thereof shall not be repugnant to the laws or statutes of this Our Realm or to the provisions of the charters of the Bank of England from time to time in force.

5. How the Court of Directors may act

The Court of Directors may act notwithstanding that a vacancy or vacancies exist among the members of the Court and shall have power to act by sub-committees and to delegate such duties and powers as they think fit from time to time, to such sub-committees and to any of their own number and to the officers and servants and agents of the Bank. The Court shall meet once in every week at the least but the Governor (or in his absence the Deputy Governor) may summon a meeting at any time on giving such notice as in his judgment the circumstances may require.

6. Meetings of the Court of Directors

At a meeting of the Court of Directors the proceedings shall be regulated as follows:

    (1)   The quorum shall consist of not less than nine members.

    (2)   The Governor or in his absence the Deputy Governor shall take the chair. If either the Directors present are satisfied that neither the Governor nor Deputy Governor will be present or the Governor and Deputy Governor are absent for fifteen minutes after the time appointed for the meeting, the Directors present may choose one of their own number to be Chairman for that meeting and the transactions of that meeting shall be as valid and effectual for all purpose as if the Governor or Deputy Governor had been present.

(3)   The Governor or in his absence the Deputy Governor or in the absence of both the Governor and Deputy Governor the Chairman chosen for that meeting shall not have any vote save where there shall be an equality of votes.

(4)   The Minutes of all orders, resolutions and transactions of the Court of Directors shall be taken by the Secretary or his Deputy or Assistant as the case may be and written in a book to be kept for that purpose.

7.   Declarations to be made

No person appointed as Governor, Deputy Governor or Director of the Bank of England shall be capable of executing or acting in the office to which he may have been appointed until he shall have made the declaration set out in that behalf in the Schedule to these presents. Which declaration may and shall be made before any one of the Lord High Chancellor of Great Britain or the Chancellor of the Exchequer or the Lord Chief Justice of Us Our Heirs and Successors or the Governor or Deputy Governor of the Bank of England or before any preceding Governor or any preceding Deputy Governor. A Governor, Deputy Governor or Director who at the date of his appointment is absent from the United Kingdom may make the declaration required by these presents before the representative of Us Our Heirs and Successors in any foreign state, before the United Kingdom High Commissioner in any of Our Dominions or before the Governor in any of Our Crown Colonies.

8.   When offices to be vacated

Without prejudice to the provisions of paragraph 4 of the second schedule to the Bank of England Act 1946, a Governor, Deputy Governor or Direector of the Bank of England shall be disqualified for holding and shall vacate his office

(a)   If he be found lunatic or become of unsound mind;

(b)   If he become bankrupt or suspend payment or compound with his creditors;

(c)   If he be convicted of an offence and the Court with the approval of Our Chancellor of the Exchequer resolve that his office be vacated;

(d)   If he absent himself from Meetings of the Court of Directors continuously for six months without the consent of the Court and the Court with the approval of Our Chancellor of the Exchequer resolve that his office be vacated; or

(e)   If by notice in writing to the Court (which notice shall forthwith be communicated by the Court to Our Chancellor of the Exchequer) he resign his office.

9.   Interest of members of the Court of Directors to be disclosed.

In all cases where the Governor, Deputy Governor and Directors or any of them shall have any interest direct or indirect in any dealing or business with the Bank of England such Governor, Deputy Governor or Director shall at the time of such dealing or business being negotiated or transacted declare and disclose to the Court of Directors his interest therein and shall have no vote relating thereto: provided that a member of the Court shall not be deemed to have an interest in any dealing or business by reason only of his being the beneficial owner of not more than one per cent. of the share capital of a company interested in such dealing or business.

10. Those concerned in debates to withdraw

Where any question shall at any time arise at a meeting of the Court of Directors touching or concerning any member of the Court such member shall have no vote relating thereto but shall withdraw and be absent during the debate of any matter in which he is concerned.

11. Exclusive services of members of the Court of Directors

(1)   The Governor and the Deputy Governor shall render their exclusive services to the Bank of England.

(2)   The Court of Directors may from time to time engage the executive services of Directors, in number not exceeding four at any time, for a period not exceeding the unexpired portion of their respective terms of office. Such Directors shall be called and known by the name of Executive Directors, or by such other name as the Court may from time to time determine.

12. Remuneration of members of the Court of Directors

The Governor, Deputy Governor and Directors shall in respect of their services on the Court of Directors receive fees at the same rate as the fees which were payable to them respectively immediately before the date of these presents for the same services that is to say the Governor at the rate of Two Thousand Pounds a year the Deputy Governor at the rate of One Thousand Five Hundred Pounds a year and each Director at the rate of Five Hundred Pounds a year.

(2)   The Governor and Deputy Governor and any Director rendering exclusive services to the Bank of England may in respect of their exclusive services receive remuneration at such rates as the Court of Directors may from time to time determine in addition to their fees for their services on the Court and the Court may pay or create and maintain a fund for the payment of pensions or capital grants to members or former members of the Court who shall have rendered such exclusive services.

13. Custody and use of the Seal

The Seal of the Corporation shall be carefully kept under three locks, the three keys whereof shall be severally kept by such three members of the Court of Directors as the Court shall from time to time empower to keep the same. The said Seal shall not be affixed to any instrument whatsoever but by an Order of the Court of Directors for that purpose first had and obtained and in the presence of three or more members of the Court for the time being. The affixing of the Seal shall be attested by the signature of any three of the members of the Court so present.

IN WITNESS whereof We have caused these Our Letters to be made Patent.

WITNESS Ourself at Westminster the first day of March in the tenth year of Our Reign.

BY WARRANT under The King's Sign Manual.

NAPIER.

SCHEDULE
FORMS OF DECLARATION

Form of Declaration by the Governor or Deputy Governor

I, A B, being appointed to the office of Governor (Deputy Governor) of the Corporation of the Governor and Company of the Bank of England do solemnly and sincerely declare that I will to the utmost of my power, by all lawful ways and means, endeavour to support and maintain the said Corporation and the liberties and privileges thereof: and in the execution of the said Office I will faithfully and honestly demean myself according to the best of my skill and understanding.

Form of Declaration by a Director

I, A B, being appointed to the office of a Director of the Corporation of the Governor and Company of the Bank of England do solemnly and sincerely declare that in the said office I will be indifferent and equal to all manner of persons: and I will give my best advice and assistance for the support and good Government of the said Corporation: and in the execution of the said Office I will faithfully and honestly demean myself according to the best of my skill and understanding.

Appendix 5
Memorandum of Understanding between HM Treasury, the Bank of England and the Financial Services Authority (FSA)

1. This Memorandum of Understanding establishes a framework for cooperation between HM Treasury, the Bank of England and the FSA in the field of financial stability. It sets out the role of each institution, and explains how they will work together towards the common objective of financial stability. The division of responsibilities is based on four guiding principles:

— clear *accountability*. Each institution must be accountable for its actions, so each must have unambiguous and well-defined responsibilities;

— *transparency*. Parliament, the markets and the public must know who is responsible for what;

— *no duplication*. Each institution must have a clearly defined role, to avoid second guessing, inefficiency and the duplication of effort. This will help ensure proper accountability;

— regular *information exchange*. This will help each institution to discharge its responsibilities as efficiently and effectively as possible.

THE BANK'S RESPONSIBILITIES

2. The Bank will be responsible for the overall stability of the financial system as a whole which will involve:

(i)   stability of the monetary system. The Bank will monitor this, as part of its monetary policy functions. It will act daily in the markets, to deal with day-to-day fluctuations in liquidity;

(ii)   financial system infrastructure, in particular payments systems at home and abroad. As the bankers' bank, the Bank will stand at the heart of the system. It will fall to the Bank to advise the Chancellor, and answer for its advice, on any major problem inherent in the payments systems. The Bank will also be closely involved in developing and improving the infrastructure, and strengthening the system to help reduce systemic risk;

(iii)   broad overview of the system as a whole. The Bank will be uniquely placed to do this: it will be responsible for monetary stability, and will have high-level representation at the institution responsible for financial regulation (through the Deputy Governor (financial stability), who will be a member of the FSA Board). Through its involvement in the payments systems it may be the first to spot potential problems. The Bank will be able to advise on the implications for financial stability of developments in the domestic and international markets and payments system; and it will assess the impact on monetary conditions of events in the financial sector;

(iv)   being able in exceptional circumstances to undertake official financial operations, in accordance with the arrangements in paragraphs 11 to 13 of this Memorandum, in order to limit the risk of problems in or affecting particular institutions spreading to other parts of the financial system;

(v)   the efficiency and effectiveness of the financial sector, with particular regard to international competitiveness. The Bank will continue to play its leading role in promoting the City. Much of this work will be directed towards improving the infrastructure.

THE FSA'S RESPONSIBILITIES

3.   The FSA's powers and responsibilities will be set out in statute. It will be responsible for:

(i)   the authorisation and prudential supervision of banks, building societies, investment firms, insurance companies and friendly societies;

(ii)   the supervision of financial markets and of clearing and settlement systems;

(iii)   the conduct of operations in response to problem cases affecting firms, markets and clearing and settlements systems within its responsibilities, where:

(a)   the nature of the operations has been agreed according to the provisions of paragraphs 11 to 13 of the Memorandum; and

(b)   the operations do not fall within the ambit of the Bank of England defined in paragraph 2 above. (Such operations by the FSA may include, but would not be restricted to, the changing of capital or other regulatory requirements and the facilitation of a market solution involving, for example, an introduction of new capital into a troubled firm by one or more third parties.)

(iv)   regulatory policy in these areas. The FSA will advise on the regulatory implication for firms, markets and clearing systems of developments in domestic and international markets and of initiatives, both domestic and international, such as EC directives.

THE TREASURY'S RESPONSIBILITIES

4.   The Treasury is responsible for the overall institutional structure of regulation, and the legislation which governs it. It has no operational responsibility for the activities of the FSA and the Bank, and will not be involved in them. But there are a variety of circumstances where the FSA and the Bank will need to alert the Treasury about possible problems: for example, where a serious problem arises, which could cause wider economic disruption; where there is or could be a need for a support operation; where diplomatic or foreign relations problems might arise; where a problem might suggest the need for a change in the law; or where a case is likely to lead to questions to Ministers in Parliament. This list is not exhaustive, and there will be other relevant situations. In each case it will be for the FSA and the Bank to decide whether the Treasury needs to be alerted.

INFORMATION GATHERING

5. Through the exercise of its statutory responsibilities, the FSA will gather a wide range of information and data on the firms which it authorises and supervises.

6. The FSA and the Bank will work together to avoid separate collection of the same data, to minimise the burden on firms. Where both need access to the same information, they will reach agreement as to who should collect it, and how it should be transmitted to the other.

7. The Bank will collect the data and information which it needs to discharge its responsibilities.

INFORMATION EXCHANGE

8. This will take place on several levels. The Bank's Deputy Governor (financial stability) will be a member of the FSA Board, and the FSA Chairman will sit on the Court of the Bank of England. At all levels, there will be close and regular contact between the FSA and the Bank. The FSA and the Bank will establish a programme of secondments between the two institutions, to strengthen the links and foster a culture of cooperation.

9. The FSA and the Bank will establish information sharing arrangements, to ensure that all information which is or may be relevant to the discharge of their respective responsibilities will be shared fully and freely. Each will seek to provide the other with relevant information as requested. The institution receiving this information will ensure that it is used only for discharging its responsibilities and that it is not transmitted to third parties except where permitted by law.

STANDING COMMITTEE

10. In addition to the above arrangements, there will be a Standing Committee of representatives of the Treasury, Bank and the FSA. This will meet on a monthly basis to discuss individual cases of significance and other developments relevant to financial stability. Meetings can be called at other times by one of the participating institutions if it considers there to be an issue which needs to be addressed urgently. Each institution will have nominated representatives who can be contacted, and meet, at short notice.

11. In exceptional circumstances there may be a need for an operation which goes beyond the Bank's routine activity in the money market to implement its interest rate objectives. Such a support operation is expected to happen very rarely and would normally only be undertaken in the case of a genuine threat to the stability of the financial system to avoid a serious disturbance in the UK economy. If the Bank or the FSA identified a problem where such a support operation might be necessary, they would immediately inform and consult with each other.

12. Each institution (the 'lead institution') would take the lead on all problems arising in its area of responsibility as defined in paragraphs 2 and 3. The lead institution would manage the situation and coordinate the authorities' response (including support operations). The form of the response would depend on the nature of the event and would be determined at the time.

13. In all cases the Bank and the FSA would need to work together very closely and they would immediately inform the Treasury, in order to give the Chancellor of the Exchequer the option of refusing support action. Thereafter they would keep it informed about the developing situation, as far as circumstances allowed.

CONSULTATION ON POLICY CHANGES

14. Each institution will inform the other about any major policy changes. It will consult the other in advance on any policy changes which are likely to have a bearing on the responsibilities of the other.

MEMBERSHIP OF COMMITTEES

15. The FSA and the Bank will cooperate fully in their relations with international regulatory groups and committees. They will both be represented on the Basle Supervisors' Committee, the EMI Banking Supervisors' Sub-Committee, and on other international committees where necessary. Where only one institution is represented, it will ensure that the other can contribute information and views in advance of any meeting; and will report fully to the other after the meeting. This will promote cooperation and minimise duplication.

16. The FSA and the Bank will keep HM Treasury informed of developments in the international regulatory community which are relevant to its responsibilities.

17. The FSA and the Bank have agreed the following arrangements for chairing domestic market committees:

— Sterling Markets Joint Standing Committee: the FSA
— Foreign Exchange Joint Standing Committee: Bank
— Derivatives Joint Standing Committee: the FSA
— Stocklending and Repo Committee: Bank

18. The FSA and the Bank will each use best endeavours to facilitate contacts by the other with overseas central banks and/or regulators, where necessary to discharge their respective responsibilities.

PROVISION OF SERVICES

19. In some cases it will be more efficient for a service to be provided by the FSA to the Bank, or vice versa, rather than for both institutions to meet their own needs separately. In these cases, service agreements will be established between the two institutions setting out the nature of the service to be provided, together with agreed standards, details of timing, charges (if any), notice periods, and so on. These agreements will in the first instance cover: provision of facilities (premises, IT etc.) during the transitional phase; the provision of analysis on domestic and overseas financial markets; the provision of research; and the processing of statistical information.

LITIGATION

20.   The Bank will retain responsibility for any liability attributable to its acts or omissions in the discharge or purported discharge of its banking supervisory functions prior to the transfer of these functions to the FSA and shall have the sole conduct of any proceedings relating thereto. The two institutions will cooperate fully where either faces litigation.

RECORDS

21.   The FSA will be responsible for the custody of all supervisory records. It will ensure that, within the framework of the relevant legislation, the Bank has free and open access to these records.

28 October 1997

Index